Oh
My Dog

Oh My Dog

HOW TO CHOOSE, TRAIN, GROOM, NURTURE, FEED, AND CARE FOR YOUR NEW BEST FRIEND

Beth Ostrosky Stern

with Kristina Grish

GALLERY BOOKS

A DIVISION OF SIMON &

NEW YORK   LONDON   TOR

Note to readers regarding pronoun use: The author uses "he" for dogs as well as for vets and other generic pet care professionals, in order to avoid confusion.

Gallery Books
A Division of Simon & Schuster, Inc.
1230 Avenue of the Americas
New York, NY 10020

First Gallery Books trade paperback edition May 2010

GALLERY BOOKS and colophon are trademarks of Simon & Schuster, Inc.

For information about special discounts for bulk purchases,
please contact Simon & Schuster Special Sales at 1-866-506-1949
or business@simonandschuster.com

The Simon & Schuster Speakers Bureau can bring authors to your live event. For more information or to book an event contact the Simon & Schuster Speakers Bureau at 1-866-248-3049 or visit our website at www.simonspeakers.com.

Designed by Joel Avirom and Jason Snyder

Manufactured in the United States of America

10   9   8   7   6   5   4   3

Library of Congress Cataloging-in-Publication Data

Stern, Beth Ostrosky.
Oh my dog : how to choose, train, groom, nurture, feed, and care for your new best friend / by Beth Ostrosky Stern with Kristina Grish.
   p. cm.
   Includes index.
1. Dogs. I. Grish, Kristina. II. Title.
SF426.S728 2010
636.7—dc22   2010005743

ISBN 978-1-4391-6029-9
ISBN 978-1-4391-6866-0 (ebook)

This book is dedicated to all dogs without homes.
My greatest wish is for each one to feel the love,
warmth, happiness, and joy of a "forever home."

Until one has loved an animal,
part of his soul remains unawakened.

—ANATOLE FRANCE, POET

CONTENTS

INTRODUCTION

The Best Kind of Pet Project

Something tells me you're about to become a dog person, if you're not one already. Maybe it's the way your face lights up when you hear the word "puppies!"—or the fact that you're two sentences into a lengthy canine compendium. Either way, you're in good company, because I'm passionate about dogs, too. After all, the only thing a dog owner adores more than her pet is an audience who will listen to her seasoned insight and animated stories about raising him. And as you'll soon learn by being the new kid in the dog park, the act of gathering friendly guidance from those in the know is a sensible rite of passage for both you and your dog.

And do I have a world of advice to pass on.

When a dog becomes part of your life, you automatically become part of a community that knows how to spot-clean carpets and neutralize puppy breath. We've spent time vetting our vets and begging trainers to "stay"—and most of us don't realize how much we have to share until you ask. Curious about barking? We'll talk your ear off.

Interested in holistic diets? Let's swap recipes. It may sound a bit over-whelming now, but when your dog's eyes are bloodshot and the vet's in Hawaii, you'll be grateful someone's done the homework for you.

Adjusting to a dog owner's lifestyle can be hard in the beginning, and I know from personal experience that you can ask a pro only so many questions before you start to feel like an incompetent mess. That's part of the reason why I wanted to write *Oh My Dog*: to share my own dog experiences, and most important, to relay guidance from talented experts you may not already have on speed dial. Raising a new canine family member isn't a task that should make you feel alone in your confusion (or in any way, really), so consider the words in this book a first resort, a friendly second opinion, a strong support system—or all of the above. Here, you'll find dog-rearing essentials, according to my own experience and a handful of wonderful experts, to help make your new adventure as simple, fun, and fulfilling as it can be. Long walks and playtime are the stuff of great memories, but growing and learn-ing with your dog can be difficult, and time-consuming as well. If I can help skim the fat from an extensive how-to process to leave more hours for you to smother each other with love, then I'll have done my part as a fellow dog owner.

Owning a dog is so much more than, well, owning a dog. It's a series of physical, mental, and emotional exercises: a time-suck one minute and a heart-tug the next. Anyone with a new puppy or full-grown dog will agree that there's nothing fun or funny about those first loud nights he spends crying in a crate near your bed or those lit-tle needle-teeth snags he makes in your new tights. But treat and train your dog well, and he's bound to become the embodiment of the best friend you've always hoped for. As you and your dog get to know each other better, it's comforting to realize that so many others have been in the same boat—many of them with fewer resources than you have in your hands right now. As my pregnant friend used to tell herself to keep from freaking out about motherhood: "Dumber people have done this." The mantra isn't so different when raising a dog, and the more time you devote to learning the basics, the more intuitive the process will become.

I'll never forget the moment Howard and I decided to get a dog together. Early in our relationship, we spent Sunday afternoons at the neighborhood dog park, just watching people interact with their pets. After a year of this, Howard suggested we get one of our own. We'd both been dog owners in the past, so we knew what a life-changing event it would be. I was panicked at first: I knew those four-thirty A.M. walks would be my duty in the middle of frigid New York City winters, since Howard had to rush to be on the air by six A.M. My family always rescued our pets from local shelters, but Howard and I were determined to find an English Bulldog. We were drawn to every one we saw! It became an obsession. In fact, we were known to chase English Bulldogs (and their owners) down city blocks just to look at them. We spent an entire year researching breeders in our vicinity, since at the time I didn't realize that there was such a thing as a breed rescue. When we finally met with our breeder, Shelly, we were excited to meet the mommy Bulldog who had our puppy in her belly.

But something happened when we arrived at Shelly's house that afternoon. She had eight grown Bulldogs running around her home, including the one about to give birth. There was one dog in particular, Reba, who just adored Howard. She immediately sat in his lap and then sauntered over to me to give me kisses. After that, I only wanted my baby Bulldog to have Reba's personality. So I asked Shelly what the story was with this particular dog, and she told me that Reba was about ten months old and was a former top show puppy until she developed a wiggle in her walk. Reba was of no use to her anymore, because she wasn't perfect and couldn't be shown. Needless to say, Reba came home with us that day, and we renamed her Bianca Romijn-Stamos-Ostrosky-Stern. It's a mouthful, I know, but it suits her.

In case you're wondering: the Romijn-Stamos part came from our friends Rebecca and John, whom we consider two of the most beautiful people in the world. When Rebecca married Jerry O'Connell, lucky Bianca took on the addition of O'Connell to her name, too!

Oh My Dog is the guide I wish I'd had when we brought our baby girl home. Howard and I think she's just about perfect, but Bianca has been very needy from the start. She follows me to the bathroom, watches me put on makeup, and when I make dinner, there's always a fifty-four-pound lump at my feet. She also farts! A lot. Very stinky ones. And during her first year with us, her gas was just rancid. I now know this isn't so strange for her breed, but it was still pretty vulgar. If friends came over for dinner, Bianca would pass gas after appetizers and before the first course. When Howard and I watched *American Idol,* Bianca would stink up the apartment before Ryan and Simon could pick their first fight. She's not much of a lady, our Bianca, but she does have a gorgeous face, a sloppy tongue, and a piglike waddle; and though she couldn't help her flatulence issues, they threw me nonetheless. I remember looking for answers online and in my own dog guides, but none ever gave me the solutions I sought. It took me a good year before I finally broke down and asked our vet about the embarrassing situation—which was helped enormously by simply tweaking her diet. If I'd had a quick and unintimidating reference to let me know how *normal* her gas was, and why it happened, I wouldn't have felt so mortified on her behalf.

As a longtime dog owner, shelter volunteer, and spokesperson for the North Shore Animal League America (NSALA), I can't tell you how many people ask me the most random questions about owning a dog—with topics ranging from breed-specific behaviors to socialization techniques. Bringing home a dog is full of so many "now what?" moments, and if I can address some of your questions before you even have them, all the better. That said, in no way do I intend to replace or undermine the roles of vets, trainers, and other schooled experts. I'd actually feel relieved if you'd consider this book an informed starting point for continued conversation with someone who holds a degree in animal care. It often takes a village, as you'll soon learn.

More than anything, I've always loved dogs and the community they promote. From puppies to adult dogs, purebreds to mutts and rescues: Each one brings its own special charm into our lives, especially when we keep an open mind and realistic perspective. So determine what you need from this book, ignore what you wish, and most important, enjoy the process. In no time, you'll be doling out advice to clueless owners, too.

1

So You Want a Dog?

I'm really excited for you! According to the Humane Society of the United States, there are 74.8 million dogs owned in the U.S.—and you may be about to boost that number. Dogs can be affectionate, loyal, spunky, and respectful companions. Some make great exercise buddies, while others offer an endless source of affection. Come to think of it, dogs can be any jumble of qualities based on their background and breed, so the trick to finding one that's right for you is being able to combine research with instinct and a whole lot of love. When deciding on what kind of dog is best for your home, you'll need to think hard about what makes you tick and the canine qualities that are the right fit for your lifestyle. And remember: This is a commitment that you'll be making for approximately fifteen years. Then again, the oldest dog on record lived to be twenty-nine, so you may want to plan for a bit longer . . .

Before you even get a dog, it's important to know exactly what you want from the pet and what you hope to get from your relationship with him. So in this chapter, I'll help you figure out your best canine match by suggesting specific ways to emotionally and mentally prepare for the new relationship. I'll take you through questions like:

What are the benefits of full-grown dogs versus puppies? How active would you like your dog to be? Is anyone in your home allergic to dogs, and if so, what breeds lend themselves to hypoallergenic traits? I'll also go into the best and worst places for you to get a dog. Never forget that owning a pet requires an open mind and a welcoming heart. So let's get to it. You have some reading to do!

Where Do Dogs Come From?

According to Mary Burch, PhD, CAAB, an animal behaviorist with the American Kennel Club (AKC), the dogs that we know and love today are called *Canis lupus familiaris* to the researchers who study them. In fact, "lupus" is the word that indicates that dogs are connected to the ancestral wolf (though some dogs, like Shih Tzus, look more like descendents of the Muppet). Science tells us that dogs evolved from a group of domesticated wolves in East Asia about fifteen thousand years ago, with earlier ancestors documented as far back as forty thousand years. Through selective breeding for specific characteristics, modern dogs have evolved over the last five hundred years.

It took a long time to create the 160-plus breeds that the AKC recognizes today. If an owner had a large brown-and-white dog and wanted a smaller version, he'd breed the smallest female in that litter to the smallest male he could find. He would continue breeding smaller and smaller dogs until he actually created a mini-version of the dog he started with generations earlier. So, from the 180-pound Mastiff to the 2-pound Chihuahua, all breeds came from a common ancestor—including mixed breeds, an even more colorful variation on the domesticated-dog theme. How interesting is that?

Studies Show How Dogs Can Improve Your Life

When people talk about why they want a dog, they usually cite emotional benefits: company, love, a way to add a little fun to their current lifestyle. Dogs are thrilled to see you after a long day, they always want to hang out with you, and their positive spirit rarely fails to make you smile. But studies tell us that dogs add so much more to your life than games of fetch and slobbery kisses. In fact, dogs can benefit your physical and psychological health, in some cases even more so than human relationships. I've combed through a bunch of dog studies and found a few interesting perks that you can look forward to:

DOGS DECREASE STRESS

▶ Dog owners have lower blood pressure, a slower heartbeat, and more relaxed muscles. It can take days or weeks before you benefit from meds, yet with only five to twenty-four minutes of petting or simply being in the moment with their pet, owners can relieve stress.

▶ Dog owners live longer, since they deal with anxiety better and fight depression easier.

▶ Dog owners have lower cholesterol and triglycerides and are at less risk of developing heart disease and other cardiovascular problems. These positive effects continue even when you're away from your dog.

▶ Heart attack victims have a higher survival rate when they spend time with a dog. They may feel a need to recover quickly so they can care for the pet, who then buffers them from future stress.

▸ Dog owners walk about 300 minutes per week compared with nondog owners, who exercise an average of 168 minutes per week. Dog walking lowers stress more than walking alone.

DOGS HELP PREVENT DISEASES

▸ Dogs help slash the risk of many terminal illnesses, plus slow down the disease's progression.

▸ Dogs can sniff out disease long before a high-tech machine or blood test, thanks to the body's chemical cues. A dog's sense of smell is up to a hundred thousand times times more sensitive than a human's.

▸ Dogs can also detect certain health issues in humans and alert their owners to the illness's onset through various behavioral cues. These conditions include changes in blood sugar and blood pressure, melanoma, migraine headaches, and heart attacks.

▸ Household dogs can be trained to detect early breast and lung cancer between 88 percent and 97 percent of the time by sniffing a human's breath. Dogs can also smell ketones on the breath and in the urine of diabetics when blood sugar is high; they detect this smell when glucose levels drop.

▸ Seniors who own dogs make fewer visits to the doctor and are more physically active. Pet owners over age sixty-five make almost a third fewer visits to their general practitioner than those who don't have pets.

▸ Elderly dog owners are four times less likely to suffer from depression than those without dogs.

Dogs Chase Away Loneliness

▶ Playing with a dog and holding his gaze can cause a hormone surge of oxytocin that makes you and the dog happier; it also reduces anxiety. The hormone is linked to friendship, infant care, bonding, and romantic love in humans; plus, it quiets stress, fights depression, and breeds trust. People who hold their dog's gaze for longer than two and a half minutes consider their relationship to be more satisfying than short-term gazers.

▶ Dogs, like humans, often look left toward the right side of human faces, since it exhibits emotions more accurately and intensely than the left. This behavior is called left-gaze bias, because the left side of the brain controls these displays of emotion. Some think dogs adapted this behavior during hundreds of years of domestication, in an effort to make sense of their owners' emotions. When we look into the eyes of a dog that trusts us, we feel less lonely because we see a creature that's trying equally hard to connect right back.

▶ Some dog owners can fondly discriminate between their pet's smell and that of a dog that isn't theirs. When blindfolded, study participants correctly identified the blanket on which their dog slept for three consecutive nights, when compared to stranger dogs of a similar sex, age, and breed. (Bianca's blanket would smell like fresh biscuits. I'd know her scent anywhere!)

▶ Nursing home residents feel less lonely after visiting with a dog alone, versus with other people.

Dogs Look Out for Kids

▶ Studies show that kids who care for pets are more nurturing, empathetic, and socially competent; at school, they're more popular with peers.

▶ Children who live with dogs are less likely to develop animal-related allergies later in life and less likely to develop eczema, asthma, and allergies to dust and pollen. Five- to seven-year-old dog owners also have fewer sick days at school, since pets may help boost a child's immune system.

▶ Five- and six-year-olds are 50 percent less likely to be overweight or obese if they own a dog, compared to those of the same age who don't own one.

Ask Dr. Z!

What does it mean when my dog . . .

Q: *Cocks his head when I talk to him?*

A: Dogs receive slightly different signals from each ear due to the separation between them. Cocking their heads may enable them to get the best "stereo" sound from all angles, so they can better understand what it is you're trying to tell or ask them.

Stephen L. Zawistowski, Ph.D., CAAB, is a certified animal behaviorist and an executive vice president and science adviser for the ASPCA. Lucky for us, he also offered to answer every quirky dog behavior question I could think to throw at him. You'll find these questions, and his answers, in the "Ask Dr. Z!" boxes that are sprinkled throughout this book. Dr. Z's assessments are based on his expertise and experience. Remember that every dog is different, but I was thrilled to see how many of the explanations applied to Bianca and her friends.

How to Emotionally Prepare for a Dog

Of course, it's important to choose a dog based on your practical life-style: where you live, how active you are, if there are children in your home, and so on. And we'll devote time to these scenarios later in the chapter. But what most people don't do, and should do, is take a really good look at their emotional expectations to help inform their dog decision, too. A dog takes up space in your life *and* in your heart. You don't want to feel disappointed when the dog you've chosen for its convenient size and polished looks also acts aloof or stubborn.

To that end, I asked Irene Deitch, Ph.D., a psychologist who works with pet owners, to outline what you should know about yourself before sharing your life with a dog:

> **Recognize your own emotional needs.** Are you a bleeding heart? Looking for a patient and attentive confidant? Personally, I appreciate a little empathy in a dog. Last year I fell down the stairs while wearing a new pair of heels, and Bianca ran over and began to aggressively lick my left foot. Sure enough, that was the foot that was broken.

> **Anticipate the dog's role in your life.** Would you prefer unconditional love or an exercise partner? Are you controlling or relaxed? If you've just left your parents' home, are an empty nester, or don't plan to have children, you may want to choose a dog that satisfies a need to nurture. If you'd like a status symbol to show off at parties or carry in your bag, an exotic breed may be the way to go.

Be ready to share your expectations with a breeder or rescue facility. Acknowledge and welcome another person's role in helping you find a dog that's right for you. When the time comes, you'll need to openly volunteer your needs and wants, but realize that experts can help you choose a dog that suits your lifestyle and personality.

Trust your instincts. In most relationships, we spend time with people before we decide what roles they'll play in our lives. But with dogs, most of us don't have this opportunity (unless you foster first), so let self-recognition fuel your research and decision. Being able to follow your own intuition is also really important when forging a rapport between you and your dog, so consider this prep work for bonding efforts down the road.

Why Do People Look Like Their Dogs?

How often do you see people who look or act like their dogs? I don't think many people would say Bianca resembles either Howard or me . . . but then again, Howard does snore loudly, like Bianca, and some days I feel really chubby. No surprise, then, that Dr. Deitch says a lot of people subconsciously cozy up to animals that share related traits. She says the reason for this is no different than it is for couples who look alike or friends who share mannerisms. Like attracts like, and this creates an immediate and automatic comfort zone, even if we don't realize it at the time.

Solving Seven Dog Debacles Before They Occur

If you have any fears about what to expect as a dog owner, Dr. Deitch says it helps to feel that the problems you anticipate are realistic but manageable. I pulled a survey from PetPlace.com that asked users: "What's the worst thing about owning a dog?" Below are my top seven answers to those problems, using some help from Dr. Deitch. Use this list to resolve common issues before they happen to you. You'll have seven fewer worries to keep you up at night.

7. **Pet Odors:** "Dog smell" is a hindrance only to the very sensitive. Even then your nose will adjust, much like it does when you work in a place with a distinct smell, or get used to a roommate's perfume after you've moved in together. Remember the study about owners who recognize their dog's scent? They identify it *fondly*. But when your dog's isn't so positive, Dr. Deitch says practical sprays and DIY remedies are a simple solution. For accidents, I've personally had amazing success with Nature's Miracle pet stain and odor remover, which works quickly, and is easy to use. As with any odor, the secret is to remove the smell's source and not cover it up with a Glade PlugIn.

6. **Aggression:** This is a complex issue that's best resolved by a professional called in to specifically modify your dog's temperament (see "When to Hire a Trainer Versus a Behaviorist" on page 146 for more). But in general, Dr. Deitch wants you to realize that a dog's behavior is both nurture and nature; pit bulls, for instance, can be very gentle if they're properly trained and reared by a warm soul (chaining and physical punishment are never the solution, no matter how aggressive your dog is).

If you detect hostile tendencies, behavior modification can be very effective. Dr. Deitch adds that you should be aware of dog aggression, but don't worry unless it becomes a setback—and know that most of the time, there is a practical solution that doesn't involve the pound.

5. **Barking or Whining:** Dr. Deitch says this may be more problematic in an apartment building than in a house, simply for noise reasons, but know that all dogs are territorial—and barking when a dog hears a noise or someone at the door is *normal*. Of course, stopping when you ask him to stop is also expected. When you eventually meet with the adoption counselors at shelters or breeders, ask them which dogs are more prone to barking than others and what situations might provoke this (some dogs bark at birds, others at the TV). If you find that your dog is barking for food or attention, or if barking accompanies separation anxiety or aggression, a trainer can help you resolve it. Eventually, you'll learn to understand what your dog's barks mean without help. (See "Listening to Your Dog" on page 139 for more on how to decode barks, whines, and howls once he's in your care.)

4. **Potty Mistakes:** If he's not already housebroken, you'll need to housebreak your dog shortly after you bring him home. Creating a regimented potty schedule will help this process. Dr. Deitch says dogs can make potty mistakes for any number of reasons, but once you get to the root of the problem, it's rarely a situation that can't be resolved.

3. **Cost of Medical Care:** If you're nervous about money matters, start by taking two initial precautions: 1) save for your dog and 2) buy pet insurance. Dr. Deitch says singles and couples without kids may be more liquid and may not need to make changes to their budget, but if your dog is part of a more financially taxed unit, you may want to save. See the box on "How Will I Deal with Time and Cost Concerns?" on page 18 for more on this.

2. **Pet Hair:** Dr. Deitch suggests researching hypoallergenic dogs if you're concerned about allergies. (President Obama, for instance, chose a Portuguese Water Dog because one of his daughters is allergic.) If you're worried about a hairy mess, you should look for low-shedding dogs. Note that hypoallergenic dogs and low-shedding dogs are not the same. See "What You Should Know About Hypoallergenic Dogs" on page 34 for more.

1. **Boarding or Finding a Sitter:** In my experience, this is a problem only if you wait till the last minute to find a dog sitter or an open kennel. Instead, Dr. Deitch recommends designating a few pet sitters before you even bring a dog home. Beyond professional facilities, I've found that responsible teens are game for dog sitting, as are friends from out of town who don't mind watching a dog in exchange for an informal "vacation" at your house. Some dog walkers are associated with boarding facilities, too, and will fill in, in a pinch. For more on this topic, see "Collect Your Contacts Before You Need to Use Them" on page 67.

How Will You Deal with Time and Cost Concerns?

Dr. Deitch says the two most typical concerns that her clients discuss with her before getting a dog are related to time and expenses. She adds that the best way to handle your angst is to tackle the problems logistically. The therapist's take on both:

PROBLEM #1: MANAGING TIME

Dr. Deitch says: Before getting a dog, recognize that he can live up to an average age of fifteen years and require stimulation throughout the day. The degree to which a dog needs this can depend on his breed, age, sex, and temperament. It may feel like a lot at first, but will soon become part of your routine. Research the needs of breeds you like, and think about how they relate to your schedule, so there are few surprises. (See "Choose a Dog with the Right Activity Level for You" on page 30 for more on exercise demands, if that's part of your concern.)

PROBLEM #2: MANAGING COSTS

Dr. Deitch says: This is a personal issue that's often dictated by where and how you live. According to the ASPCA, in most cities, new dog owners spend about two thousand dollars during their pet's first year at home. (It does not include the cost of the dog.) This cost includes food, medical care, insurance, training, and accessories. Future expenses, however, won't include initial expenses like training or a crate, so expect this number to slice in half (about $700 to $1,000) after the first year. If money is a concern, consider shelter adoptions, which will be less pricey. At shelters, dogs cost only a few hundred dollars (at most) and are often spayed or neutered when you get them (some shelters, like NSALA, throw in additional exams, tests, and classes for free; in exchange, many appreciate a donation, though it isn't necessary). Dogs that come from breeders often start around $1,000, depending on the breed; this cost includes initial health screenings, plus official paperwork about your dog and his breed. Finally, be sure to choose indulgences wisely (think: Burberry dog coat versus an American Apparel tee). For updated information about how much food, medical care, and other expenses cost annually, visit ASPCA.org's "Pet Care Costs" page for small-, medium-, and large-dog breakdowns. To review specifics about health insurance, see "Why Health Insurance Is Important" on page 192.

How to Mentally Prepare for a Dog

Before you even decide where to get your dog, figure out how basic lifestyle, care and maintenance, financial, and pet characteristic considerations will impact your day-to-day life. Julie Shaw, senior animal behavior technologist for the Animal Behavior Clinic at Purdue University's School of Veterinary Medicine, kindly offered us the questionnaire she uses when counseling people on how to choose a dog (below). Your adoption facility or breeder may ask you to fill out a similar form or review some of the same topics before you meet, but spend time answering these in advance. If you're raising the dog with another person, ask him/her to participate so you're on the same page.

LIFESTYLE

Are there other pets in your household? _____

Have you had pets in the past? _____

How often do adults visit? _____

How often do children or teens visit? _____

How hectic would you say your current lifestyle is? _____

Does anyone in your family have special needs?   _____

Is anyone in your home allergic to animals?   _____

Are there any major family changes in your near
future? Think: new baby, moving, divorce, etc.   _____

CARE AND MAINTENANCE

Do you live in a house, an apartment,
on a farm, or elsewhere?   _____

What is your approximate yard size?   _____

What type of fencing is around your yard?   _____

Where will your dog spend most of its time?
(indoors, outdoors, 50/50)   _____

How will a dog be managed in your backyard?
(fence, tie, not sure)   _____

What will your pet's indoor areas include?
Access to what rooms and furniture?   _____

Where will your pet sleep?   _____

How long will your pet be left alone
during the day?   _____

Where will your pet be kept when
you're not home?   _____

How much time do you plan on interacting with
your dog daily? (training, playing, exercise, etc.)   _____

Prioritize three activities you'd like to do
with your pet. (jogging, swimming, agility
training, etc.)   _____

How often will you walk your pet off your
property for mental stimulation?   _____

Who will be in charge of feeding your dog?   _____

Who will be in charge of cleaning up
after your dog?   _____

How often do you plan to work with
your pet on training?   _____

If you're acquiring a puppy, will you take
him to socialization classes?   _____

Do you plan on crate training your dog?   _____

Who will be responsible for administering
your pet's medical care?   _____

How would you prefer to have your pet trained?
(private, group class, at a training facility, etc.)   _____

What will you do with your pet when
you travel?   _____

MONEY CONSIDERATIONS

How much are you budgeting monthly
for your pet's food?   _____

How much are you willing to pay for
your pet initially?   _____

Do you plan on spaying or neutering your pet? _____

How much are you budgeting to spend
annually on your pet's medical care?   _____

Which of the pet sources are you considering?
(rescue, breeder, etc.)   _____

PET CHARACTERISTICS

- -

What other animals will your pet interact
with—both yours and others?   _____

What's your purpose for getting a dog?
(family pet, child's pet, breeding, show,
hunting, etc.)   _____

What breeds are you considering?   _____

Has someone in the house owned
a puppy under six months old?   _____

What age would you like your pet
to be when you acquire it?   _____

Are you interested in training your pet?   _____

How tolerable will you be of
housetraining problems?   _____

What about shyness with strangers/visitors?   _____

Aloofness with family?   _____

Excitability?   _____

Demanding attention?   _____

Jumping on people?   _____

Digging in the yard?   _____

Chewing/destruction?   _____

Excessive vocalization?   _____

How often do you plan to groom
your pet at home?   _____

How important is it to you that your pet
guards your home?   _____

What size pet do you prefer?   _____

How important is it to you that your pet
wants to sit in your lap, follow you around, etc.?   _____

Would you have your pet professionally
groomed?   _____

How much does hair on your clothing
or furniture bother you?   _____

Make Your Life Stage a Priority

Your life stage refers to your marriage, parenting, and career status, among other social details. Isabelle Hamel, head trainer and behavior consultant at North Shore Animal League America (NSALA), says that knowing the limits and freedoms of your life stage can help you make a wise dog choice. It's also smart to imagine what your world will be like fifteen years from now and what function your dog will play in it. To help with this exercise, Isabelle describes the following possible scenarios and dog care considerations. Find the situation that sounds most like yours (present and future). What kind of dog owner will you be?

You are single

What to consider: You have your own place and want your own pet. But having a dog can be time-consuming and inconvenient if you aren't used to this type of responsibility. Who will feed and walk him if you go out after work? If you want to sleep in after a late night, will you still do an early-morning potty walk? If you travel for business, do you know someone who can care for your dog? If you rent, does your landlord allow dogs?

You just bought your first house

What to consider: A change of environment can trigger temporary behavior problem in new pets. Will you be tolerant during this transition if the dog poops on newly carpeted floors or damages molding? Is your new neighborhood conducive to raising a dog? Does your homeowner's insurance cover the breed you want to get?

You are part of a couple who doesn't have children

What to consider: When couples decide they don't want children or aren't ready for a baby, they often adopt a pet. Some treat the animal as though he is a child, but so much coddling can be a problem should you decide to have a baby down the road. A pet that's been the center of attention and allowed in bed and on furniture may suddenly find that his home environment has altered—and so have the rules. Dogs are creatures of habit, and since their life is typically limited to your home and yard, they're very sensitive to change. If this is you, immediately place your dog in a routine that won't change, even if your family does. Set rules that provide a dog with stability; you can learn how to introduce him to a child when and if the time comes.

You have already started a family

What to consider: Dogs need to be taught manners and boundaries, because some can be rough with children when they're still adolescents themselves. Will your schedule allow for this? Can you afford the added expense of a dog? Is there any chance your child may be allergic or afraid of a new pet? Expose your children to a variety of animals before committing to a long-term relationship. This will give you an opportunity to monitor your children's interactions while keeping an eye out for allergic reactions. As your children grow, so do their social lives. Will you provide your pet with early socialization so he acts appropriately around all kids? Who will care for your pet when you're at work and your children are at school?

You have grown kids who are about to leave home

What to consider: You're inching close, or have already entered, the empty-nest life stage. Your kids are seldom home and will soon have lives of their own. Caring for a pet can give you a sense of purpose while providing company. But you'll also experience the freedom that comes with having time away from kids. Will you want to be home for a pet? If your teen originally wanted the pet, what will happen when he leaves for college? Will the pet have to leave home as well?

You are retired

What to consider: How will your life change now that your time is your own? Do you enjoy traveling, or do you like to stay at home? Will the dog be able to travel with you? Keep in mind that flying is a risk for dogs. (Many airlines are not equipped to safely and comfortably board them; plus, your dog may not adjust well to the altitude change.) If the dog stays behind, do you have boarding options? How well will the animal tolerate confinement and separation? Maybe your time will be divided between two homes. Are both suited for a pet? Will the dog travel well in a car?

You are a senior

What to consider: A puppy may seem like a good idea until you realize how exhausting it is to train one. Because baby dogs get into everything, a lot of time will be spent bending down to clean up papers or accidents, or retrieving objects from a dog's mouth, and if you don't choose the right dog, you could be scratched or bruised when he wants attention.

Plus, puppies tend to be fast-moving, and precautions need to be taken to prevent escape. They also need regular vigorous exercise to help avoid behavior problems (retrieving games or playdates are easy on seniors). If you like to walk, choose a dog that's easy to control—either with training devices or by choosing an older or smaller and more manageable dog. Mixed breeds, which NSALA calls mutt-i-grees, are fine dogs for seniors because they're not bred for one particularly fierce task (such as hunting birds) and can have milder temperaments due to their mixed qualities. In fact, I encourage people to consider adopting an adult dog, since they're usually trained, have all of their vaccinations, have passed the puppy stage, and will likely sleep through the night.

You are between life stages

What to consider: Being a foster parent. If you're not ready to commit to a dog, think about fostering one from a shelter to see what it's like to have an animal in your house. Test each other out. If you fall hard for this dog, you can talk to the shelter director about adopting him for good. If it's not serendipitous, don't worry; someone else will hopefully give him a loving home, and you can give another shelter pet a try!

Ask Dr. Z!

What does it mean when my dog . . .

Q: *Refuses to leave my side when I'm pregnant?*

A: Dogs can sense vulnerability, and they may recognize that the pregnant leader or role model is a little awkward while walking, and stick close by to take care of her. Dogs are very good at noticing changes in body language. Some experts also believe that dogs can smell the change in hormones that occurs in a woman's body when she's pregnant. This may cause him to stay close.

Decide Between a Puppy and a Full-Grown Dog

Though it's a great feeling to nuzzle a puppy, raising one isn't all cuddles and ear licks. Baby dogs, like baby humans, are a lot of work. And while neither puppies nor adult dogs are without their challenges, you may be more adept at caring for, and bonding with, one over the other. Julie Shaw helped break down what each option can entail:

Puppies . . .

▶ Require time and supervision, housetraining, socialization, constant exercise, and the patience to navigate normal puppy problems such as teething, destructiveness, mouthing, and nipping.

▶ Are especially vulnerable, because they've just left the smells and littermates that color everything they know. It's imperative that you have empathy for these little guys.

▶ Are most influenced by socialization between four and sixteen weeks old (this is when socialization has the biggest impact on behavior). So as a puppy owner, you'll have the most control over his behavior during this time. You should also expose the puppy to as many stimuli as possible: sounds, smells, and sights, including wheels, cats, dogs, water, and children.

▶ Are most challenging as adolescents, around six to eighteen months. A lot of adolescent dogs end up at shelters because they're most feisty during this age, so constant socialization and training are necessary.

Adult Dogs . . .

▶ May not require as much training as a puppy, since they can arrive at a shelter with some manners and housebreaking experience.

▶ Are often calmer because they've reached maturity. Three can be a magical age!

▶ Don't allow you to have control over their initial socialization, since they spent time in another home, so you must learn to understand their behavioral baggage and ultimately deal with the reasons an adult dog is no longer with his original owners. These may include bad or very little training, poor socialization, aggression, separation anxiety, and neglect.

▶ Can already be rehabilitated when they come from some rescue organizations (NSALA rehabilitates as many dogs as they can before finding them new homes). These shelters spend time with an abandoned dog to train and gather as much behavioral information as they can before placing him in a home. Not all shelters are this invested, but if rehabilitation is important to you, then find a shelter that does this or offers to work with new owners to help train their dog and modify unappealing behaviors.

FROM PUPPY TO ADULT: A BEHAVIORAL TIME LINE

If you decide to bring home a puppy, you can anticipate a number of behavioral changes that happen quickly. Katenna Jones, CAAB, CABC, CPDT, a humane educator and animal behaviorist with the American Humane Association (AHA), takes us through important milestones.

Three to six weeks: Puppies can be considered the dog equivalent of toddlers when they start to explore their environments and practice interacting with their moms and littermates.

Five to six weeks: Puppies can begin introductory training but shouldn't be separated from mom and littermates until eight to nine weeks to ensure proper social behavior.

Four to fourteen weeks: This is the optimal time for socializing a puppy with other dogs, animals, new places, and new people. Limit interaction with other animals until after the puppies have been vaccinated.

Twelve weeks to six months: Puppies are considered juveniles at this time and will start to test their independence and boundaries. This can be very frustrating, as puppies are trying to figure out what they can get away with. This is a prime period to hit training and behavior classes, since it's the most crucial time for developing a well-behaved adult.

Also around six months: Puppies begin to sexually mature, so they should be spayed or neutered by this time (if you do not intend to breed the dog) to avoid exploration of sexual behavior, such as humping and marking (peeing on an area to establish territory via scent).

Six to eighteen months: A puppy is now an adolescent, which is considered by many to be the most difficult period, since many dogs practice bad habits that they've developed while growing and changing. A lot of adolescent dogs end up at shelters because they're most challenging during this age—if they don't have adequate coaching. Never give up on a feisty dog; continue to socialize and train him, and stick to it!

Eighteen months: Dogs are considered physically and socially mature around eighteen months. After this time, some dogs will lose many of those frustrating puppy behaviors and begin developing into well-behaved, mature adults. Some breeds begin to calm down at this time, while others exhibit rambunctious behavior much longer, so it is critical to choose the right breed to suit your lifestyle early on.

Choose a Dog with the Right Activity Level for You

My good friend Joanne Yohannan, senior vice president of operations at NSALA, says that pairing a dog with the activity level you'll be able to offer him is crucial when getting a dog. If a canine isn't well exercised, he can become depressed, hyperactive, overweight, anxious, destructive, or aggressive. Note: Exercising your dog at the right activity level doesn't include short potty walks, which happen four times a day. A dog may require low, medium, or high levels of activity based on his temperament, age, size, and/or breed. Involving your dog in your daily lifestyle—for example, taking him on errands—will make his exercise needs feel like less of a burden to you. Take a look at what each of these levels mean, and assess how much time and energy you can realistically devote to giving a dog the activity he requires.

ACTIVITY LEVEL: *Low*

Needs: At least a brisk walk around the block once a day

Low exercise doesn't mean no exercise! Dogs need activity for physical and mental stimulation.

Make no assumptions about exercise needs based on a dog's size (this is a common mistake). A Mastiff and a Great Dane, both large breeds, require less activity than a Jack Russell Terrier, a small dog.

ACTIVITY LEVEL: *Moderate*

Needs: About twenty to thirty minutes of aerobic exercise a day

Moderate-energy dogs require owners to follow a consistent regime, as much as high-energy dogs do. It's tempting to fall behind if your dog's exercise needs aren't on either extreme end of the exercise spectrum.

Consider using doggie day care, a dog walker, or a private caretaker service to provide daily exercise that your schedule may not allow.

ACTIVITY LEVEL: *High*

Needs: More than thirty minutes of aerobic exercise a day

A high-activity dog doesn't "need" a yard; it only makes life easier for you.

If you live in the suburbs, consider fences and doggie doors so your dog can go out when he wants. (I hate electric fences and think they do more harm than good. They don't work on all breeds, can fail, can provoke behavior and aggression problems, and can give a dog a false sense of security.)

Don't leave a dog unattended outside. No dog will exercise alone in a yard for any length of time unless he is acting out of frustration. It's also not safe to leave a dog outside alone, since he can accidentally escape, come in contact with a wild animal, or pose a threat to a stranger who walks into his yard.

Consider using doggie day care, a dog walker, or a private caretaker service to provide daily exercise that your schedule may not allow.

> ### Tips for Owners That Apply to Dogs of All Activity Levels
>
> Be honest with yourself about your dog's needs, and avoid getting a dog that requires extensive exercise if you're not able to provide it.
>
> Pair your hobbies to your dog's physique. Really active owners who want to run or hike with their dogs should choose a dog with strong legs. Some small dogs have weak hind legs and need to limit exercise, so don't expect to win marathons with, say, a Dachshund in tow.
>
> While exercise can help a dog live a healthier life, as with people, it doesn't always determine life span. Studies show that regularly exercised dogs live up to 30 percent longer than their inactive counterparts, but on the whole, smaller dogs often live longer than big dogs.

Decide Between a Purebred, a Mixed Breed, and a Designer Breed

Once you've figured out how much energy and time you can devote to engaging your dog in activities, start researching what types of dogs might best fit your lifestyle. Here's some information that should help you narrow your search to either a purebred, a mixed breed, or a designer breed dog.

GENERAL PUREBRED QUALITIES

Dogs that belong to a recognized strain that's been established by breeding individual dogs of an unmixed lineage over many generations

Fixed and predictable dog genes

Most likely to meet both parents

The purchase price can be expensive

General Mixed Breed (AKA Mutt-i-gree) Qualities

Dogs whose parents are from mixed or different breeds

Random and unfixed genes

Unlikely that you'll meet both parents

Price will be lower

Generally speaking, mutt-i-grees have fewer genetic medical issues, since genes are mixed

Mutt-i-grees weren't bred for specific tasks, so behavior will be more difficult to predict

General Designer Breed Qualities

Also called a hybrid or a crossbreed, a designer dog has ancestry in two different purebred dog breeds

Hybrid dogs like the Labradoodle (Lab + Poodle) or Cockapoo (Cocker Spaniel + Poodle) have coined their own category, but they're considered an unpredictable "breed"

Genetic benefits often mirror those of mixed breeds; few of their characteristics are fixed

What You Should Know About Hypoallergenic Dogs

Hypoallergenic dogs are in high demand, judging by the number of people who ask me about them! Most assume a dog's coat causes an allergic reaction in humans, but there are really *three* ways people can be allergic to dogs: through coat, dander, or saliva (when a dog licks them). And when most have an allergic reaction to a shedding dog, they're actually reacting to the dead skin cells that flake onto the coat—not to the hair or fur itself.

Allergies vary from person to person and from one dog to another, even within the same breed. Though some doctors advise parents of kids with allergies not to get a dog, studies show that early exposure can strengthen a child's immune system against allergies and asthma.

While there are no breeds that don't shed at all, some breeds are less allergy-provoking than others. This is either because they're low-shedding or because they're low-dander. And if you're allergic to a dog's saliva, well, it doesn't matter what kind of hair the dog has!

People with allergies often find comfort in what are known as non-shedding breeds, which tend to be curly-coated, like Poodles, Portuguese Water Dogs, and Bichon Frises. Minimal shedders are terriers like Soft-Coated Wheatens and Schnauzers. Low-shedding dogs include Italian Greyhounds, Chihuahuas, and Malteses. Here are some of the most hypoallergenic breeds:

Basenji	Havanese
Bergamasco	Irish Water Spaniel
Bedlington Terrier	Kerry Blue Terrier
Bichon Frise	Löwchen
Bolognese	Maltese
Border Terrier	Native American Indian Dog
Cairn Terrier	Poodles
Coton de Tulear	Portuguese Water Dog

Puli	Tibetan Terrier
Schnauzer	West Highland White Terrier
Shih Tzu	Wirehaired Fox Terrier
Soft-Coated Wheaten Terrier	Yorkshire Terrier
Spanish Water Dog	

TOP TWENTY MOST POPULAR DOG BREEDS

To help match your needs to a breed, Dr. Burch broke down the pros and cons of the top twenty most popular dog breeds in the U.S. She also identified three of the more common priorities that dog owners have: which breeds are hypoallergenic, which are good with kids, and how much activity a dog breed usually requires. As with everything, these are generalizations; most key characteristics are unique to each dog. However, I hope the information below will help you in your search.

✳ High Activity   ✦ Moderate Activity   ▲ Low Activity
☺ Good with Kids   ✿ Hypoallergenic

1: LABRADOR RETRIEVERS ✳ ☺

Pros: *Highly trainable, eager to please. Popular service and agility dogs.*

Cons: *Since Labs were originally hunting dogs, they can run for hours and pull on a leash. These are high-energy pups!*

2: YORKSHIRE TERRIERS ✳

Pros: *Adaptable, bright, and perky toy breed. They're good in apartments, and they travel well.*

Cons: *Because Yorkies are so cute, they're easy to spoil. If this happens, they can be ornery and snappy.*

3: German Shepherd ✸ ☺

Pros: *Known as police or military dogs but also dependable and loving as pets.*

Cons: *Can be aggressive if trained with punishment or mismanaged.*

4: Golden Retriever ✸ ☺

Pros: *Highly intelligent, friendly, gentle. This breed's a pleaser, so it's easy to train.*

Cons: *Goldens can love you to a fault. They want constant play, attention, and activity.*

5: Beagle ✦ ☺

Pros: *You know him as Snoopy. Happy and friendly. Originally bred in packs to hunt for rabbits, beagles feel comfortable with humans and other dogs in a family.*

Cons: *Most problems for Beagles arise from being raised in the wrong setting. Because they're bred to hunt and roam, Beagles can take off for miles. A Beagle's hound bay is also noisy, and they love food, so as adult dogs, they can become overweight if their diet isn't managed.*

6: Boxer ✸ ☺

Pros: *Attractive, muscular dogs that love people. They are very athletic and can often stand on their back legs and smack toward you with their paws—hence the name.*

Cons: *A Boxer's playfulness could be a problem for someone who isn't very active. They're great with go-everywhere and do-everything families, as opposed to introverted apartment dwellers.*

7: Dachshund ✦

Pros: *There's a lot of variety here. Mini or standard, wire-haired or smooth. Dachshunds are lovable, playful, and good with children. They're also easily adaptable to various living arrangements.*

Cons: *These dogs may bark a lot and, if not socialized, can be snappy. Their bodies are long and fit easily in small, tight spaces. Since they're bred to dig tunnels and pull out badgers, they can also leave holes in the yard.*

8: BULLDOG ⅄ ☺

Pros: *Sweet, calm, gentle, great with families. Require very little exercise.*

Cons: *Because their noses are smooshed in, Bulldogs easily overheat and often have breathing problems. Enter: wheezing, snoring, drooling, gas. Bulldogs also require a lot of maintenance, especially since their folds and wrinkles require daily cleaning.*

9: POODLE ✹ ☺ ✿

Pros: *Available in toy, miniature, and standard sizes. Poodles are very smart, very active, and need lots of exercise. Since they were bred to be retrieve birds from the water, it was once thought that leaving hair only around their joints would keep them limber in the water—hence the funny pom-pom cuts.*

Cons: *If the smaller dogs aren't socialized, they can become shy. Coat requires lots of care.*

10: SHIH TZU ✦ ☺

Pros: *This Chinese dog was once the prize pet of the upper class. They're lively, alert, friendly, devoted. Bred for centuries to be a companion. Requires minimal exercise.*

Cons: *Not for rowdy children, and if training doesn't begin early, they can be stubborn. Housetraining can also be a problem.*

11: MINIATURE PINSCHER ✦ ☺

Pros: *Active, alert, obedient, friendly, willing to please. Great for seniors.*

Cons: *Noisy, yappy, barky like terriers. Can be a little argumentative with other dogs.*

12: Chihuahua +

Pros: *Devoted, loving, charming, highly intelligent, can live in an apartment, and require little exercise.*

Cons: *Chihuahuas can have housetraining issues. Sometimes they can snap at a person's fingers ("finger snapping") or bite when they're afraid ("fear biting").*

13: Pomeranian +

Pros: *Very trainable, highly intelligent, extroverted, active. Because they were bred to herd, Pomeranians are plucky, independent, and very spirited.*

Cons: *Tend to yap and can become spoiled and snappy if not socialized.*

14: Rottweiler +

Pros: *Though they were originally bred to drive cattle, Rottweilers are often police, service, obedience, or protection dogs. They need a job to do, or they can be trouble. They're adaptable, predictable, and loyal to their families.*

Cons: *If you're not in charge, they will be ("I'll sit on the couch; you sit elsewhere"). Stubborn.*

15: Pug ⚔ ☺

Pros: *As far back as 400 B.C., Pugs were kept as pets in Buddhist monasteries. They are often playful, charming, outgoing, and loving toward kids and families. They're sturdy little animals that require minimal exercise.*

Cons: *Without training, they can be stubborn. Like Bulldogs, Pugs have squashed faces, which leads to snoring, overheating, drooling, and gas.*

16: German Shorthaired Pointer ✸

Pros: *Bred to hunt birds, they require a lot of exercise from an active owner.*

Cons: *Not apartment dogs, and in the wrong setting, they can seem hyperactive; may look restless if kept indoors for too long. If bored, they can destroy furniture or bark excessively.*

17: BOSTON TERRIER ✦ ☺

Pros: *Need moderate exercise, are easy to train, love to be with owners.*

Cons: *Can have dog-to-dog aggression, problems with housebreaking. Same smooshed-face and gas issues as Bulldog and Pug.*

18: DOBERMAN PINSCHER ✷

Pros: *Once police, war, and tax collector dogs. Loyal, friendly, obedient, great with families.*

Cons: *Without training, can be territorial, aggressive, and restless indoors. Need lots of exercise.*

19: SHETLAND SHEEPDOG ✦ ☺

Pros: *Attractive herding dogs from the Shetland Islands. Loyal, highly trainable, devoted to families. These dogs are quick to learn manners during obedience training.*

Cons: *If not properly socialized, can need behavior intervention for jumpiness. Bark a lot.*

20: MALTESE ✦ ✿

Pros: *Gentle, affectionate, intelligent, playful. Great with families.*

Cons: *If spoiled and not trained, they'll soil the house. Also, irritable snapping and excessive barking can be problematic.*

Bad Places to Purchase Your Dog

Before I jump into specifics about how to work with a responsible breeder or shelter, I need to mention the sources from which you should *never* purchase a dog: puppy mills, backyard breeders, and yes, pet stores. In an ideal world, this rule of paw would put all three out of business. Lisa Peterson, director of club communications with the AKC, helps me explain why.

Puppy Mills

Though everyone's definition of a puppy mill is different, the general consensus is that they're large-scale commercial breeding facilities. Some sources cite that there are an estimated 5,000 puppy mills in the U.S. that produce more than 500,000 puppies a year! These dogs are kept in cramped conditions, including chicken-coop cages, become poorly socialized to other dogs or humans, and can have severe disposition issues as a result. Puppy mill offspring are often riddled with sickness or other genetic problems when sold to dealers, who then sell them at pet and puppy stores. Inbreeding; zero medical care, exercise, and proper socialization; and poor diets cause these problems and more. And as you might expect, financial gain is at the heart of this trend. Lisa notes that mill puppies can be sold as purebreds to obtain higher prices, though the mills' arbitrary breeding practices rarely qualify the dogs as such. Reputable breeders never sell puppies to dealers or pet stores. I have seen, firsthand during NSALA's puppy mill rescues, the damage that these places do. I remember a Maltese that had never left her cage. When we opened the door, she crawled on the ground because walking was an unfamiliar action. It was heartbreaking.

Backyard Breeders

Backyard breeders are smaller-scale breeders hungry to make cash from naive buyers. Lisa says they're usually two random owners who breed their dogs to make puppies for profit; she adds that they differ from small hobby breeders in the lack of credibility of their paperwork and their unethical standards. If you opt for any breeding route, find someone who has put thought into the breed, is intent on improving the breed, and wants to create a new generation of dogs that are sound, healthy, and well behaved.

Pet Store

Please do not buy a dog from a pet store, since industry sources say that they often use dealers who get their dogs from puppy mills. If you choose to ignore my plea, Lisa says to at least demand that the store owner discuss and provide AKC papers on the dog. The AKC is the only purebred registry that inspects breeders who register with this non-profit organization. If you see a dog at a store who is registered with kennel club names like APR, AKA, or any of the competing registries that are in the business of producing papers for profit, you shouldn't trust the vendor. (Pet stores and crooked clubs seem to bank on the fact that three-letter acronyms will confuse consumers.) The AKC, however, donates their registration dollars to public education programs for responsible dog ownership and charity funds such as disaster relief.

Another responsible kennel club is the United Kennel Club (UKC). This is an international registry that recognizes more than three hundred breeds of dogs, so if you're looking for a dog breed that isn't registered with the AKC (say, an American Pit Bull Terrier), you can check with this organization's website at UKCDogs.org to find legitimate breeders.

Internet

The Internet is a great place to *research* breed prospects, but Lisa doesn't recommend it as a spot to purchase one. If you must buy a dog from someone who doesn't live near you, ask for references and speak to others who've purchased dogs from this breeder. She says you should also ask if the breeder is a member of an AKC-affiliated club and contact that club to verify membership.

If you find a breeder through a website, you shouldn't send money without speaking to this person on the phone and checking his or her references and credentials first. Corrupt breeders and scams can present themselves through professional-looking sites that draw you in with photos of rolling hills and cute dogs that don't exist. Lisa says to also be wary of breeders who insist you wire money and call to ask for even more wired money to cover last-minute fees. Sites without phone numbers, and with credit card emblems, also point to bogus breeders, as do sites that advertise more than three breeds.

How to Purchase a Dog from a Responsible Breeder

Your relationship with a potential breeder should be long-lasting. This is the person who's bringing a new member of your family into the world, so you want to feel that she's responsive, open, and interested in you and your home. No question is off-limits for anyone in this scenario. Lisa offered these suggestions for getting started:

▶ Attend a dog show, visit AKC.org, or call the AKC at 919-233-9797. Contact the breeder referral officer for the breed's parent club to find a kennel club in the U.S. All-breed kennel clubs in your area are also a good option; these are listed on the AKC site as well. The AKC recognizes 161 purebreds, each of which has a national breed or parent club that's comprised of the breed's owners. As members, these breeders sign a code of ethics about responsible standards. If you'd like to rescue a purebred, the happy medium between breeders and adoption, visit the "Purebred Rescue Groups" directory on AKC.org.

▶ Don't be offended if a breeder isn't immediately responsive to your initial call or e-mail. Most hobby breeders have full-time jobs and don't always have available puppies. Be selective. Find a breeder who's knowledgeable and makes you feel comfortable. On the flip side, don't be put off if your breeder seems to care too much! You want her to ask where you live, your work hours, if you have children, etc. Talk about what you expect from a dog so she can suggest a sex, housebreaking tips, and the like. This shows she's invested in you and your dog's future together.

▶ Visit the breeder's home or kennel—if she doesn't invite you over, invite yourself. You may not be able to visit the puppies during their first eight weeks to keep exposure to sickness minimal, so don't see this as a danger sign. Instead, make sure the breeder's home or kennel is clean, odor-free, and responsibly maintained. A breeder should appear proud of what she does and want to show you around. Dogs and puppies should be clean, well fed, lively, and friendly. Look for signs of malnutrition such as protruding ribs, or illness such as runny nose or eyes, coughing, lethargy, and skin sores. Ask to meet at least one of the puppy's parents to get an idea what your dog's future temperament and appearance will be. Half of a puppy's DNA comes from his mom, so a good feeling about the mom should translate to a good feeling about the puppy. Don't be alarmed if the dog's father doesn't live with the breeder, but do ask to see photos and AKC documentation and health clearances.

▶ Pay attention to how the dogs and puppies interact with their breeder. Does the breeder seem to genuinely care for the puppies and adult dogs? Neither dogs nor puppies should shy away from the breeder; they should also be outgoing with strangers.

▶ Ask about the health of your puppy and his parents. Breeders should be honest about the breed's strengths and weaknesses, and knowledgeable about any genetic diseases that can affect their breed—plus what's being done to avoid them. Breeders should share proof of health screenings of the parents and the puppy, including OFA (Orthopedic Foundation for Animals) and CERF (Canine Eye Registration Form) certificates.

▶ Establish a rapport with the breeder. This person will be a resource and mentor throughout the dog's life. Six years later, I still call Bianca's breeder to ask Bulldog-related questions, and she still calls us to check in on Bianca. Don't be afraid to contact the breeder with even the simplest question; he or she wants to hear from the owners and learn how they're enjoying their puppy.

▶ Don't expect to bring a puppy home until he is eight to twelve weeks old. Puppies need ample time to mature and socialize with their mothers and littermates. During this time, breeders should be willing to answer any questions you have and should ask many of you, too. They should want to make sure their dogs are headed to wonderful homes with people who've made the necessary preparations.

▶ Don't leave the breeder without the appropriate documentation of the dog's pedigree: The words "American Kennel Club" as well as the AKC logo should be clearly visible on the document. Among this paperwork should be an application to register your dog with the AKC, which you'll need to fill out and mail in on your own. Question a breeder who refuses or hesitates to give you papers, wants to charge you more for AKC papers, offers papers from a registry other than the AKC, or tells you he will mail the papers at a later date. You should leave with health certificates for the puppy and his parents, a family tree, and a bill of sale. A breeder may also ask you to sign a contract that says if certain care conditions aren't met or you become unable to keep the puppy, the breeder will reclaim him.

▶ The AKC inspects about five thousand kennels a year, and breeders found to have major kennel deficiencies may lose AKC privileges (the ability to register dogs or compete in events). In some cases, they can incur fines, with an indefinite suspension of privileges; the AKC may also contact law enforcement. A quick call to AKC customer service will ensure your breeder is in good standing.

▶ Beware of breeders who seem preoccupied with the financial aspect of the transaction. A reputable breeder will be more concerned with how appropriate your home is for the dog than when he's getting paid. However, make sure everyone knows how and when the puppy will be paid for—in writing. If he's shipped long distance, pay for half up front and half upon receiving the dog (after your own vet signs off on the puppy's health).

▶ Beware of websites that offer 1) more than three breeds that 2) can be purchased right away. First, Lisa says that most responsible breeders tend to focus on one or two breeds. Second, since gestation and socialization of a litter take months before individual puppies can be placed with new owners, it's highly unlikely that your perfect puppy will be available for shipping the very day you call.

SHOULD YOU TAKE A BREEDER SERIOUSLY IF SHE HAS DOG DECOR?

Lisa says that you shouldn't be scared off by random dog paraphernalia in and around a breeder's home or kennel. Though Norwich Terrier flags, garden gnomes, and hand-woven tapestries may not be your taste, they don't make a breeder's pedigree any less credible. In fact, since the majority of responsible breeders receive trophies and porcelain bells for their efforts, these should be signs of encouragement! Lisa assures me that dog decor demonstrates a breeder's passion for his or her animals.

How to Adopt a Dog from a Shelter

I have a place in my heart for shelters. Suzydog, our first family mutt, came from a Pittsburgh shelter, and some of the most generous people I know are responsible for rescuing, rehabilitating, and finding first-class homes for abandoned or mistreated dogs. Though each shelter does as much as its funding allows, spay/neuter programs, vet services, disaster relief, adoptathons, fostering, and hospital and senior outreach are regular priorities. Here, Joanne from NSALA answers basic questions about how to rescue a dog of your own.

Q: *Are some shelters better than others?*

A: While some shelters have more resources than others, this should not impact the inherent quality of the animals. Many shelters operate on a shoestring budget and depend largely on the help of volunteers. They aim to provide maximum help and as much information on their animals as possible. In the end, all shelters have the noblest of intentions: to help others adopt homeless animals and save their lives.

Q: *What information should I trade with a shelter worker?*

A: When you meet with a shelter worker or volunteer, share and gather as much information as possible. Explain what you're looking for and ask for suggestions. Find out what kind of medical screening the shelter applied to the dog, and ask if he's been vaccinated and spayed/neutered. At most shelters, you can expect to adopt an animal that's been medically examined, vaccinated, temperament-tested, and spayed/neutered. Inquire about the kind of pet behavior screening process the shelter employs. Then, once you've made a selection, ask for as much background information on the specific animal as the shelter can provide.

Q: *How much time can I expect to spend at a shelter?*

A: Adopting an animal is an important decision that could end up being a fifteen-year commitment. Plan to spend three hours at the shelter to allow time for the selection, dog interaction, and application process. Since there are so many dogs under one roof, and it's only natural to want to rescue all of these lost souls, it's important to form an idea of the type of pet you're interested in *before* you visit the shelter. Most shelters have adoption counselors or volunteers who can help you select a dog that's right for you. Share what you're looking for, the details of your lifestyle, and your expectations—and they'll guide you through the process.

Q: *What should I bring to the shelter?*

A: Once you make your selection, most shelters have their own process, which usually involves an application and references. To facilitate it, come prepared with your references' names, addresses, and the phone numbers at which they can be reached at the time of adoption; potential adopters should also bring identification with their name and current address for the shelter's records. Facilities like NSALA encourage all potential adopters to make this a household affair and to bring all members of the house to the adoption. If you rent your home, you may also want to bring your landlord's phone number or a copy of your lease to prove that you can keep a pet.

Q: *Can I bring a dog home with me the same day I meet him?*

A: Most animal shelters do have a screening and application process that must be completed before an animal goes home with his new owners. This is to help ensure that the adopter and animals are matched properly and that the relationship will last. Some shelters and rescue organizations do not do same-day adoption (they conduct home visits and interviews before approving adoption), while others will allow animals to go home the same day the application is submitted and approved. In any case, you should allow two or three hours to make the selection, bond with the animal, and receive all paperwork associated with the adoption.

Q: *What paperwork can I expect to receive?*

A: Sylvia Mariani, shelter director for NSALA, explains that while each shelter has its own paperwork, you can hope to leave with a receipt of adoption, at the very least. At NSALA, this receipt reviews any medical or behavioral conditions they've noticed in the dog and a discharge note from a vet that details the vaccinations and certifications he's had, plus other medical history that will be helpful for the dog's new vet. Care guides are typical, as they explain tips related to behavior, feeding, training, housebreaking, and medical care, among other topics. Behavior training pamphlets are also common. Not every shelter will explore medical history, but as an adopter, you should know if the dog has vaccinations or been spayed/neutered. In some states, such as New York, it's law that a dog must be spayed/neutered before he leaves a shelter.

Q: *How can I foster a dog?*

A: Fostering programs are a great alternative to adoption. You can foster any variety of pets, from nursing babies to seniors in need of special care to everything in between. Fostering can be a very emotional experience, should you choose to part with the pet, but it is a vital resource to shelters and saves countless animal lives. If you're interested in fostering a dog, a shelter volunteer will interview you about your intentions for either a long- or short-term arrangement.

Addressing the Top Three Hesitations About Shelter Dogs

When dogs are given to a shelter, some will already be trained and ready to join your family. Others, however, have received minimal training—which is why some agitated and willful dogs tend to be in shelters to begin with. These dogs, in need of additional coaching, tend to bark, jump, and resist a leash *because* their original owners never took the time to correctly train them. And while some shelters teach manners before putting dogs up for adoption, not all do. If you adopt a rescue that needs training, don't expect him to coach himself or adjust to his new home overnight.

According to Mike Malloy, manager of the pet behavior department at NSALA, a shelter dog takes four to six weeks to settle in to his new home. During this time, expect deliberate tests of authority and accidents if he's not already housebroken (the dog may want to mark his territory in a new environment). Group classes, a private trainer, or a training manual can correct specific problems, though Mike says indoor peeing and pooping, challenges with a leash, barking, and separation anxiety are typical dilemmas that benefit from work with a professional. Mike took the time to describe the three most common problems a shelter dog might have and how to deal with each:

HOUSEBREAKING

Housebreaking a shelter dog can be less of a predicament, even with trainable animals, if you use a crate. Dogs are "den animals," which means that they like having their own small space to go into or under. Crates double as housetraining tools, since dogs won't eliminate where they eat and sleep. The proper size, location, bedding, food, and water will help your cause. When introduced properly, crate training can address and help you avoid other behavior problems, such as chewing and separation anxiety. We'll discuss crates and training more thoroughly in Chapter 3, but trust that your trainer will be able to give you the best and most personal direction for your dog and home.

BARKING

To avoid incessant barking, don't leave a dog alone for longer than eight hours (especially not a puppy!), and arrange your schedule so you can visit during lunch and after work. This goes for dogs that come from a shelter *or* breeder! Mike says barking can develop in all dogs when they experience separation anxiety and are trying to communicate— but it's especially a problem in shelter dogs. It's normal, however, for a dog to bark if he hears something strange, as long as he stops when you ask. Barking is also a natural reaction to other dogs. Only when barking turns to aggression do you really need to worry. For more on barking, see "Listening to Your Dog" on page 139.

SEPARATION ANXIETY

This holds true for shelter dogs and puppies from breeders: Mike says that when you leave the house, you shouldn't make a big deal out of it. Grab your keys and go. Your dog will become used to this pattern and begin to feel more comfortable in your absence. When you get home, don't make a fuss when your sixty-pound dog greets you, or he'll understand this excitement as a reward for jumping on your leg. Believe me, your friends won't find it as cute as you do, and it's unfair to get upset with the dog when you essentially trained him to enjoy the attention. To help your dog feel secure when you leave, and to assure him that you're always coming back, use a gradual approach that's less jarring to a dog and to you, too. This measured process is just one reason why it's a good idea to bring your dog to his new home over a weekend—more ideally, with a few vacation days tacked onto the end.

Good News About Dogs with Special Needs

As with humans, dogs that lack one major faculty tend to compensate with others that shine. Mike says NSALA often sees blind, deaf, and three-legged dogs that are very resilient and adaptable. Blind dogs need a strict routine, but rely heavily on their noses and ears to make sense of the world. For instance, if a blind dog is in a house with barking dogs, he'll follow their lead. Deaf dogs can be taught hand signals for basic obedience and are especially receptive to reward training. Dogs with only three legs can go on to chase squirrels and compete as agility dogs, or if their back legs are missing or damaged, they can be fitted with custom aluminum carts. Mike says you don't need to be hesitant to adopt a dog with a deformity, disability, or injury, but most will require time with a professional trainer and a little patience on your part. In general, they bounce back very quickly.

Should You Keep a Stray Dog?

It may seem tempting to keep a stray, but this is unfair to his previous owner, who may miss him very much. Plus, you don't want to expose yourself or your pets to possible health concerns. A stray dog may have a contagious disease, fleas, parasites . . . It's also illegal in some states to take a dog anywhere but to a shelter, which will do its best to locate the owner. If you're really interested in keeping the dog, let the shelter know that when the stray holding period is up, it should contact you about adoption. (A stray hold could last anywhere from twenty-four hours to five days, depending on the city/state.) Because more dogs are likely to be abandoned than to simply wander off, like the unassuming dog from *Annie,* it's best to let an expert administer a professional temperament test before you commit to him. After the stray hold, the shelter will know if the dog has issues and can reveal to you the assessment results. At that time, you may consider adoption.

Afraid of Making a Bad Match? A Trainer, Behaviorist, or Shelter Can Help

Whether you purchase a dog from a breeder or adopt from a shelter, there may be times when he misbehaves and you wonder if you've made a bad match. When this happens, Katenna suggests that you call a professional.

Katenna says that if you need to improve your dog's manners or skills—like when he runs away, won't stop peeing on the rug, or turns your shoes into Jimmy Chews—call a trainer. If you are facing much more serious problems—like aggression, anxiety, or fear—contact a behaviorist.

In the vast majority of scenarios, Katenna believes that the problems you experience can be resolved with patience, time, work, and professional help. In some cases, however, the match between you and your dog may just not be the right one, and it could be time to contact your local humane society, animal shelter, or breed rescue group for advice on placing your dog in a new home.

Please note that most dogs that land in a shelter or are thought to be ill suited for a home are simply misunderstood: 50 percent "act out" because they're underexercised, 40 percent because they're not intellectually stimulated, and 10 percent because they're paired with the wrong owner. With proper training, your dog may become a better dog for you and him.

And Now, a Word About Your Future Pet

When you head out to find a dog and move into a new life chapter as his owner, please remember that having a dog isn't about possession—it's about nurturing a valuable relationship. As your dog's role model, you'll soon be asked to demonstrate trust, forgiveness, empathy, understanding, patience, consistency, kindness, and solid communication skills for your bond to grow and for your dog to truly respect and love you. This might feel demanding at times, but try to enjoy the process as much as you can! It won't be long before you and your dog mean the world to each other.

Ask Dr. Z!

What does it mean when my dog . . .

Q: *Lets out a sigh or a deep breath just before he goes to sleep?*

A: He's simply relaxing. This behavior would be similar to the sigh that you might make after you've had a hard day and are dropping into a lounge chair with a cold beer in your hand.

2

You're Getting a Dog!

Congratulations on making such a big, important, and life-changing decision! As a dog owner, you're about to join the ranks of people who personalize mugs, hoodies, and holiday cards with their dog's faces (and with only the slightest hint of irony). Owning a dog also means you'll become the most significant figure in an animal's world, so brace yourself for lots of licking, laughing, and loving ahead.

From here on out, I intend to fill this book with rights and wrongs about humane dog rearing based on personal experience, expert insight, and commonsense tips on raising your dog. Please know that following directions won't earn you a gold star, and there's no such thing as one "correct" way to rear your dog. If I've learned anything from our experts, it's that for every theory, there are at least two more that passionately challenge it. That said, your main concern should be to give your dog boundaries and affection that help him become an ideal pet *for you*. If you don't want to teach him fancy tricks, then don't. If you'd like him to snuggle with you in bed, then by all means, let him. But as you move forward, let your individual dog, personal priorities, gut instinct, and trainer's advice inform your judgment and decisions for a fantastic life together.

Shop for Your Dog Before He Comes Home

No matter what type of dog you decide to get, or where you decide to get him, please put things in order *before* he arrives. Prepping your home in advance decreases the inevitable upheaval of exposing an untrained animal to a new environment. Though you may prefer to wait on size-specific items like a collar, try to stock the house with as much as you can ahead of time.

To that end, I've asked celebrity dog trainer Steve Brooks, a certified personal dog trainer and founder of the reward-based training program K9U, to suggest must-buy items for your shopping list. He usually saves his advice for clients like Sheryl Crow and Robert Downey, Jr., but now you can benefit from it, too.

> **Crate:** A crate gives your dog a safe place to sleep at night and take unsupervised naps during the day. It also helps your dog relax, learn self-control, and master potty training. At some point in your dog's life, he'll need to be crated or confined (like at the groomer or vet), so teaching him tolerance now is important for good behavior in the future. At the start, don't bother with blankets or pillows for the bottom of the crate, since they absorb pee and odors. You can add these nuances once your dog is potty-trained.
>
> **Food bowls:** Porcelain and stainless-steel options are sturdy and sanitary. Don't use plastic bowls, which dogs can chew or destroy.
>
> **Collar and harness:** Invest in a buckle, head, or martingale collar in soft cotton, nylon, or leather. Buckle collars fit a dog's neck, while head collars loop around a dog's snout and behind the back of his ears to leave the neck free. A martingale collar won't

slip off a dog's neck if he tries to back out of it, since two rings pull snug behind his ears without choking him. Prong, chain, choke, and electric shock collars are not my or Steve's first choice (punitive collars should be reserved for special cases and as a last resort after more humane options have been exhausted). Also, no collar should be left on a crated dog, since it can become caught in the bars. Ask your trainer whether he suggests that you buy a front-attaching harness for your dog, especially if he's prone to trachea or neck issues, so that he doesn't feel choked should you accidentally pull on his collar. Harnesses also help you comfortably lead your dog on walks.

Leash: A six-foot leash made of leather, cotton, or nylon should do the trick. Stay away from retractable leashes, which can pull and snap (they also have weight limits, which some owners don't realize). I like the collars and leashes at FoundMyAnimal .com. All proceeds go to rescue.

D.A.P. plug-in diffuser: For puppies and full-grown dogs, dog-appeasing pheromones (D.A.P.) can help a dog feel less anxious, calmer, and safer—especially if he has vocalization, house-soiling, nervous, anxious, or destructive tendencies. Small enough to plug in to a light socket, D.A.P. mimics the properties of the natural reassuring pheromones of a lactating female dog.

Lavender spray or oil: Find a safe place to keep it, and burn or spray this natural relaxer to calm anxious puppies or rambunctious dogs before you put them in a kennel.

Bitter apple or tea tree spray: Spray these pungent "flavors" on furniture legs to deter biting.

Shampoo and grooming essentials: When it comes to products, Steve prefers all-natural options. During your first vet visit, ask which brushes and nail tools are best for your dog. (For Bianca's nails, I've always used a Dremel with the sander attachment. If you start using it while they're young, dogs won't freak out from the sensation and the noise.) Ask about ear solution, plus a canine toothbrush and toothpaste, and how to carefully use each. Studies say that brushing your dog's teeth can extend his life up to five years, so I brush Bianca's teeth at least four times a week. If you have a puppy, you can also ask about oral products to eliminate puppy breath. Note that mints and gum are out of the question, as is human toothpaste. All vet recommendations will depend on the dog's size, breed, and temperament. See Chapter 6 for a comprehensive look at how to groom your dog.

Baby gates: These are helpful for blocking off different rooms during or after training, with puppies and adult dogs. Baby gates should be made of plastic, wire, or wood.

Pooper scooper: It's illegal in many states not to scoop on the street. If your dog deposits in your yard, scooping will help you determine where your dog poops (you'll return to this area when potty-training him) and avoid ruining your shoes. Plus, some parasites can live in dog feces for an indeterminate amount of time, so you can avoid repeat illness by scooping.

Doggie bags: After you scoop, be sure to dump the doodie in environmentally safe bags. Experts estimate that it will take five hundred to one thousand years for plastic bags to biodegrade, which means that using these bags for poop will also keep the poop from decomposing. Look for earth-friendly bags that won't harm the environment, like Flush Puppies or FlushEze, which dissolve in the toilet.

Pee pads: Steve likes pee pads if you have a puppy younger than three months and/or if you have no regular outdoor access. Your goal, however, should be to teach your dog to use the bathroom outside the house. If a small dog must do his deed *in* the house, sod litter boxes for dogs are a fine option (you can even put them on a balcony). This way your dog won't ever confuse the pee pad with a throw rug or bathroom mat, and will learn to go on outdoor surfaces when he's outside.

Dog bed: A lot of puppies or new dogs will gnaw a bed to pieces. So until he's trained or you really know the dog's temperament, let him use the bed only while supervised—not overnight or when he's home alone. Eventually, a dog bed will become a safe "home base" for your dog outside the crate.

Premier Ultimate Puppy Tool Kit: Not that you want a lot more reading material, but puppy training and socialization are so specific that this additional resource will be tremendously helpful to have on hand. The kit includes socialization, games, junior obedience, and housetraining tips in six easy booklets. Buy it at pet stores, online, or at your local bookstore. Alternately, seek out puppy-training books at your nearest library or bookstore.

Three Types of Toys to Buy

Steve breaks dog toys into three categories that I've taken the liberty of renaming: owner-interactive toys, alone-time toys, and natural toys and chews. It's really important not to throw them all into an available basket for your dog to retrieve as he wants. This can cause unsafe, undisciplined, and understimulated behavior. Instead, rotate these toys out according to how you structure your playtime.

Bear in mind that dogs can choke on just about anything that will fit in the opening of their trachea, though the most typical culprits are small balls (like golf and squash balls), rawhide, real bones, cellophane, and children's plastic toys. Kong toys that aren't tough enough for a strong-jawed dog have sent many dogs to the animal hospital, too.

Here, Steve describes what toys qualify for each category, with the help of Melinda Miller—who consults with clients at Smith Ridge Veterinary Center in South Salem, New York, on diet and nutrition—to fill in a few blanks about which natural chews to buy and which to avoid.

Owner-interactive toys: These toys are anything your dog can swallow or destroy (think soft, squeaky, and small). With owner-interactive toys, your dog is allowed to retrieve the toy or carry it on a walk, but it is important that you control the games by initiating and ending them on your terms, not his. Supervised toys also protect a dog from potentially ripping or shredding the toy, or swallowing and possibly choking on a small chunk of it when you're not looking (your dog's stuffed hot dog seems durable, but hours of play can cause the toy to break apart). Keep your pet away from stuffed animals, too. To a dog, there may be little difference between this and your throw pillows or a favorite childhood toy, minus a price tag he can't read or respect.

Alone-time toys: This includes a Kong toy, which lets you stuff food inside it (peanut butter in a Kong can keep dogs busy for hours). Kongs are great for teething and solo playtime, depending on the toughness rating (Kong ranks its toys' destructibility, since some strong-jawed breeds like Labs and Boxers have been known to ingest them). Inedible Nylabones, which promote good dental hygiene, mental fitness, and positive behavior, also fit into this group. If your dog has a lot of energy, Buster Cubes and Kongtime dispensers keep him out of trouble: Buster Cubes hold food that tumbles out during play, while Kongtime dispensers automatically shoot out food-filled Kong toys while you're away. I also like Busy Buddy toys, a line of treat-dispensing chew toys. When the dog's home alone, they entertain your pet and give him something to look forward to beyond a nap. In addition to acting as a babysitter, they can also quell separation anxiety and keep dogs busy.

Natural toys and chews: Natural toys are great for your dog if you give him the right ones. Speak to your vet before giving your dog any natural chew, since they can cause diarrhea or vomiting in some canines. Most experts really like bully sticks (hard, durable chews that resembles thin sticks but are made from a bull's penis—they also help clean and scrape a dog's teeth); bully straps (like bully sticks but flat); and pigs' ears (natural chews that are exactly what they sound like). According to Melinda, bully sticks provide dental benefit and are easy for your dog to digest; in fact, the longer-lasting bully sticks yield a lot of psychological satisfaction for dogs, since chewing is a pleasing behavior for them. Bully straps are also an excellent chew, though they don't typically last as long as bully sticks. Pigs' ears are more of a treat than a chew, but as an occasional indulgence, they're fine.

What to avoid? Rawhides, since, unlike bully sticks and straps, they don't break down well in the digestive system and can cause obstructions. Melinda says that a lot of rawhide is imported from outside the U.S. and is "cured" with horrible chemicals, including formaldehyde! She adds that marrow bones are also a bad idea; they are made worse once they've been processed (cooked), since this makes them brittle—dogs can damage their teeth on them; plus, they're really fattening. When buying natural treats, note that they should always be big enough that your dog can't swallow them whole. Melinda notes that if your dog's a gulper, you may want to avoid natural chews altogether. As a dog owner, you should always be around when your pet is enjoying natural toys. Please realize that any kind of chew can be a problem in the right circumstance: raw bones, pet store bones, bully sticks, bully straps, etc. For more on natural bones, see "Is It Safe to Feed My Dog Natural Bones?" on page 284.

Ask Dr. Z!

What does it mean when my dog . . .

Q: *Chews bones or plays with his toys in play-bow position?*

A: The play-bow position is an all-purpose behavior that shows a dog is having a good time. It's also an invitation for others to join! A play-bow is when a dog's rear is in the air, his front legs are lowered, his eyes are relaxed, and his ears are generally up and forward.

BEHAVIORAL ISSUES AND NATURAL TOYS

In the past, experts have assumed that some natural toys create behavioral issues, like a predatory instinct in dogs. However, Melinda says this is a misunderstanding. A better way to describe the way some dogs guard and covet their treats is to compare the scenario to a human's relationship with money. Consider: if someone were to place a penny in your hand and then try to snatch it right back, you wouldn't really care because it's just a penny. But if someone put a hundred-dollar bill in your hand and then took it away, this time you'd very much "defend" it. After all, it's a hundred dollars! The bill has real value and is worth defending, so you'd be more willing to take a stand in order to keep it. Likewise, to a dog, a natural chew can seem like a hundred-dollar bill—something of "value" to them.

While natural chews like rawhide don't *cause* behavior problems, they are certainly a potential trigger for some dogs and should therefore be used with caution—especially around children or dogs you don't completely know, like a friend's dog or a dog you've just adopted. However, keep in mind that while many dogs won't guard anything at all, some dogs might guard items other than natural chews, like beds, bowls, toys, or even their owners!

Melinda adds that owners should be very careful when giving any dog that you don't know well anything that it can possess, especially if the dog has shown possessive tendencies in the past. This is especially true if children are nearby, since they are often unable to notice aggressive signals from a dog. If your dog develops this tendency, also called possessive aggression or resource guarding, address the issue with a behaviorist or trainer right away. *All* owners should have the ability to take *any* object away from a dog at *any* time.

Ask Dr. Z!

What does it mean when my dog ...

Q: *Gets scared and hides when there's thunder, lightning, or fireworks?*

A: Loud and unexpected noises can be frightening to dogs. This is especially true if early experiences with loud noises have been surprising or associated with other stress-producing events. You can work with your dog by gradually desensitizing them to loud noises. Look for a CD that features the sounds of firecrackers or thunder, and play it at a very low volume while the dog is eating. Over a few days, you can increase the volume, and the dog should begin to associate the loud noises with something good—like dinner! If this does not help, you may need to consult a veterinarian about a drug that could help reduce your dog's anxiety, and combine the drug treatment with desensitization techniques.

Puppy-Proofing the House

Puppies are curious and feisty, with a special knack for chipping at your heirlooms *and* your patience. Puppy-proofing isn't something you want to postpone until your dog has dug an escape route under the fence or chewed down the leg of your new couch. Countless experts say that if you can train yourself to see the house through the dog's eyes, your whole family will be better off.

The goal in puppy-proofing is to figure out which items may become chew toys or choking objects, then remove them from the puppy's path. Lifting electrical cords, moving small trinkets, and securing cupboards and toilet lids with childproof locks are all good ideas. If a puppy gets his mouth on risky items, an accidental injury could turn fatal. I once heard about a puppy who ate a pair of panty hose, and when he tried to throw them up, the nylons became entangled inside his digestive tract. A vet removed them during surgery, but had the dog's owner seen this as a risk, it could have been avoided.

Popular puppy-proofing fixes include moving toxic houseplants like philodendrons and poinsettias to a place your dog can't reach them (for a full list of toxic plants, go to ASPCA.org), running cables under carpets, concealing wires behind furniture, using plastic cable covers, covering exposed cables, and lifting small objects out of a dog's reach, especially those that cause choking, poisoning, and intestinal blockage—such as yarn, ribbons, rubber bands, coins, pencils, shoes, socks, and children's toys.

Medications, automotive and cleaning supplies, and tobacco products (nicotine gum, cigarettes, tobacco, and patches) can also be lethal to dogs, so these should be put away, too. Dogs have a determined ability to jump, paw, or strategize to remove items from low tables and shelves, so place potential risks on high ledges or behind cabinets and doors. This includes trash cans, which can contain hazards—especially in the bathroom. Feminine products and dental floss are particularly problematic, because they can expand, absorb body fluids, and wind around organs.

Unattended tubs and sinks full of water are drowning risks. The word "unattended," here, is the essence of puppy-proofing. Don't leave your puppy unsupervised, but if you do need to leave him, put him in a dog playpen or gated-off area. Keep windows and doors shut or blocked with a screen or gate. Stairwells, porches, and raised decks should be sectioned off, too. A simple guideline is that if you wouldn't allow an infant access to an item or area, you shouldn't grant it to a puppy, either.

Adult Dogs Require House-Proofing, Too

According to Greg Kleva, trainer and behavioral therapist for Bark Busters and host of the Sirius XM radio show *It's a Dog's Life*, adult dogs that are brought into an unfamiliar environment need to be taught what is acceptable and what is off-limits in your home. Transitioning to a new environment can create anxiety and stress in any dog, which may cause him to act out when you're not looking, so it's smart to puppy-proof your home for adult dogs, too. (Though most dogs tend to act out when they first enter a new home, sometimes a dog will take about two weeks to settle into his home before he relaxes into displeasing behavior. Puppy-proofing for adult dogs will minimize potential problems).

With puppies and adult dogs, you can return the items in your home to their original place a little at a time, with supervised trial and error. Be patient and gentle when teaching an adult dog his new boundaries, giving him time to learn. Don't expect a dog to catch on right away, since his prior home may have had different rules than yours.

Ask Dr. Z!

What does it mean when my dog . . .

Q: *Acts like I've been gone for weeks when I come home after being out for only a few hours?*

A: Dogs don't wear wristwatches, and they can't tell time. They don't know how long you've been gone. Each time you leave, to them it is forever—and when you return, it seems like a miracle.

Collect Your Contacts
Before You Need to Use Them

Research a vet, trainer, dog walker, and kennel before your dog comes home, since life will become hectic very quickly. For each of these, I highly recommend asking dog lovers in your community for suggestions, plus checking references for each expert. Write all names and numbers on an emergency-contacts page that can be affixed to the fridge or over your desk, then added to your cell for when you're on the go.

Vet

Scope out the healthiest and happiest-looking dogs in a nearby dog park or among your friends (search for energetic dogs, with bright eyes and a shiny coat), and ask owners which vets they like best in the area. If you survey at least three people, names will begin to overlap, and you'll know who to seek out and who to ignore. Dog owners have strong opinions about who cares for their dogs and will be more than happy to share names with you. Or you can visit the websites for the American Veterinary Medical Association (AVMA) at AVMA.org; American Animal Hospital Association (AAHA) at AAHANET.org; American College of Veterinary Internal Medicine (ACVIM) at ACVIM.org; American College of Veterinary Surgeons (ACVS) at ACVS.org; and American Holistic Veterinary Medical Association (AHVMA) at AHVMA.org for referrals. Finding a good vet is vital, since this person will monitor your dog's health for years to come. He'll also recommend specialists if your dog needs to see a surgeon or acupuncturist. Consider your vet a GP of sorts, and ask about a twenty-four-hour dog hospital in the area in case he's not available during an emergency.

BE SURE TO BRING:

A fresh stool sample

Paperwork and health records from the breeder, shelter, pet store, or previous owner

A list of any questions or concerns that you may have, as well as descriptions of any health-related issues you may have noticed

Trainer

The easiest and most efficient way to find a trainer is to ask a friend, neighbor, breeder, breed club, local humane society, boarding kennel, or groomer for a referral. Do not assume that a trainer's membership in a dog trainer association qualifies him as a suitable instructor. According to the Humane Society of the United States, no government agency regulates or licenses trainers, so research a trainer's qualifications before you hire him or enroll your dog in his class. What is the trainer's experience? How was he educated? What methods does he use? The Association of Pet Dog Trainers (APDT) can also suggest a trainer in your area at APDT.org. I prefer reward-based training, since no trainer should endorse yelling, jerking, hitting, or aggressive handling. Your dog should listen to you because he wants to, not because he has to, and your trainer should refer to you as a "leader," "role model," "guardian," or "parent," relative to your dog. The Association of Pet Dog Trainers, the International Association of Animal Behavior Consultants (IAABC), the Delta Society, the American Society for the Prevention of Cruelty to Animals (ASPCA), the American Veterinary Society of Animal Behavior (AVSAB), and the American Humane Association (AHA) all have formal positions and/or publications that support humane dog training methods, if you'd like to investigate this topic further on your own.

BE SURE TO BRING*:

Six-foot leash made of cotton, leather, or nylon

Flat buckle collar and/or harness

Treats

Favorite toy for motivation

Optional: long leash for distance and recall work (ask your trainer about length, since this can range from twenty to a few hundred feet)

*Most trainers provide new clients with a list of items they'll need for their first meeting; if yours doesn't volunteer this, ask about it! The above, however, will get you started.

Dog Walker

If you're not home during the day, ask friends and neighbors for suggestions or research your town's dog walking services online. The National Association of Professional Pet Sitters (NAPPS) website, PetSitters.org, is a good resource. Before you meet with potential walkers, determine whether you'd like your dog walked alone or with others. It's more expensive for your dog to walk solo, but if he likes extra attention or is better behaved without other dogs to compete with, you have options. You should also decide if you'd like a short (potty) or long (exercise and potty) walking schedule. Certification from NAPPS is a bonus. Since your dog walker will have keys to your home, be sure he's trustworthy, reliable, flexible, organized, and puts your dog's safety and happiness above all else. Like a reliable babysitter, a great dog walker can be a lifesaver.

WHEN YOU DO MEET . . .

> *Provide the dog walker with a feeding schedule,*
> *special instructions, and a daily journal to record:*
>
> > *What your dog ate (food and non-food)*
> >
> > *Unusual physical problems (if he limped, licked his*
> > *paws obsessively, etc.)*
> >
> > *Unusual behavioral problems (barked aggressively,*
> > *had a skirmish with another dog)*
> >
> > *Bathroom habits (how often did he pee and poop and*
> > *the times of each)*

Boarding Facility or Kennel

A lot of dog walkers are affiliated with boarding facilities, so you can kill two birds with one stone here. Others will privately watch your dog when you're away (my friend's dog walker even sleeps with her dogs when she goes on vacation). If you prefer a kennel, check it out first to decide whether it's right for you. Clean kennels that offer safety, security, sanitation, health care, and exercise are basic requirements. Also make sure the kennel has a relationship with a veterinarian, and check for accreditation from the Pet Care Services Association (PCSA), formerly the American Boarding Kennels Association (ABKA). Their website, PetCareServices.org, is another good place to research kennels in your area.

WHEN YOU DO MEET . . .

ASK ABOUT:

- -

> *Cleanliness*
>
> *Ventilation*

Roominess

Comfortable bedding

Whether dogs are separated by size

Feeding schedules

Regular exercise

Bathing and grooming, if necessary

Access to outdoors

Walking routine

Required vaccinations

Also, you may want to take your dog on a tour of the facility before you board him, and pay close attention to how he reacts to the environment.

A Word About "Helpful" Websites

A careful online search for dog-related resources in your area should be a starting point and not your only stop or last resort. I'm almost willing to bet that there are as many dog-related websites on the Internet as there are dogs in this world, so please be selective about where your fingers roam. Generally speaking, keep an eye out for 1) any mention of bogus or unseasoned associations and 2) websites that appear to recommend an edited list of professional services but are truly filters for pet care advertisers. Read through a few sites to learn how to discern which are credible and which are best deleted from your bookmarks. Use common sense: the site's design and the specificity of the info it offers are two cues as to whether its advice and affiliations are trustworthy.

What does it mean when my dog . . .

Q: *Yawns?*

A: Sure, yawning can mean a dog is tired. But it can also be a sign of stress. If you have company or the dog is visiting a new location when he yawns, it means that he is feeling stressed out and you should cut the visit short or provide him with a quiet place to chill. Yawning can also occur during sessions with a professional trainer. If your dog is being taught new rules and learning a new dynamic from a stranger, he can feel anxious.

Break Old Habits Early On

Bringing a dog into your life is a terrific reason to change your bad habits, since smoking two packs a day or leaving your garden untended can be just as harmful for your canine as it is for you. Studies say that it takes about twenty-one days to develop new behaviors, so it's never too soon to start addressing the following vices in your own life in order to become a more careful role model for your pet.

Stop smoking: Dogs can have allergic reactions to secondhand smoke, and being repeatedly exposed to cigarette smoke also diminishes their natural pep. According to the American Legacy Foundation, which funds research about tobacco use, secondhand smoke impairs the ability of an animal's heart muscle to convert oxygen into adenosine triphosphate, which is used for energy. It's been linked to nasal and lung cancer in dogs, too, and when exposed to secondhand smoke, long-nosed dogs were more than twice as likely to develop nasal cancer as those with shorter snouts (though these dogs are certainly susceptible, too).

Don't be a slob: An old coaster left on the table or a remote stuffed between the sofa cushions can quickly become a chew toy if you don't pick it up. Lift electric cords, and put away cleaning products before your curious pet gets to them. Remember, too, that leaving dirty socks and underwear around makes you unsanitary *and* negligent. Old take-out containers, especially those made from plastic or Styrofoam, are very dangerous.

Weed your garden: Before you introduce a puppy or a full-grown dog to your backyard, be sure it's properly tended. You may want to fill in holes, which could easily become the start of an escape route for ambitious diggers. Also, uproot all poisonous plants, such as hydrangea, foxglove, and Boston ivy. For a complete list of toxic plants, visit the "Animal Poison Control Center" page on ASPCA.org.

Be a good "role model": Since you're the one researching dogs, you will probably become your dog's leader or role model. Without you as his leader, this position could otherwise be assumed by anyone—another dog, neighbor, housekeeper, nanny, or dog walker. While the people who interact with your dog should be expected to help with and reinforce training, *you* should be the designated teacher of manners. You'll also be the one to teach your dog that he can't destroy things when he's left alone and that he will need to be housebroken to earn rewards.

Don't be a pushover: Rules about furniture use are the hardest to maintain and enforce, so decide what your position is on this before you get a dog, and stick with it! If you decide to let your dog sleep in your bed or hang out on the sofa, it's best to grant this privilege once your dog has mastered basic manners and potty training.

Ask Dr. Z!

What does it mean when my dog . . .

Q: *Sleeps in the closet since we had a baby?*

A: Dogs are natural den animals. The baby's arrival probably resulted in a variety of schedule changes and even changes to the home environment, with the addition of cribs, playthings for the baby, and maybe even a new sleeping space for the dog. The closet is like a little cave or den where the dog can feel safe from the crazy and very sudden stuff that's happening in the home.

On Your Dog's First Day Home, Make a Positive First Impression

It's normal to compare your relationship with your new dog to the dog-owner bonds of neighbors, friends, family members, or even dogs you've owned in the past. But this judgment—and the accompanying self-doubt—won't do you any good. Instead of focusing on your dog's shortcomings, get to know how your personalities mesh. What games do you two like best? How is your bond really special? How does he make you proud?

My trainer friend Greg Kleva says the most immediate way to

connect with your new dog is to crawl inside his head. This isn't about acting like a dog. It means realizing that dogs will never understand life from our human perspective, so it's your job to look at it from his. Such thinking should limit your frustration and create a better relationship with your pet. It took me about a year to really understand Bianca's habits and behaviors, but now I often feel like I can read her mind.

In this section, Greg addresses some of the more typical questions that owners have about their dog's behavior on the first day home.

How do canines think?

Dogs make choices based on what works and what doesn't, according to rules you enforce. When dogs misbehave, they're not doing it to be "dumb" or "spiteful." These are human terms, and dogs don't know what they mean. Dogs want to be part of a family that meets their needs and makes them feel comfortable. So when your dog jumps on the linen sofa, it's not because he wants to test your patience; he does it because you're part of the same family, and since the sofa is where you sit, he thinks it's where he sits, too (plus, it's comfortable). Same goes for when dogs beg to eat from the table. They don't want to take something that's yours; the table is where food comes from, and it smells yummy. Try to understand why your dog makes the decisions he does, so you can curb behaviors you don't like. It's okay to feel frustrated in your first few weeks together, but you can't blame the dog for too long if he's not behaving. It's your job to enforce the rules for your house.

Will we bond immediately?

Some new dog owners treat their new dogs like new family members of the human variety, which can confuse the dog and force owners to be too critical about their initial bond. Remember that attachments take time, and dogs need to learn your verbal and body language first. So if a dog dodges hugs, it doesn't mean you chose the wrong dog because you're tactile and he isn't. It means that he innately finds them overbearing and potentially threatening, but eventually he can be trained to accept hugs from you. Bear in mind that throughout your relationship, your dog will use your actions to shape his behavior—all while trying his best to make sense of your feelings.

How should I first greet him?

Body language sends strong messages to a dog and can signal calm or confidence. Erratic physical moves like finger waving, pointing, or rushing toward a dog may make him jumpy. Your tone of voice can do the same, so use light, happy tones when a dog makes a good choice, and lower, more guttural ones to correct his mistakes (dogs growl in a low pitch, so they read negative commands better from humans when they're spoken in a voice that's low pitched). When you first meet, your voice and body language will establish your role as the leader who influences behavior.

Will my dog tell me what he wants?

He'll definitely try! Since a dog or pup comes into your life with an established personality that's foreign to you, your instinct may be to accommodate him. But if you let your dog tell you when he'd like to be touched, fed, walked, and played with, he may see himself as the rule maker. The funny thing is, your dog doesn't *want* to be a leader; he wants someone else to enforce the rules so he can feel safe. It's similar to how children need sleep, potty, and feeding schedules, plus social boundaries. Without boundaries, children feel disoriented and act out—and so do dogs.

Name Your Dog

After interacting with your pet for a few hours, Greg suggests giving him a name that reflects his personality, appearance, foibles, or quirks. Be creative, and have fun! Just choose a name wisely, because it's natural for strangers to initially judge your dog by his name before they get to know him. Moms sure don't want their kids petting a dog named Killer . . .

▶ Some experts recommend a two-syllable rule, though Greg says that dogs initially respond to the sound and rhythm of a name and not always the word itself. Fun two-part names like Charlie Brown, which can be shortened to Charlie, are a great way to get around this strict rule.

▶ Choose a name that doesn't sound like other words, including terms you'll use to teach him manners. "Clown" may be too similar to "down," which can confuse your dog. If you must name your dog Clown, use another word for the "down" command. Also avoid names that sound like the names of other pets or people in your family. If your son's name is Joe, avoid the name Bo, etc.

▶ If your shelter, rescue, or inherited dog comes with a name you don't like, you can change it. (Bianca's breeder gave her the name Reba, but that changed the day we brought her home.) And if this *new* name doesn't resonate, try another one; have at least three in mind, so you can try them all. If you purchase your dog from a breeder, tell him the dog's name in advance so he can use it from birth.

▶ Use a happy vocal inflection when saying your dog's name. When he responds by looking up, making eye contact, or walking toward you, reward him with lots of positive feedback, like a treat, verbal praise, and/or affection. Dogs don't have a sense of self, so they need to know that when they hear their name, something good will happen next; this makes them want to respond.

▶ Never overuse a dog's name or use it in a negative way. When he associates his name with repetitive, harsh, frustrated, or punishing tones and situations, he'll become less likely to respond.

▶ Give your dog a nickname to use when you talk about him in the same room; this way he won't think you're speaking *to* him. A nickname will also help his real name retain its value.

▶ When training your dog, always use his name in conjunction with commands and happy tones: "Bianca, come!" "Good sit, Bianca!"

NEED NAME INSPIRATION? CONSIDER USING YOUR FAVORITE . . .

Sweets: Clementine, Ginger, Snickers

Cartoon characters: Ariel, Daffy, Sully

Musicians: Floyd, Mick, Bruce

Designers: Marchesa, Louis, Calvin

Book characters: Atticus, Huck, Eloise

Divas: Mariah, Beyoncé, Aretha

Strippers: Bianca, Candy, Cristal

Grandfather names: Seymour, Martin, Lester

Grandmother names: Ethel, Carmella, Eleanor

Flowers: Daisy, Petunia, Posey

Silly Names I Love

Bianca isn't the most feminine dog, so sometimes it surprises people that her name is so girlie. Maybe it's because of her that I always smile when I meet dogs with unexpected names, like a poodle named Steven or a Great Dane called Tiny. I've collected a few other names that make me laugh. I hope you like them, too:

Winnie the Pooch	Air Jordan
Jennifer Lopez	Argus
Boozer	Dracula
Sushi	Woofgang
Smelly Pickle Juice	Charles Bark Lee
Barstool	Lowke (as in "low-key" for a laid-back dog)
Cannoli	
Bob Fosse	Baron Bartholomew Von Oontyhausen
Fancy Pants	
Useless	Princess Pigster

Your First Day Together

Although you'll want to throw a party when your dog finally comes home, your first day together should be relaxed, calm, and relatively uneventful. Greg says that you don't want to overly excite your new dog, especially since he'll already be stimulated and a little confused by such a strange but interesting turn of events. A few suggestions:

▶ Bring your dog home over a weekend or extended break. This will give him a few days to become comfortable with his new family. Your dog will need time to acclimate, because he won't know where he is, who you are, and how the pieces fit until you show him what's appropriate.

▶ Realize that your new dog wants you to lead and will appreciate a routine as soon as you can provide one. Dogs crave companionship, so use his attentiveness to show him the lay of the land.

▶ If your dog is from a shelter, take him for a long, calm walk outside your home to introduce him to new smells, sights, and sounds. Next, walk him around in your yard on his leash.

▶ If you got a puppy, *only* guide him on a leash in the backyard. He won't have all his vaccinations when you bring him home, so stay within a secluded outdoor area to keep him healthy.

▶ When you bring your dog inside, keep stress levels low. Let him sniff around and meet family members at his own pace. On a leash, guide him to various spots in the house: show him his water and food bowl, walk him through his sleeping area, and guide him in and out of the door you'll use to housebreak him. Establish your dog's new home as a place of safety, calm, and comfort.

▶ Once you've given the dog a tour, partition off a small but main room with a gate, and finally take off your dog's leash. Sit on the floor, play with a toy, and spend time with your dog in the gated-off area. Keep activities light and fun, with no pressure to perform. Call your dog's name with light, happy tones and pet him gently. When you reach for him, use a cupped hand and softly pet beneath his chin. This will help your dog recognize your smell. Avoid hovering or other actions that your dog may interpret as menacing. Hugs and kisses may intimidate him while things are still new.

▶ In the gated room, introduce your dog to his crate during playtime. Keep the door open, and encourage him to go in and out of the crate with toys, treats, and other positive associations. Do *not* shut the crate door. (If this room isn't where the dog will sleep, move the crate right before bedtime.)

Ask Dr. Z!

What does it mean when my dog . . .

Q: *Runs and hides from laundry?*

A: A dog may be associating laundry with the noise and clamor that's caused by the washer and dryer. This is the dog's way of avoiding the commotion that he associates with it.

▶ After playtime, guide your dog back toward his eating area and fill his water dish. When your dog eats, he does not need to be on the leash. (Adult dogs typically eat twice a day, while puppies eat three or four times a day. Larger breeds that are prone to a gastrointestinal condition called bloat may be given multiple daily meals to help deter it.) Establish a consistent routine in the following days so your dog knows when to expect his meals. Your vet or trainer can help, as all dogs are different.

▶ Begin to put your dog to bed in his cage or kennel about fifteen minutes to a half hour before you usually go to bed. This allows time to address any of your dog's anxieties before you both turn in.

Never Take Your Eyes off a Puppy (or Adult Dog, in Some Cases!)

Puppies are wily and mischievous, though new adult dogs can also be very nosy animals. For this reason, please don't take your eyes off your new dog, especially if he's still young. If your puppy isn't with you, he should be eating or inside his crate. Otherwise, experts say that he should be on a leash, tethered to a table leg near you or to your body (for some training regimes), or in a crate that lets him stand up, turn around, and lie down at all times. Playing, grooming, and feeding are obvious exceptions. Keeping a puppy close will cut back on the number of ways he can misbehave. For instance, he can't roam, chew, pee, or act out under your supervision. In addition, puppies and small dogs should never be allowed under beds or couches or in other tight spaces, since they can be full of harmful objects to lick, chew, swallow, or choke on.

Your Dog's First Night Home

Whether you've brought home a puppy or adult dog, his first night with you is also his first night without his mom, littermates, or shelter-mates—in a new environment, no less. Greg recommends how new doggie parents can help their new pets get a good night's sleep:

DO: *Keep him close*

It can be very stressful for your dog to be in an unfamiliar new space—and then left alone in another part of the house. Let him sleep in your bedroom for at least the first few weeks he's home, even if you don't want him to sleep there for good (if he doesn't seem upset, crate him in the room he'll eventually sleep in; but more often than not, a new dog will want to be near you). Place his crate within arm's length of your bed, with the door closed, so he can sense you're nearby. Hang your hand over the crate to help him adjust, since dogs huddle together when they sleep. He'll stop whining sooner this way.

DON'T: *Worry that he'll sleep here forever (unless you want him to)*

Once your dog sleeps through the night in his crate, begin to make small transitions each subsequent night toward the room where he'll eventually sleep. Move him first toward the door, then to the hallway, and then to the landing on the stairs . . . until you've moved the crate to where you want it to stay. As your dog becomes better trained, get a feel for where he prefers to sleep. Does he retreat to small spaces, like his crate? Is he happier on a cool kitchen floor?

DO: *Make your dog feel comfortable*

A warm water bottle and ticking clock wrapped in a blanket or towel is a great tool for puppy comfort, because these items mimic the body heat and heartbeat of a littermate. (Note that the clock should stay near but outside the crate so he doesn't eat it.) Your trainer may also know where you can find stuffed animals with heartbeat simulators and microwaveable beanbags to keep a new dog company. When you pick up your dog from the breeder or shelter, ask if you can take one of his blankets or toys to help ease the transition from old bedroom to new. The familiar smells will trigger fond memories.

DON'T: *Assume he'll sleep in your bed*

Before you let your dog sleep in your bed, make sure he realizes that a queen-size mattress is a privilege, not an entitlement. If he takes over the space or pushes your legs into an uncomfortable right angle, move your dog to the floor until he respects his position above the covers.

DO: *Expect your puppy to whimper and whine*

If your puppy makes a fuss, take him out of the cage and carry him outside. He may be telling you that he needs to use the bathroom. During your first few weeks, consider sleeping in sweats or keeping flip-flops near the bed so you can scoop him up and take him outside quickly. Puppies experience a brief window in which they feel a pang in their bladder, and then they relieve themselves.

DON'T: *Throw a party, play together, or overly encourage your dog when he uses the bathroom in the middle of the night, or else he'll think the whine-'n'-pee routine is worth revisiting for fun.*

Instead, quickly praise him and put him back in the crate. If it turns out that your puppy didn't need to go outside, let him cry it out. Most puppies will stop in fifteen minutes or so.

DO: *Expect your dog to find your sex life fascinating*

Having sex with your partner will excite a canine of any age, but not because he's randy or thinks you look good naked. Your playful movements, unexpected noises, and the strange smell of sex are what make your dog want a closer look.

DON'T: *Let him watch*

Dogs love a good wrestling match, so he'll either sniff curiously or want to jump in on the action and take control of the scenario. Your dog doesn't think your partner's hurting you, but he does think it's time to play. Give him a Kong in another room to keep him busy while you get busy.

DO: *Tire your dog out*

The more physically and mentally stimulated your dog is, the more he'll relax during the day and sleep soundly at night. As the bumper sticker says: A TIRED DOG IS A HAPPY DOG . . .

DON'T: *Expect him to do this without your help*

Games and training exercises help to exhaust his brain and body until he's ready for bedtime, but unless they're acting out of frustration or stress, few dogs will exercise on their own.

Ask Dr. Z!

What does it mean when my dog . . .

Q: *Circles his bed, or turns around in it, before settling down for sleep?*

A: This is a common behavior among animals in the dog family. There's no clear sense of purpose behind this circling— it may simply be to make the place where they lie down more comfortable. Think of this as being similar to fluffing your pillows before *you* go to bed!

How to Introduce Your Dog to Other People and Other Dogs

The right introduction can make or break the comfort level between the new people and animals in your dog's life. Kim Guerin, owner of the pet care service Loving Your Dogs, gave us some meet-and-greet tips, and Greg weighed in for good measure.

Meeting Other People

Greg says dogs should spend their first several days with only their immediate family unit. This allows them to feel settled into their new environment. If your friends and family insist on meeting your dog, limit group activity to two faces at a time. While you may want to instantly invite your friends and family over to greet him, a large welcoming committee may frighten him into a stressed-out state.

When an outsider meets your dog, Kim says to ask him to not reach over or pet the top of your dog's head, since some dogs perceive this as a threat. Instead, ask that he greet the dog with a cupped, open hand, and gently rub under his snout or muzzle. This way your dog can smell the sweat glands on the stranger's hand and identify him by his smell. If your dog backs up, your visitor shouldn't force himself on the dog. Feel free to inform your friend that dogs like to be stroked behind their ears and on their chest, shoulders, cheeks, and face. This will put your friend in good standing with your pet!

Kim says it's important to gradually teach your dog that his new world is safe and enjoyable. To avoid behavioral problems, she suggests socializing a puppy (after he's fully vaccinated) at play-training classes, dog parks, or private playdates. Introduce him to new sights and smells during walks and backyard games. Just be sure to use caution with an adopted adult dog, since you're new to his behavior and quirks.

Because your new dog will follow your example, set an overly good one for everyone who enters and exits your home. Greg notes that an overly excited greeting on your part can encourage your dog to pounce on you, guests, and the delivery man. Be respectful of your guests, and teach your dog to stay down.

Meeting Other Dogs

There's no easy way to predict which dogs will get along best with yours before they meet. Most people assume that size and breed point to compatibility, but this isn't necessarily true. And if a large dog is too exuberant or rough, different sizes can cause safety issues and physical damage to the smaller dog.

Your dog will look for body language cues from other dogs, so Greg says it's best to match the energy levels of two dogs when you set up playdates (energetic with energetic, calm with calm). It's a myth that large dogs are afraid of small dogs and that small dogs think they're big dogs.

Before you let two random dogs sniff each other, Kim says you should first ask the other dog's owner: "Is your dog friendly?" If the answer is yes, say, "Hi!" and exchange small talk while your dogs get to know each other. Do not feel like this is an intrusive request, and always be honest about your dog's temperament.

Dogs are territorial, and they like to take care of their home and family. So if you want to introduce your dog to a friend's dog, or if you plan to send your dog to a sitter who has his own dog, Kim suggests first letting all dogs meet outside the home and on neutral territory: down the street, outside the gate, or in a dog park. Also avoid walking the two leashed dogs right up to each other and then standing still. This greeting can be too intense for the dogs. Instead, walk the two dogs side by side, down the street, and allow them to sniff around until some of the novelty and stress has worn off. At that point, you can allow them to really stop and sniff each other. Without this initial meeting, the home dog's instinct will be to protect his family unit, and the new dog may cause him initial anxiety when entering the picture. When dogs show they're happy and don't see each other as a threat, bring both dogs into the home. Here, one dog will establish who is boss in a healthy way; you'll know that all is well by the dogs' relaxed eyes and body language.

If one dog is aggressive with the other and a fight ensues, see "How to Break Up a Dog Fight" on page 165 for more on how to safely and confidently intervene. I don't want either you or your dog to be hurt because you were too afraid, unaware, or intimidated to step in.

You Know Your Dog's Happy When He . . .

Pants and smiles (it sounds funny, but you'll know a smile when you see one!)

Relaxes his body language and facial expressions

Wags his tail enthusiastically, horizontally, slightly lowered, or so it thumps on the floor*

Body hair lays flat

Lies with one paw tucked under him

Gets into the play-bow position: rear end up, front end down, tail wagging

*Note: don't assume all tail wagging is good. A lowered wagging tail in conjunction with a lowered head, direct stare, closed mouth, held-back ears, and wide-open eyes is a warning to back off.

Dominant Dog, Submissive Dog

When two dogs meet each other, experts say that they immediately establish rank as either the dominant or submissive animal. And if you can read your dog's body language, you'll be able to forecast the two canines' behavior and intervene on your own dog's behalf if you sense trouble.

A dog's tail, ears, eyes, neck, and posture are very telling of his intentions. If you feel you need to make a move, be careful not to pull your dog up and back to restrain him if he's on a leash; this may lift an otherwise submissive dog's head and carriage, which will appear to challenge an already dominant dog.

Easy-to-Notice First Impressions

Staring: A dominant dog stares directly at a submissive dog; the latter averts his gaze and exposes his neck. A dominant stare, head high, with rigid neck and motionless body all point to dominance.

Head high: The dog that holds his head higher as two dogs approach each other is considered dominant; the submissive dog must lower his head and refrain from eye contact. If they make deliberate eye contact and challenge each other with raised heads, the meeting can end in a fight.

More Typical Dominant Dog Clues

Staring down another dog

Tail up

Ears up

Growls at another dog's movements, no matter how innocent

Puts his chin on other dog's shoulders

Puts his paws on other dog's back

Tenses his muscles

Sniffs the other dog

Urine marking (peeing on an area to establish his territory via scent)

Overmarking another dog's urine (peeing over another dog's urine)

Mounting

MORE TYPICAL SUBMISSIVE DOG CLUES

Ears flat and back against head

Head down

Tail down or between his legs

Eyes look away

Rolling over with belly up and exposed

Licking lips

Looking to owner for guidance

Submissive urination (peeing when he feels powerless, intimidated, and/or fearful)

Lifting one paw

Your First Trip to the Vet

Make an appointment to see your vet within the first two weeks of your dog arriving at home. In an ideal world, your vet will double as a mentor and friend at all times. During your first visit, he'll cover lots of territory that'll help you avoid harried calls and frequent follow-ups, and invite you to ask questions. Before all visits, I like to jot down questions about Bianca's health on a pad of paper so I can remember to ask them; I also write down everything the vet tells me so I can review it later. The process keeps me on track and slows down the vet so he doesn't overload me with information. Sometimes it's even helpful to bring a friend or partner; four ears are better than two!

With the aid of Kenneth D. Fischer, DVM, of the Hillsdale Animal Hospital in Hillsdale, New Jersey, I've listed a few talking points for your first visit that should make sure all bases are covered.

ASK YOUR VET ABOUT: *His time*

Most vets consider fifteen to thirty minutes the norm for a first visit, though Dr. Fischer spends at least forty-five minutes with a dog and his owner during their initial visit. If your vet is of the speedier variety, ask the staff and other techs at the vet's office to answer questions your doc doesn't have time for. I'm a fan of extra attention from veterinarians, especially since owning a new dog can be a lot to handle. Guidance from an objective source who knows good from bad, and normal from abnormal, is invaluable.

ASK YOUR VET ABOUT: *Medical provisions*

Your vet will provide you with a specific vaccine and booster schedule, but your dog should receive his first round of shots at eight weeks, his second at eleven or twelve weeks, and his third booster at fifteen or sixteen weeks of age. Since there are several diseases that rarely exist anymore, some vets offer only distemper and parvovirus vaccines; and given that so many diseases are geographically determined, let your vet tell you which boosters your dog will need in the future. You should also let your vet know if your dog attends day care, a boarding facility, or dog parks so he can suggest the necessary vaccines. During your visit, your vet may administer a liquid topical flea and tick medicine that is absorbed into your dog's skin to repel and/or kill fleas and ticks. After that, it's up to you to do this once a month (ask your vet to suggest a brand, or see "Parasite Control" on page 202 for advice). And no, you can't just get away with giving your dog a flea collar to wear in woodsy areas. If he wears one around his neck, it doesn't do anything to discourage fleas that make a home near his tush.

ASK YOUR VET ABOUT: *A stool sample*

Your vet will want to check for worms and parasites, so bring a fresh stool sample from that morning, or one that's been refrigerated for no longer than twenty-four hours. This will be studied for parasites or small worm eggs. If your vet finds parasites in your dog's stool, pick up past and future poops from the yard soon after he deposits them. Some eggs resist environmental breakdown from rain and sun, so the parasites will keep their family's life cycle going for as long as they exist in your yard, which can lead to recurring problems for your dog. (Don't allow your dog to sniff random droppings from other dogs on the curb and in the park, since these can also transmit harmful parasites.)

ASK YOUR VET ABOUT: *Dog-to-human conditions (zoonotic diseases)*

Zoonotic diseases, the term given to conditions that are transmissible between animals and people, are worth a quick talk with your vet. Many of these diseases are most harmful to young children and people with existing medical conditions, but some can affect anyone. There are two types of zoonotic diseases: those that can be transmitted from dogs to humans (like leptospirosis, a disease contracted through infected urine; ringworm and giardia are also common zoonotic diseases) or diseases that infect both pets and people (like Lyme disease). You can't catch a cold from your dog (they have their viruses, and we have ours), but it may be foolish to kiss your puppy on his snout after he's licked his bum. Most infectious diseases prosper in specific geographic areas, so ask your vet about this.

ASK YOUR VET ABOUT: *Spaying and neutering*

As Bob Barker insisted on every episode of *The Price Is Right*: "Help control the pet population. Have your pet spayed or neutered!" Ask your vet when to have these procedures done, especially if you have a female puppy, since a female dog should be "fixed" at approximately six months old to lower her risk of mammary cancer and eliminate her risk of ovarian or uterine cancer. If you miss this window before her first heat, schedule an appointment to have her spayed when she's finished her cycle. You'll know she's coming into heat when the folds of her vulva become puffy, she licks her private parts a lot, and a small drop of blood hits the floor. Your dog may need to wear dog diapers during this time, since her period can be messy; however, some dogs experience "silent heat," which means they have subtle or nonexistent signs. Schedule a spaying at least six weeks after she starts spotting.

The larger the breed, the older she'll be when this happens. Male dogs can be neutered at any age, though your vet will recommend when it should be done. Spay and neuter your dog early on for optimal health and behavioral impact; for more information, see "Spaying and Neutering," on page 198.

ASK YOUR VET ABOUT: *Housetraining*

Your vet will explain how long your dog should physically be able to refrain from going potty until he can go outside and what your dog should expect from you as his teacher. (Dr. Fischer says the longest most dogs can wait between bathroom breaks typically correlates to the number of hours the dog can wait overnight without relieving himself. Waiting longer than seven hours on a regular basis can result in a urinary tract infection or worse.) Talk to your vet about bladder strength for your dog's specific age and breed. Please note that your dog requires more intense training and socialization from a trainer or group class, but your vet is the first education opportunity you'll have to really ask important questions.

Ask Dr. Z!

What does it mean when my dog . . .

Q: *Sniffs crotches?*

A: To dogs, sniffing crotches is like saying hello and asking, "Baby, what's your sign?" Dogs can seek and gather a wide range of information by sniffing. Here, they're looking for a way to associate the sniffee with one of his/her many smells.

ASK YOUR VET ABOUT: *Nutrition*

Vets mostly talk food when asked about dry versus canned, or if a dog is experiencing a health problem related to his diet. Yet as with humans, much of a dog's wellness is tied to nutrition. If diet is important to you, consider a vet with holistic interests in fresh, frozen, and raw foods. Holistic vets consider the dog's evolution as it relates to his health when creating a food plan. Ask your vet for his take on nutrition and where he suggests you start. If you'd like to stick with more traditional vets and their dog food suggestions, be sure to ask the vet about a feeding schedule for your dog. These can vary depending on a dog's specific size and age. For more on how to feed your dog a healthy and well-balanced diet, see Chapter 5 on nutrition.

ASK YOUR VET ABOUT: *Teething*

By the time a puppy is eight weeks old, he has thirty baby teeth. But around four to five months old, he'll start to lose them all and grow up to forty-two teeth until he's six to seven months old! That's a whole lot of change and soreness in a short period of time, so ask your vet to confirm when your dog needs to start chewing soft toys and frozen ropes to ease irritation, rawness, and occasionally bleeding gums. In the meantime, know that allowing your dog to gum hands and fingers while he's young can lead to a bad habit when adult jaws are stronger; and stay away from hard plastic toys that can damage teeth, since dogs need a little give in order to massage their gums. Your vet may also suggest washcloths that are soaked, wrung out, knotted, and frozen to sooth your dog's mouth, and small bowls of chipped ice are a cool comfort. Contrary to popular belief, any shoes and socks are a bad "toy" idea, since puppies can't distinguish between old and new Converses.

ASK YOUR VET ABOUT: *Vomiting and diarrhea*

Puppies vomit a lot, so don't be scared if yours does, too, but do tell your vet about it. Your dog will spend a lot of his puppyhood licking and eating random stuff off the floor that isn't food, so "floor scores" are a likely source of stomach upset. A puppy can also vomit from an immature digestive tract, so his body may not be able to handle the food you're giving him (ask your vet about changing it). If your puppy has diarrhea, bring a stool sample to your vet to check for parasites and consistency. Because few diagnoses are concrete, keep your eyes and nose open for upsets even after your dog is home.

ASK YOUR VET ABOUT: *Your dog's feet, face, and ears*

These three sensitive areas need to become familiar to human touch, so ask your vet to demonstrate the best ways to handle each part. To make nail care a breeze, start to handle your dog's feet at an early age to avoid jumpiness when it's time to clip and file. With your dog's face, familiarize him early on with having his mouth pried open, plus teeth and gums examined, should anything become stuck in his teeth or across the palate. Ask your vet how to check for a yeast smell or ear infection by lifting the ear flap, turning the ear inside out, and wiping it clean. You'll want to do this after you visit the groomer or give your dog a bath.

ASK YOUR VET ABOUT: *Grooming*

Some dogs require more grooming than others to maintain their coat, but try not to bathe your dog more than twice a month, since bathing strips protective oils from his fur that keep it shiny. Save frequent washes for skin therapy with medical shampoos, and even then, only at your vet's request. Also review toenail filing or clipping tips, if you plan to do it on your own, during this visit.

ASK YOUR VET ABOUT: *Teeth cleaning*

Every regular exam should include a quick dental exam. This may introduce the need for dental cleaning under mild anesthesia, about once a year, though not every dog will need it this often. The regularity of dental cleanings varies from dog to dog, since frequency is due largely to the dog's natural defenses against dental disease (genetics) and how much care you provide at home. Dog owners should actively engage in preventative dental care, which involves any or all of the following: toothbrushing, dental rinses (some are simply added to your dog's water), protective gels, appropriate chew toys, or prescription dry food with a mild abrasive that helps clean teeth. For dogs that amass more than a normal amount of tartar, special dental diets help keep teeth clean. For most, brushing every other day is the best way to help your dog avoid dental disease and tooth extraction. Ask your vet to show you how to brush your dog's teeth, and be on the lookout for bad breath; yellow-brown crust on teeth; a change in chewing or eating habits; red or bleeding gums; loose, chipped, broken, or missing teeth; a change in behavior; or uncharacteristic drooling, which are all signs of dental disease.

How Often Should You See the Vet?

After the first trip, visit your vet at least twice a year to help detect, treat, and prevent health problems before they become serious. Disease prevention is based on your pet's lifestyle and the threats in your area, though biannual checkups are helpful, since owners tend to "save up" their dog's problems during the course of a year, which can result in overly involved visits down the road. When you compare what a vet does to what a human PCP does, the average vet can be presented with a year's worth of problems that might require the care of additional specialists. It's unrealistic to think that one person can take care of so many problems in one trip, so if you sense something is wrong, make an appointment.

ASK YOUR VET ABOUT: *ID'ing your dog*

Some owners have their dogs microchipped so they can be easily reunited if their dogs get lost, which I highly recommend. It can be done when your dog is spayed or neutered. During the quick procedure, an alphanumerical, scanable chip (it's the size of a very large rice grain) is implanted under the canine's skin between his shoulders. I had Bianca microchipped, and I've never regretted it. However, some holistic vets feel that it raises the possibility of cancer. Discuss this with your vet, and if you're wary, consider an ID tattoo as an alternative. This consists of numbers and characters, and the sequence is registered with a national database; the dog's ink appears on his ear (inside the flap) or inner leg. *All* dogs should also have an ID tag on their flat buckle collars, with their name and owner's phone number.

ASK YOUR VET ABOUT: *Emergency clinics*

Your vet may not always be around if your dog is sick on weekends or during off hours. Ask him what you'll need to do in an emergency, i.e., whether you should call the vet directly (often on his cell or pager) or go to a specific emergency clinic or hospital. As veterinary medicine becomes increasingly sophisticated, specialists and emergency practices have become more prevalent. Program the clinic's number into your cell, keep it posted by your home phone, and provide it to anyone who cares for your pets.

ASK YOUR VET ABOUT: *Pet insurance*

A multitude of plans are available, so shop around for one that accommodates your dog's age, treatment needs, and any preexisting conditions. The ASPCA claims that the cost of veterinary care has more than doubled over the past ten years, while specific treatments like surgery and chemotherapy have risen even faster. Health insurance protects your pet in case of accidents and illness, and it covers routine preventative care from licensed veterinarians such as dental cleanings and vaccinations. Reimbursement fees vary, and some come with a money-back guarantee.

Keep a Health Folder

Keep all your vet records in one place. I like to store the following in a small portfolio.

Registration, identification, and pedigree records

Rabies and vaccination records

Microchip information

Dog photos

General health and wellness pamphlets and information

Health insurance records

Helpful dog articles pulled from magazines

Vet receipts and miscellaneous forms, papers, and pamphlets

3

Training and Behavior

A lot of dog owners think that housetraining, crate training, and teaching your dog manners are the three most important things you can do for your budding relationship. And in many ways, they're right! But the problem is that they *stop* at the how-to part and never take the time to learn about the behaviors that motivate their dog's actions. So once he's trained, what causes accidents? And if he's often quiet, what does it mean when he barks? Without some background on dog behavior to complement training, too many confusing scenarios can send innocent dogs to shelters. And when you commit to owning a dog, I believe you commit to raising him to be a great family member—not a boarder whose behavior is "good enough."

When Howard and I got Bianca, I had no interest in raising a good-enough dog. From the start, we considered her part of our family, and that required teaching her the manners and boundaries she'd need to feel secure in her new home; plus, we had to learn her natural tendencies in order to understand the methods behind her occasional mishaps. So you can do the same, I've asked experts to review training and behavior basics here, but you'll need to go deeper on your own and with your trainer, since you'll want to use techniques with your dog that speak to his specific personality.

I will say, however, that whether you work with a private trainer or enroll your dog in a class, make sure the program includes verbal communication, reading your dog's body language, and behavior modification (techniques used to change a dog's undesirable actions for the better). Visual communication like special hand signals is also helpful, and an absolute necessity if your dog is deaf. Avoid trainers who believe in dominance-based training, and find one that uses caring words and positive reinforcement to coach your dog to practice good manners. Essentially, you want a trainer to show you how to be a predictable and trustworthy leader or role model for your pet. A good trainer also teaches you how to speak the same language as your dog, using a shared vocabulary and various communication techniques. Though training can be expensive, it's the best money you'll ever spend. If you're interested in less expensive options, ask a shelter volunteer about potential classes at rescue facilities in town. She may even host or teach a training class herself!

How Nature and Nurture Influence Training

A dog's personality, as we typically think of it, is established at birth. In a litter, says Mary Burch, PhD, CAAB, an animal behaviorist with the AKC, there will always be the active, outgoing puppy and the quiet, subdued puppy. These traits will stay the same for the dog's lifetime. But even among purebred dogs, no breed trait is set, and Dr. Burch says that socialization plays a very large role in the types of behaviors your dog demonstrates throughout his life. As your dog's owner, you can identify certain behaviors you don't particularly like and, with training and reinforcement, change them.

For example, you can teach a very active, athletic dog that evenings are for cuddling in front of a movie. A quiet, subdued dog can be taught that playtime is fun, thanks to running and play training. Agility training is a great confidence builder in timid dogs, and if your dog is leery of other people, exposure to strangers will improve his reactions to those he doesn't know.

The fact that puppies are "hardwired" to have different personalities, just like their owners, is the reason that responsible breeders and shelters do temperament testing to match pups and dogs with the right owners. It's also the reason that you should spend time with a good trainer to make the most of your dog's breed traits. For instance, we may think of a Maltese as clingy and docile because people carry them as an accessory. However, Malteses also make impressive obedience, agility, and therapy dogs because they come from an intelligent and warm breed.

Ask Dr. Z!

What does it mean when my dog . . .

Q: *Chases his shadow?*

A: Some dogs are highly predatory, and moving shadows will stimulate their chase behavior. Their visual system is especially sensitive to moving shapes. A high prey drive, anxiety, and boredom may also contribute to this behavior.

Housetraining Your Dog

Howard and I were lucky enough to acquire Bianca after she'd been housetrained, but I know from training our family dogs when I was young just how challenging this process can be. What's more, housetraining requires as much effort and discipline on your part as it does the dog's. With the help of Stacy Alldredge, owner of Who's Walking Who dog obedience and behavioral training, I've laid out below the factors that influence potty training—but talk to your trainer about customizing these tips, since every dog, owner's schedule, and home environment is different.

Scheduled Food and Water

When housetraining, most trainers suggest putting down food and water for only a half hour during each of the dog's regular feeding times, then picking them up until his next mealtime. This may seem like a limited window to eat and drink, but if you leave food and water down all day, his belly will remain full, and he'll never learn to "hold it." Stacy says that if you schedule all food and water, you can better monitor your dog's input/output. However, I'd prefer that you ask your trainer about the water part, because dogs' needs vary (for instance, dogs that live in hot climates or require a lot of exercise may need to drink more). Once your dog is housetrained, Stacy says he should always have access to fresh water; you'll want to establish a lifelong schedule for food at this time, too.

During housetraining, small or young dogs need to eat three to four times a day, while large or adult dogs over twelve pounds can eat twice a day. Do not give your dog food or water three to four hours before bedtime, but if you're housetraining your dog during the summer, or if

Smart Dogs Aren't Always Easier to Train

If you chose a dog based on his breed's perceived "intelligence," you may be in for a challenging training experience. Just because a breed is deemed smart doesn't mean the dog is highly trainable. According to Julie Shaw, an animal behavior expert for the Animal Behavior Clinic at Purdue University's School of Veterinary Medicine, trainability simply means a dog's desire to learn. In fact, the dimmer the dog, the easier he will be to train: He won't react to every single cue—both negative and positive—that he receives from humans and animals, which can confuse the process.

there's no air-conditioning in your home and it's warm outside, give your dog ice cubes and use common sense about his thirst level.

SET A HOUSETRAINING SCHEDULE FOR YOU AND YOUR DOG

▶ When you first wake up, take your dog out for a quick pee and poop. Use a verbal prompt, like "Go potty!" or "Hurry up!" until he does his deed. To teach him these terms, say them while the dog is going to the bathroom, so that he associates the word with the behavior. These cues will help your dog know when to act on a command in the future, the same way that "sit" urges your dog to sit and "stay" prompts your dog to stay.

▶ Give your dog ten minutes to use the bathroom. Once he's successful, calmly reward him with praise and gentle petting—and, if your trainer suggests it, a treat—to show him how well he's done. Too much excitement may distract him. Don't bring him in until he's done number one *and* number two (he should poop once or twice a day).

▶ A dog may not go on command right away. If this happens, bring him back inside to a garage or apartment lobby, not into the actual home, and wait fifteen minutes. Take him out a second time, and repeat the process if he doesn't go. It may take him up to three days to catch on.

▶ After he goes, let your dog play freely in your home for fifteen minutes while you get dressed.

▶ Give him food and water. Once he's finished, take him outside again to relieve himself, then guide him to his crate just before you leave the house for the day. He should always use the bathroom before entering his crate to avoid accidents there. (I'll discuss the role of crates in housebreaking later in the chapter.)

▶ Take your dog out as frequently as his age dictates. In general, puppies need to go out every three hours, while adult dogs go out every four to five. If you can't meet these needs, a reputable dog walker can be a great support during housetraining. Note: The number of times your dog will need to be taken out depends on his breed, age, size, diet, and temperament. In general, know that puppies need to use the bathroom four to eight times a day. Also, it's better to be proactive about taking the dog out more often to start, then scale back to your dog's individual bladder needs—versus spending the housetraining period cleaning up accidents and wondering where you went wrong. If it helps, keep a notebook with your dog's hit-and-miss potty times to track and adjust progress.

▶ Once your dog is trained, he should have four opportunities to use the bathroom each day, including a walk in the morning and a walk at night before bed.

▶ Remember, *short potty walks aren't exercise.* Exercise your dog according to his temperament, age, size, and breed.

▶ Train your dog to go to the bathroom on various outdoor surfaces. While he's still young, introduce him to grass, grates, pavement, and mud. Some dogs innately hate the rain, but if you're calm during rainy walks, he'll feed off your energy and become more tolerant, too.

▶ Train your dog to do his business on or near the curb. Nobody likes to step over puddles and smudges in the middle of the sidewalk.

What About Pee Pads?

Pee pads are popular among urban apartment dwellers who have small dogs, or owners who don't have regular access to the outdoors. I should mention, though, that Stacy finds them unsanitary in the long term (they're also expensive). A dog's natural instinct is to live in a clean environment, and using pee pads past three months of age may cause him to confuse the pad with a rug. If you start with pads, your trainer can show you how to transition the puppy from going potty indoors to always going outside. Or, if your dog doesn't have regular outdoor access for the long term, try a litter box for canines. These can even be placed on balconies if you live in an apartment building (just make sure your balcony is safe for your dog!).

Bear in mind that your dog won't like to eat where he potties, so if you do opt for pee pads, you should put them far from his dog bowls and separated from the food area by a wall (and out of sight for guests and young children). Change them after a few pees or one large pee. Your dog won't want to use an overly saturated pad and will seek out other alternatives if you don't provide a clean place for him to eliminate. Regular changing also minimizes the urine odor.

How a Healthy, Balanced Diet Affects Training

The healthier your dog's diet, the less output there will be from the dog. A lot of canned and dry foods sold in grocery stores are high in salt, which makes dogs drink more water. Canned foods can also contain a high amount of moisture, which can make your dog pee a lot. If your dog is having digestion problems, he may also experience constipation or diarrhea, which may require changing his diet. See Chapter 5 to learn how to choose a dog food that's right for your pet. If problems persist, ask a vet for advice. (Low-quality foods are often packed with indigestible fillers, which makes more—and stinkier—poop!)

While we're on the subject of diet, be sure to change your dog's water a few times a day (I change Bianca's up to five times a day), and always provide fresh food during his designated mealtime, even if your dog didn't previously clean his plate. Food that's left out can become crusty and inedible, not to mention harbor bacteria and mold. This topic affects training because your dog needs to learn when and how he can rely on fresh water and food, relative to his body's impulses.

Clean House

Stacy says it's never a surprise to her that dogs with *housetraining* problems tend to have owners with *housecleaning* problems. The cleaner your environment, the easier it is to housetrain a pet. Immediately tidy any accidents your dog has, so he won't seek out the area a second time. And while this may seem obvious, Stacy says a lot of people become used to their dog's feces and let them sit for a while (yuck!). Dogs have an innate desire to be clean, so they won't eat or sleep where they've used the bathroom; it's one reason that housetraining works. Leaving trash, clothes, or other random stuff on the floor can also slow the housetraining process.

Ask Dr. Z!

What does it mean when my dog . . .

Q: *Occasionally snubs me when I ask him to come?*

A: The good news is that your dog's not a snob. The bad news is that there's a good chance he doesn't have a great recall response. If there are sights or sounds distracting him, he may not respond to the call. Keep working with your dog until he comes when you call him—all the time.

Verbal Praise

When your dog correctly uses the bathroom outside, lay on heaps of calm congrats. In light, happy tones, commend him with a "Good potty! Good potty!" or "Good girl! Yay, Bianca!" Positive reinforcement right after a job well done confirms good behavior. Stacy says this is one instance when you should not reward with food, because it can stimulate another bathroom use. Some trainers disagree on this last point, so you'll want to ask yours what he prefers, but if you do use treats, it's best to stick to nibbles the size of your pinkie nail.

Yard Training

Dogs in training should never leave the house independently or be left outside alone. When housetraining, take him into the yard so you can be there to praise him when he does his good work. To celebrate, let your dog off the leash to run around (as long as you're in a secure fenced area). Leave his previous poop on the grass to stimulate his next potty; this way, your dog will recognize the area's smell and location the next time he goes out, and he'll soon consider it his designated pooping place. When your dog makes a new poop, scoop up the old one. (Localized potties also keep your dog from sending you on a hunt for his feces, which happens if the entire yard is fair game).

Accidents

If you come home to an accident, Stacy says you should tweak your dog's schedule. It's your responsibility, not your dog's, to make his housetraining work. Do you need to take him out longer or adjust his schedule or food portion? Remember that accidents are very normal during the first few days, because the dog's routine is still new, and with puppies, their bladders are still small. But if you're concerned that your dog's accidents aren't training-related, or if your previously trained dog suddenly starts having them, ask your vet to rule out health issues like bladder infections or parasites.

Should you catch your dog squatting in mid–pee stance, calmly but firmly say no or use another stop command (some people like to clap their hands once). Quickly pick your dog up and take him outside, praising his final potty. Ask yourself: When was his last walk? When did he eat? Stacy says it usually takes about two to three weeks of vigilant housetraining before your dog is aware of his schedule. Be patient.

Don't punish your dog if you don't catch him in the act. Your dog won't know what he did wrong, and sudden discipline may create anxiety. Never yell, hit, rub your dog's nose in the mess, or point or wave your finger at your dog; threatening him while he's still learning right from wrong will make him more nervous. Use positive affirmation only: it really works!

Cleaning an Accident

Everyone makes mistakes, but not everyone's mistakes smell like pee or poop. To discourage future accidents in the same spot, experts suggest neutralizing the area by lifting the smell from your floor entirely.

Clean the carpet or floor as soon as you see the problem, so the smell doesn't soak through to the rug, its pad, or your wood floors. Not only does an accident smell bad to you, but it also encourages your dog to continue peeing in this area. When cleaning pee from your floor, rug, or carpet, use a solution with pet-neutralizing enzymes to kill the smell (I like Nature's Miracle pet stain and odor remover); it should not contain ammonia or vinegar, since these chemicals smell like urine to a dog. You should also avoid bleach, which is toxic to canines. Follow the solution's cleaning instructions, and shampoo or steam your carpet or rug again if the stain leaves a shadow or if the solution doesn't eliminate the problem. If you still detect a rancid scent, try steaming the carpet again to lift the odor and repeating the cleaning process. A Bad Air sponge can be used as a last resort since it will further absorb the smell in the immediate area, but alleviate the odor only for humans—dogs will continue to smell it and go to the bathroom there.

Crate Peeing

Experts say that it's not natural for your dog to pee in his properly sized crate, since dogs innately want to keep clean sleeping and eating environments. However, sometimes puppies will do this if they're raised in a pet store, dirty kennel, puppy mill, or other inappropriate condition. Speak to a trainer about how to resolve this issue, as it's likely individual to your dog.

Refrain from dressing the crate in bedding until your dog is housetrained, since this encourages urination. A crate that's too large and lets a puppy move around too freely may cause crate peeing, since jostling the bladder can stimulate his bladder; a crate that's too large also allows space for a sleep area as well as a potty area. A crate should be large enough for the dog to stand up, turn around, and lie down comfortably, but no larger. If you are crate-training a puppy, you may need to get additional crates as the puppy grows or limit the amount of available space inside the crate with a divider.

Not All Random Pees and Poops Are "Accidents"

Even after your dog is housetrained, he may have an unexpected potty mistake. For instance, experts say a dog that suddenly starts going to the bathroom in the home after years of doing it outdoors may have a medical problem, may have experienced a breakdown in housetraining, or may be undergoing some type of anxiety. If a dog eliminates only when you're away, he may have separation anxiety.

Observe your dog's behavior before and after the incident so that you can discuss it with your vet, in case his unusual bathroom use isn't a housetraining or behavioral issue. Is your dog lethargic? How often do accidents happen, and how much does he pee or poop? Do you take him out when he first wakes up and before he goes to sleep at night? Be as specific as you can about your dog's elimination habits in the event that your vet needs to prescribe meds or change your dog's diet. Spaying and neutering can also help with random elimination issues.

POINTS ABOUT ACCIDENTS TO KEEP IN MIND

▶ Inappropriate urination can be related to housetraining and urine marking, but no vet or trainer should ever suggest behavior modification without ruling out a medical problem first.

▶ Marking, stress, or old age can cause random pees. In the last case, you may want to confine your dog to a small area of the house during the times when he usually does this.

▶ If you suspect that your dog is marking from separation anxiety, call a behaviorist.

▶ Accidents may be due to an immature bladder, a urinary tract infection (UTI), or another health issue.

> ▶ A dark color, pungent smell, and small but frequent
>   urinations are signs of a possible UTI.
>
> ▶ Accidents can indicate that your dog may be drinking too
>   much water or eating too much moisture-rich food. Talk to
>   your vet about your dog's thirst because his accidents may
>   be masking a more serious problem.

Not-So-Happy Peeing

When a dog frantically welcomes his owner or visitors at the door with a tinkle, some people call this a "happy pee." Yet experts say the excitable pee is really a form of submissive urination and is not a housetraining issue but an emotional problem caused by how you and your dog relate.

Submissive urination is a way for dogs to tell us that they know their place is at the bottom of the family hierarchy, which they demonstrate by peeing when they feel intimidated, fearful, overexcited, and/or out of control. It can be an inherited trait or, more commonly, can come from being corrected too severely in the past—with loud, angry, or physical contact. The memory of this interaction may cause a dog to pee when he first sees his owner. Submissive urination occurs at the time of excitable greetings, arguments, guests entering your home, loud noises, and reprimands. It can also come with a naturally skittish personality, so be careful not to jump to conclusions.

If your dog makes a submissive urination, he may lack confidence. The best way to boost his self-esteem is to draw as little attention to the pee as possible. Ignore it, clean it up, and move on. The next time you enter the house, Stacy says, you should establish a calm and relaxed energy in the room. Calmly say hi, read the mail, and let the dog settle down before you engage him with a loving and gentle hello. Never correct submissive urination, since your dog could begin to associate greetings with negativity; that will only make him feel more nervous and, consequently, have more accidents.

Sneaky Peeing

Though it may seem that your dog is being sly or modest by sneaking a pee in the guest room or behind the sofa, the truth is that he may not see these areas as part of the house or even indoors. Because they're seldom-used spaces, your family hasn't established its scent here, and your dog doesn't recognize them as part of his family unit's home. A sneaky pee-er has learned not to pee near people, but he must be taught not to pee inside. You may see this sneaky peeing in adopted dogs that weren't properly trained in their previous home. Severe punishment, such as spanking or yelling, teaches dogs to fear and distrust humans, so it is never advised.

To avoid private pees, neutralize the smell as advised in "Cleaning an Accident" on page 110. Then spend time with your dog on the floor, in the exact problem area, to establish your scent. Because dogs don't like to pee where they eat, try feeding him in this space for a few days. Run through small exercises and tricks in this area to reestablish that the space is also "home." Don't forget to reward him in light, happy tones when he pees outside, to reinforce right from wrong. As with accidents, it's pointless to correct his actions after the fact. Train him to do better going forward.

Signs That Your Dog Needs to Go Out

How do you know when your dog needs to go? He'll exhibit one or more of these signs:

Walks in circles while sniffing the ground

Paces, can't sit still, looks uncomfortable

Sits near the door

Barks or whines

Stares at you

Pants heavily

Anus puckers

How to Retrain Your House-Soiling Dog

Dogs can experience a breakdown in housetraining for any number of reasons, some of which may be related to behavior issues. Here, Nicholas Dodman, BVMS, director of the Animal Behavior Clinic at Tufts University's Cummings School of Veterinary Medicine, explains how to retrain a dog when his accidents are not caused by a medical condition.

1. Take your dog out on a leash at regular times: morning, noon, evening, before bed, and when he transitions from one activity to another (for instance, sleeping to walking).

2. Walk him outdoors for fifteen minutes during each potty time while verbally encouraging him to focus on the deed with verbal cues. Don't let him become distracted by people or events on the street or in the yard.

3. Praise and reward your dog right away for pees and poops well done. Dr. Dodman suggests doing this with small treats that are of high value, so they're worth waiting to go outside for (some experts discourage rewarding with treats during potty training, however, so ask your trainer which rewards he feels are best.)

4. If your dog doesn't do his deed in fifteen minutes, bring him back inside and confine him for fifteen minutes, tethered to a furniture leg on a short leash or enclosed in a gated area, to prevent accidents. You can also attach the dog to your belt with a short leash for fifteen minutes. Take him outside again for fifteen minutes to try a second time. Repeat this process until your dog successfully potties where he should, then reward him with praise and treats, and give him some freedom somewhere in the house where he's still under your watchful eye.

5. If you catch him urinating in the house, create a loud noise (such as clapping your hands once) to distract him, then lead him outdoors to finish his business.

6. Properly clean the soiled area.

7. Please be consistent and understanding until your dog is properly housetrained again. Even older dogs that were never carefully housetrained in the first place can learn with great success!

Marking Territory

Stacy says dogs mark their territory on household items or outdoor areas like hydrants, street curbs, and garbage bags as a way of saying "mine!" When another dog sniffs the urine mark, he can learn a multitude about the dog that left it—including his age, health, and mating details (urine contains sex hormones). If marking happens inside the house, it's not a house-soiling issue. Dogs often mark to establish territory on a doorway or new furniture with an unfamiliar smell, Stacy adds. Dogs that feel stress may also mark, since it establishes confidence, and they can mark if they see dogs outside the window. Male dogs, dominant female dogs, small breeds, two dogs competing for dominance in a household, or unspayed/unneutered dogs are among those that mark most. Female dogs may also pee on an existing mark to claim territory (this is called over-peeing). Consult a trainer to help correct indoor marking if it's a persistent problem.

Ask Dr. Z!

What does it mean when my dog . . .

Q: *Stares intently into space as if he can see something I can't?*

A: This may happen when the dog hears or smells something that you are unable to detect. If there is no associated visual stimulus, the dog may appear to stare into space as he concentrates on the sound or odor. I know what you're thinking, but don't worry. You don't have ghosts!

Scratching

Stacy says that scratching is a continuation of scent marking. Dogs sweat through their feet, which are equipped with scent pads, so they'll often scratch their back paws on the ground to mark it. This usually happens after a dog pees or poops to emphasize their "I was here!" status. Howard and I stand clear of Bianca when she does this on the beach, or we'll get sandblasted. Our girl is one enthusiastic scratcher.

Crate Training

To a person, a crate may seem like a claustrophobic and uncomfortable place to relax and spend alone time. But to a dog, a crate is his "den"—and when you travel, it's his home away from home and a cozy place where he feels protected. The crate also serves as a housetraining tool, since dogs don't like to eliminate where they eat and sleep. Brandon Solotoff, certified master trainer and owner of Pets at Play Resort and Spa in New York City, says wild dogs like to burrow under rock crevices and in caves where it's cool. Before long, your dog will enjoy his crate in a similar way.

According to Brandon, a crate or kennel gives your dog a place to sleep and take unsupervised naps during the day. It also helps your dog reduce stress and learn self-control and housetraining. At some point in your dog's life, he will need to be crated or confined—like at the groomer or vet—so teaching him crate tolerance early on is important to good behavior in the future. Just don't blanket the bottom of the crate with too many soft throws or pillows until your dog is potty-trained, since they encourage peeing and absorb odor.

Ask your trainer which size and material will be best for your dog's crate—this likely will be based on your dog's breed, size, and previous home. Whether your dog came from a breeder, shelter, or pet store will impact the crate he needs for housetraining, since previous metal runs, wire crates, or private homes can all influence a dog's housebreaking aptitude. Brandon notes that dogs from pet stores are the hardest to train, because they were taught to use the bathroom in the same place that they slept—in their kennel. Since so many pre-you scenarios yield different housetraining regimes, help your trainer by asking your breeder or shelter where your dog was kept before you got him. This will limit your frustrations, too.

At night, initially keep your dog's crate in your bedroom. During the day, keep it in a central sunny location like the kitchen or family room so your dog is in the middle of activity. Push it against a wall, preferably in a corner. The crate's locale will be your dog's favorite spot once he's fully housetrained, since it's here that your dog will become most familiar with the sights, smells, and sounds of your house. Never leave a dog in an isolated area, such as a basement or laundry room (his loneliness could manifest in behavioral problems), and don't allow kids to play in the crate or bother the dog while he's in there. It's supposed to be a peaceful place where he feels safe and can be alone to unwind.

Ask Dr. Z!

What does it mean when my dog . . .

Q: *Buries bones or treats?*

A: This is a common behavior among wild canids, which tend to hide food or carcasses from other hungry predators like jackals and hyenas. Other times they simply hoard it for future consumption. Many domestic dogs retain the natural survival instinct to bury or cache food items so they can consume them later.

Choose Your Crate

Wire, metal, or plastic crates are all fine for puppies and adult dogs, though Brandon warns that some dogs can get their jaw or paws stuck between the bars of metal or wire crates, in the same way that a child's head can get caught between banisters. However, wire crates do provide plenty of ventilation and have a removable plastic tray on the bottom that's easy to clean. They usually fold up for easy storage and transportation, and they have dividers so you can adjust the size as your dog grows. Experts say you can cover a wire crate with a blanket at night to make it feel more like a den.

For puppies, plastic crates allow small squares of air and light to flow through, though they don't provide as much ventilation as wire crates. They create shade to keep dogs cool and cozy in the dark, which Brandon prefers. To help you decide which type of crate to choose, consider the amount of time your dog will spend there, plus the temperature of your home.

Once dogs are housebroken and crate-trained, most can graduate to a canvas kennel in six months if you'd like, but these aren't good for young puppies, since they can be chewed or destroyed. After your dog turns one (or if you've brought home a trained dog), move the canvas kennel to the next room over from your main living space so he can find solace in his private den. Brandon says that dogs love peace and quiet away from their owners; this is a relaxing break for you, too.

A housebreaking crate should be large enough for your dog to stand up, turn around, and lie down in. The goal is to limit the dog's space, since that will keep his bladder from expanding and contracting with movement. For a housebroken adult dog, buy a crate or kennel that lets him fully stretch out or lie on his back. Your head and torso should fit into this space, too. Initially hanging out with your dog in here helps reinforce the family bond.

If your dog digs, tries to escape his crate, or damages it in any way, don't just buy a sturdier crate. Contact a professional, because your dog may be experiencing a larger problem like separation anxiety or other behavioral issues.

Create a Relaxing Environment

Puppies sleep up to eighteen hours a day, so they use their crate a lot. Brandon suggests laying a shirt you've worn or a pillowcase you've slept on in the bottom of the crate to limit separation anxiety when you're not there. Although Bianca is grown now, I always leave the T-shirt I slept in the night before on her bed the next day, since it smells like me. Remember: don't add blankets or pillows to a dog's crate until he's housetrained; they only absorb smells and subtract from the cool feel of plastic under your dog's belly. Brandon likes to download CDs that play a dog's heartbeat, nature sounds, or even bass-driven jazz to lull the dog to sleep. He says that Nat King Cole, for instance, is a favorite among puppies and adult dogs because of the rhythmic bass that resembles a heartbeat. A subwoofer (your bass on the stereo) can also cause the floor and kennel to vibrate a bit, which helps the dog relax. Studies show that heavy metal, rap, and talk radio are not relaxing to pets, whereas soothing classical music, like Bach, has the most calming effect. A CD with city sounds or outdoor noises will help your dog feel more comfortable when he plays and walks outside, because he'll already feel familiar with them.

Experts say to feel free to leave the TV on while you're away, unless it's turned to Animal Planet. The sounds of other animals (especially barking dogs!) may trigger a response you aren't able to see, control, or understand. Bianca barks when she sees dogs on TV, so we leave the local news on for her when we go out.

Don't Leave Food or Water in the Crate

Some trainers encourage food as positive reinforcement, but Stacy says it can pass through your puppy's digestive system a little too quickly while he's still young and throw off your training agenda. A bone or stuffed and frozen Kong toy, however, will keep him occupied for hours in his private den. You can use a treat to lure him into the crate, along with a cheerful voice and lots of praise, to make the crate a positive space.

Never Use the Crate as Punishment

Your dog should view the crate as a happy place and a pleasant retreat, and for this reason, a crate should never be used as punishment. If your dog misbehaves or acts rambunctious when guests visit, don't put him in the crate to alienate him from the group. This only teaches your dog that when people come over, he doesn't need to behave. Instead, coach your dog on how he should greet guests. Put him on a leash and tell guests how to pet your dog (open hand, under the snout). When we meet dogs with an open palm, they can smell our sweat glands and identify us by our smell; if a dog backs up, he doesn't want to be touched. Believe me, your guests much prefer to experience a well-trained dog than to hear a crated one bark through a dinner party.

"But he's crying in the crate!"

Though your dog may whine or cry in his crate when you first introduce him to it, I tend to think of this ornery phase as the canine version of Ferberizing a baby. Hearing your child cry when you put him down to sleep is often harder on you than it is on him; similarly, hearing your puppy fuss can be harder on you than it is on him. He should stop in fifteen minutes if you don't give him any feedback. Putting your dog in his crate once he's tired will also move the process along.

What does it mean when my dog . . .

Q: *Chases his tail?*

A: This is usually a compulsive disorder (and a stereotype, in many cases). Some research with Bull Terriers suggests that tail chasing may be inherited, since compulsive tendencies are highest in breeds with a high prey drive. Frenzied tail chasing can also happen after neuter surgery or following a geographical move. Some dogs are affected when they're between five and nine months old, but a few develop the behavior when they are fully mature. Stressful situations may exacerbate the problem. It can become serious if the dog begins to injure himself while spinning.

Gates for Working Puppy Parents

If you work all day and can't come home every few hours, a crate is too confining for a puppy to stay in all day. Instead, set up a plastic, wire, or wood baby gate in a part of the kitchen or another small room so the puppy has room to play. This room becomes a supplement to—not a substitute for—crating when you're not home.

Brandon says to make sure the dog gets a good workout while you're outside together during his morning potty walk and before confining him. Then ask a spouse, friend, or roommate to take your puppy out during the day, if you can't afford a dog walker. Tell this person not to get really excited when she greets the dog, so your dog has an easier time being left alone again so soon.

Using a Gate to Teach Limited Access to the House

Brandon favors the following exercise that teaches your dog to live in your home without supervision. In two weeks, he should be able to handle an eight-hour stay alone and in multiple rooms of the house. Start this exercise on a Saturday, so you can fit in two days of training.

▶ Exercise your dog before leaving him alone.

▶ Give your dog the freedom of one room (or a half-room, depending on the size of your dog and home) that's been gated off with an exercise pen. This is a room separator made from wire or plastic that can bend to be made round, octagonal, or straight. Your choice of room shouldn't be a kitchen or bathroom, since we store too many chemicals in these areas.

▶ Split the room in half with the exercise pen, which needs to be stabilized against or between objects, so it doesn't fall onto your dog or something valuable in the house.

▶ Put your dog in the gated-off room with a few safe toys to keep him busy. Don't leave food in this area, but you can leave a bowl of crushed ice, which will quench a dog's thirst while you're out and give him something to play with.

▶ Leave your dog alone for an hour in his new play area.

▶ When you get home, calmly greet him as you would any other time you enter the house.

▶ If he's done well—seems calm, hasn't chewed furniture, hasn't scratched the walls, etc.—then you should repeat the one-hour duration two more times before increasing his alone time to two hours.

▶ If he does well for two hours three times in a row, then you can progress to four hours. Repeat the process, doubling the time your dog is left alone, until you reach eight hours or other desired (but realistic) time duration for this exercise.

▶ If you come home and he's misbehaved, cut the time in half and restart the process.

▶ If the dog gets into trouble while you're out, don't try to correct his behavior after the fact. Remove or cover whatever items he got into, and slowly reintroduce them in a trial-and-error way.

When your dog has mastered an eight-hour stay alone, it's time to expand the house.

▶ Start by giving the dog two rooms for eight hours. Use an exercise pen, baby gate, or wire gate to section off larger rooms. Do not include the bedroom, since this is where you spend most of your time, and therefore, where a dog will act out in your absence.

▶ If he does well, open two more rooms every eight hours. Do this each time you leave.

▶ If your dog doesn't do well, limit your dog's free space to one room.

▶ Use common sense when controlling your dog's environment by opening and shutting rooms, depending on his behavior.

What does it mean when my dog . . .

Q: *Poops in my husband's office after we fight?*

A: Dogs may poop when they're stressed, and they will usually try to avoid pooping in a place where they can be seen. It is likely that your husband's office is off-limits to folks most of the time, so it's a place where the dog can sneak off and poop without being caught.

Teaching Your Dog Manners

Who doesn't love a polite dog? When deciding on a trainer, training class, or written guide, look for options that primarily use reward and motivation techniques—whether it's affection, praise, clickers, food, toys, games, or anything that encourages a strong relationship between you and your dog. When teaching your dog manners, it's not so much about differentiating between good and bad as it is about encouraging love, trust, and respect. "Obedience" is a really loaded term, so let's just say that training should be about encouraging your dog to behave in a way that lets your family live in harmony.

Once you understand the basics of most humane training techniques, you'll start to see how easy it is to make smart and intuitive decisions about how to further a great relationship with your dog. I can't discourage you enough, however, from working with trainers who endorse or focus on dominance, force, fear, "hanging" (raising the dog off the ground by his collar), physical pain, social isolation, or emotional manipulation. These tactics are often—though certainly not always—used by the same people who lean on physical exhaustion, choke chains, prong collars, dominance rollovers, or stressful aggression of any kind. In my mind, a happy, well-mannered family member is preferable to a fearful, submissive pet.

Because there are so many training techniques in the world, and such heated debate about each (right down to who uses what commands, treats, rewards, cues, *oy*), it's really important to trust your gut when adopting a school of thought for your dog. Should you find yourself intuitively questioning a trainer, there's likely a reason for it. And if you sense that your dog is afraid, in pain, or not understanding the rules in a clear and happy way, it may be time to move on. You should also expect your dog to make realistic progress; over the years, I've learned that no training regime is black and white. If your dog doesn't seem to advance, expect your trainer to try customizing his techniques for your dog. Every dog, environment, training, and socialization period is very individual; and even when three dogs are from the same pack, each one's role and training needs can vary because they're simply not the same dog. Customized techniques will yield the most progress with your dog—second only to the patience, consistency, clarity, and follow-through that you'll provide. All your dog asks is that you be a supportive leader, so do him a favor and look for the good in his behavior. It's easy to notice when a dog does something wrong, but how often do you reward your dog when he's calm, content, and respectful?

Finally, I think books and DVDs such as Ian Dunbar's *Sirius Puppy Training* can be very helpful supplements to early, individual, or class training, but I don't advise them as the only means of dog training. In-person guidance is irreplaceable. Have fun with it!

Decoding and Debunking Dominance/Pack Talk

The term "pack" describes a group of dogs or wolves that live together. However, some trainers uphold the theory that your family unit, including all dogs and humans, is also one pack—and that humans must be the "alpha" of their pack in order to "dominate" subordinates. But for so many reasons, it's important to avoid trainers who support this archaic theory. Here's what Katenna Jones, CAAP, CABC, CPDT, a humane educator and animal behaviorist with the AHA, taught me about the subject.

Dominance-based training theory sprang from wolf behavior observations in the 1940s, and it led some people to assume that dogs acted the very same way as these animals. Such observations were made of captive packs that had been forcibly created by humans and resulted in unnatural, volatile pack behavior. More recently, observations were made of natural wild wolf packs, and it was discovered that the alpha-beta-omega linear hierarchy first observed was not an accurate description of wolf behavior, much less that of dogs. (Domestic dog behavior is far more fluid and far less linear.) Dominance-based training theory does little more than teach your dog to distrust, fear, and ultimately dislike you. In the end, the dominance-based training theory ignores ten thousand years of dog domestication, as well as the natural behavior of their wild ancestors. It also disregards current scientific research, which has shown that normal, natural pack behavior is much less aggressive and confrontational than once thought.

What This Means for You

Dogs are not wolves, and wolves are not dogs—even if your dog is an ancestral relative of the wolf (this thinking ignores thousands of years of domestication). And while some trainers like to refer to a dog's family unit as a pack, rest assured that your dog is fully aware that humans aren't canines, even if you do share the same family. After all, humans don't look, smell, taste, or act like other canines. And no matter how many times you refer to yourself as a pack leader, a dog won't treat you like a fellow dog, even if he lives in your home and sleeps in your bed. To wit: When was the last time your dog playfully grabbed your throat and pinned you to the floor? This is an example of normal pack behavior among dogs, but I sure wouldn't expect it from a healthy dog/owner relationship.

Rather than adhere to the wolf paradigm, think of raising your dog as one might parent a child. Love, consistency, guidance, predictability, structure, socialization, and health care are all musts for a thriving life. If your dog displays aggressive or another undesirable behavior, he's definitely acting out, but he's not tapping into his wolflike instincts. Contact a qualified professional who understands how to correctly train your dog without relying on force or fear.

Ask Dr. Z!

What does it mean when my dog . . .

Q: *Grabs underwear and tries to eat it?*

A: Underwear is a treasure trove of odors, especially to a dog that uses his nose and mouth to investigate objects. Sweat, pheromones, and other remnants of you are all over your undergarments. Though this behavior may seem amusing at first, you should discourage it in puppies and adult dogs, since underwear can cause GI issues if swallowed—or deeply embarrass an overnight dog sitter when you're not around.

How Can I Find a Dog Trainer?

Ask for referrals from your vet, family, and friends. Once you find a trainer, you should be comfortable talking about the details of your lifestyle without feeling judged or belittled. Never work with a trainer who mentions the word "guarantee" or one-size-fits-all methods, since there are so many variables in dog breeding, temperament, owner commitment, and experience—although an instructor can and should be willing to ensure satisfaction with his services.

For a lead on certified dog trainers, I'd start with the website of the Association of Pet Dog Trainers (APDT.com). Its member directory lets you research the requirements for certification, plus a member's skill and education level. To be accepted and certified by the APDT, a trainer needs to abide by their code of ethics. Because no certification is mandated by the training community, it's important to notice if your trainer is a member of any other educational organizations and whether he's pursuing ongoing educational opportunities. A conscientious trainer will stay updated about dog training innovations and behavior tools and techniques. This person should also believe that you can teach an old dog new tricks. It may take longer for a dog that's older than six months to learn or even relearn information, but it's doable!

The best way to assess your trainer is to gauge your dog's reaction to him. Is he sad to see him go? Did your dog seem like he enjoyed your time together? Are you seeing positive results? These are fantastic signs!

Choosing a Personal Dog Trainer

Personal dog trainers are more expensive than group classes, but with a personal trainer, you can make your own schedule and design training techniques that are specific to your dog. According to Katenna

Jones, a personal trainer will teach your dog basic manners and skills, including general commands. The trainer will also help with house-training and crate training if you need it. Consult your friends, vet, local humane society, and APDT.com for suggestions, and with each training candidate, please take some time to understand the different types of behavior and play-training techniques that are employed.

Choosing a Group Dog Trainer

In the mind of my friend Tamar Geller, best-selling author and game-based "life coach" for dogs, you should avoid classes that wave two red flags: dogs in choke collars and people walking in circles (literally).

Choose an instructor who uses training tools and methods with which you feel comfortable. The APDT insists that a skilled and professional dog trainer use humane methods that aren't harmful to the dog or handler, such as beating, kicking, slapping, shocking, or employing devices that cause stress, pain, or imminent physical harm. Cruel treatment includes choke collars, which inspire fear and pain during the

Ask Dr. Z!

What does it mean when my dog . . .

Q: *Sleeps all the time?*

A: Most predators focus their efforts on finding food and then mating. After that, they save up their energy for the next hunt, since activity uses energy and exposes them to possible dangers. This is a trait that's been carried over from wild to domesticated canids. Older dogs will sleep for much of the day simply because they're old. Changes in sleep patterns may indicate medical problems, however, and a veterinarian should be consulted if you're concerned.

teaching process. If at any point your dog isn't immediately receptive to your commands, examine what you or the coach may have done to miscommunicate intentions. Examine how your dog replied, and react specifically.

Tamar also says to avoid group trainers who focus too much on the "heel" command with collar-snapping techniques ("heel" basically means "walk beside me until I tell you to stop," and this is often done in a circular pattern). She finds this too regimented and prefers a group teacher who's flexible, uses games to have fun, and customizes her techniques to suit the individual needs of each owner and dog. She also suggests classes in which each owner and dog have a generous space for exercises that include standing, leaning, and lying down together. According to Tamar, you should choose classes that encourage a bond with your dog above all.

A good instructor will also insist that all puppies and dogs are vaccinated prior to class and will tell you which vaccines are required. You and your vet should be comfortable with the mandates. If you opt to go

---

Ask Dr. Z!

What does it mean when my dog . . .

Q: *Looks up at me as the trainer tries to teach him new tricks or manners?*

A: You are the one your dog trusts in this unfamiliar scenario, so he is looking at you for reassurance! Encourage him by giving praise when he does respond to the trainer. For the most part, both you and your dog will get the most benefit if *you* do the training under the guidance of a trainer. It's also important that other members of the family participate in training, so the dog is comfortable responding to people other than you (or the trainer).

Evaluate a Trainer Before You Take His Class

A competent dog trainer will use humane training methods that aren't harmful to the dog or handler. Ask to observe a session before you pay for a class, to make sure the instructor is approachable and adheres to the APDT standards below, even if he isn't a member. If I were you, I'd take this checklist to a class, rate the trainer on a scale of one to five, and if he rates lower than a four in any of these categories, express your concerns before officially enrolling. You have every right to question and learn more about training techniques that will be used on your dog.

A SKILLED CLASS INSTRUCTOR WILL

☐   Provide a clear explanation of each lesson.

☐   Demonstrate the behavior(s) that students will be teaching their dogs.

☐   Provide clear instructions and written handouts on how to teach the behaviors.

☐   Give students ample time in class to begin practicing the day's lesson.

☐   Assist students individually with proper implementation of techniques.

☐   Encourage dialogue and be courteous to dogs and human clients alike.

the class route, consider home-training your puppy with a book or DVD for the first month, since he won't be able to participate in a class until he has all of his vaccinations, and there may be a waiting list for attendance. Choose a class only if you have the time to attend every session, practice at home, and own a dog with no behavior issues. Look for a small class, unless the room has generous space and provides special attention to dogs and owners. Before you officially enroll, ask to attend a group class; this gives you the opportunity to ask clients if they're enjoying the experience and instructor, and if they feel their overall training goals are being met.

After your dog learns his basic manners and commands, you may want to look into group classes that encourage bonding, agility and advanced training, and socialization opportunities. For suggestions specific to your dog's innate breed qualities, see "Bonding by Breed" on page 377.

Ask Dr. Z!

What does it mean when my dog . . .

Q: *Sings or howls to music?*

A: Howling is a social gathering call for dogs. Some types of music may mimic the acoustic signature of typical dog howling, so your dog will join in, just to be social. Dogs have a much wider hearing range than humans (60 to 50,000 Hz, compared to 60 to 25,000 Hz for humans). They hear about as well as we do at the low end of the tonal scale, but they hear much more at the upper end. They will often react most strongly to high-pitched voices or instruments (think guitar feedback or fiddles). But if you reward his behavior with praise or happy verbal cues, there's a good chance he'll continue to do it!

Teaching Basic Commands

Tamar says that an adult dog's reasoning skills can be akin to that of an eighteen-month-old child, and science contends that dogs are more like toddlers than chimpanzees. To be honest, I'm not too surprised to learn that dogs can understand more than 150 words each, since I've met some pretty smart canines who can differentiate between their toys, bones, balls, and sticks—all because they identify words, tones, and cadences. Here are some basic tips from Tamar and my own experiences with Bianca:

▶ For everything your dog does, give it a name. If your dog drinks, say "water" when he drinks; if he stretches, say "stretch." Create a vocabulary for a running dialogue with your dog. This helps strengthen your bond and teaches him a very limited but mutual language. Try to consistently and carefully put these words to use at very specific times.

▶ Be exact about what you say, plus how and when you say it. Rambling doesn't compute with a dog. Use words he knows, at the exact time when you need him to know them. Repetition out of context can devalue a word, similar to what I said earlier about misusing your dog's name.

▶ Light, happy tones encourage activity, while long, drawn-out words like "gooood" either praise or sooth; and a low-pitched, growly voice connotes authority. The lower your voice, the more serious the command's intention. A low voice that comes from your chest mimics how dogs challenge each other. Practice various commands in appropriate tones with your trainer and dog.

▶ As with many people, yelling doesn't generate results. It only causes stress and dissolves trust.

▶ Give your dog a break. If he understands his commands 95 percent of the time, it's still impressive. Even the best professional baseball players get a hit only three out of ten times, and baseball is all they do!

Can I Send My Dog Away to Be Trained?

This really expensive option is surely preferable to not training a dog at all, but I don't think it's the best idea to send your dog to another person to train him for you. Katenna says that most behavior problems are the result of interactions between the animal, caregiver, and environment. So giving your pet to an expert to learn manners or "fix" a problem is rarely an ideal solution, because these three elements aren't addressed.

In an ideal world, all owners would work directly with their pets in their home environment. If you don't have time to train your dog, and you're committed to perpetuating the good manners and respectfulness that the trainer has introduced, then this is a fine solution. I'm seldom one to judge! But you must also be willing to earn your dog's respect by working with him when he gets home, since he'll have learned to see the trainer as his leader or role model. The far-from-home trainer will grease the wheels, but you'll need to be the one to see things through.

Six Behaviors Every Dog Should Know

You may use different words to name certain commands, but here are the standouts that every dog must master at the very least. Dogs are hungry to learn and can become bored, anxious, or stressed if they're not mentally stimulated. So use these commands as a starting point, but know that ongoing lessons will make your dog feel happier, smarter, and more connected to you.

Also, please ask your trainer when to use these commands, if they should be coupled with other words, what vocal tone is best, what body language to use, how to reward and praise success, and when it's okay to move on to new words and behaviors. Most important, enjoy the bonding time. If training feels rewarding to you both, your dog will never want to stop learning.

1. *Sit:* One of the easiest commands to teach, this helps your dog sit still and in one place.

2. *Come:* The most important behavior your dog can learn. Coming when called will keep him out of trouble, off guests, and within your line of vision.

3. *Down:* Keeps the dog in a lying-down position for pets and visits.

4. *Off:* Means "keep your paws off that" (person, couch, etc.). Used most during greetings, this command helps when guests visit or when you're wearing tights.

5. *Stay:* Often used in conjunction with "sit" or "down," no matter what the distraction is.

6. *Walk:* There are multiple interpretations of this, some with variations on "heel," but in general, walking on a loose leash yields no pulling, tugging, or stalling when you walk.

What does it mean when my dog . . .

Q: *Digs in pillows and blankets?*

A: Wild dogs needed to dig a den or move around piles of leaves before lying down to sleep. Domesticated dogs may show a vestige of this behavior by messing around with blankets or pillows before they settle down for a rest, nap, or long night of cushioned sleep. (Cushions should not be used in a crate while a puppy is in training, but they are a must once a dog has learned to control his bladder and bowels.)

Praising Your Dog

For a job well done, dogs can't get enough positive reinforcement. This includes affection, verbal praise, toys, and treats. How much and what kind will differ from one trainer to the next, so it's important to be consistent with whatever method you choose.

Tamar likes to give food treats during the first few weeks of training, and once your dog is ready and begins to catch on, she advocates using them randomly, as a "jackpot"—so that your dog constantly anticipates, and gets really excited about, his next score. She also suggests tempering your dog's food treats once he's shown significant progress, but it's always a good idea to consistently show him praise and love.

Tangibile positive reinforcement is also priceless to a dog. Rub him behind his ears, under his chin, between his shoulders, on his back just above his tail, on his chest, and on his belly to show you're proud. Reaching over his head can appear to be a threat. Couple positive touch experiences with verbal cues. Using light, happy tones and drawn-out words, and verbally linking praise with your dog's accomplishment like "Good *sit*" and "Good *stay*," are effective ways to tell your dog he's a star.

No matter what your immediate goal, praise your dog for trying and for succeeding, and be sure to reward him after his action so that he connects it to a positive result. Ask your trainer about his own techniques so that you're on the same page about when, how, and how often to give praise. If your dog doesn't seem happy when you praise him (no pert ears, wagging tail, panting, smiling), or if he's not making reward-driven progress, talk to your trainer about customizing his techniques and potentially turning the day's lesson into a cooperative game. Play training lets you work with relevant training tools, but in a way to which dogs are often more receptive.

Listening to Your Dog

Since we don't speak the same language as dogs, we should at least try to interpret their barks, moans, yelps, and groans. Katenna explains that at birth, dogs can whine, scream, grunt, and mew. By the time they're adults, they can also yelp, yip, growl, whimper, and bark. These are voice sounds that carry over a distance, ranging from close proximity (as with yelps and whimpers) to a more far-reaching span (as with howls and barks). The sounds mean either approach (come closer) or withdraw (go away). Dog vocalizations are controlled and influenced by emotions and can occur alone or in combination with other sounds, like a bark-whine. That's why it's essential for you to notice dog vocalizations in tandem with behavior. Here, Katenna breaks down typical dog sounds:

> **Barking:** Domestic dogs bark in a variety of contexts, such as threatening, alarming, aggressive, play, greeting, call for attention, when alone, care-soliciting, or during group interactions. Deeper barks tend to mean a dog feels threatened, and high-pitched barks are typically more beckoning or playful.

Deep, rapid, repetitive bark: warning that something is invading the dog's territory

Repetitive, medium tone; equally spaced barks: boredom, doesn't want to be alone

Short bark: dog may want something from you (like a cookie or to go out)

High-pitched, happy bark: excitement and an interest in investigating what a dog hears or sees; this is nonthreatening and may be interchangeable with "short bark."

Excited, quickly packed, high-pitched bark: hears other dogs outside, harmless

Sneezing: excitement or stress (rapid, combined with relaxed, investigatory behavior, outside the context of sickness). Dogs examine the world with their noses, so if they sniff a lot in a new place, they'll also sneeze to clean out their nose so they can keep sniffing.

Whining: A way for a dog to draw attention to himself, either because he's in pain or because he's begging. Translation: Pet me, love me, feed me, notice me, I want to go outside. This can also mean "I'm emotionally upset," perhaps afraid or anxious. When the whine isn't related to pain, the response is conditioned and can be eliminated with a trainer's help.

Yelping: Distressed, startled, in pain. Dogs yelp if they're stung by a bee or if you step on their tail. Similar to "ouch!" yelps can also be in response to movements or noises that are startling.

Moaning: Pleasure sound. Dogs moan when you are doing something that makes them feel really good, like rubbing behind their ears. Most often this happens when they're relaxed, looking at you, and/or have closed eyes. It's similar to when a cat purrs.

Growling: Warning, go away. A deep growl can come from the chest, a more shallow growl from the throat (this is less threatening). Also used when playing with you or another dog: If your dog is in a play bow or his body is wiggling, it's fine. Katenna compares a play growl to a child who screams on a playground. Screams mean excitement but, in another context, signal danger.

Howling: A way to communicate with others, signal the time of day, or express how he feels. Pack-hunting and wolf-type breeds are more prone to howling. Some dogs also howl to music, whistling, or sirens.

Is Your Dog Stressed Out?

Dog owners and experts talk a lot about stress or anxiety in a dog, which can lead to a variety of unwanted behaviors ranging from house accidents to tail chasing to aggression. Katenna says a stressed dog is similar to a stressed human: Dogs experience a physical and emotional state of anxiety that elevates heart rate, blood pressure, and causes an adrenaline release. Simply put, dogs feel stress when they are in an uncertain situation. Stress also occurs when a dog finds himself in a fight, flight, play, pounce, or run situation. When a dog feels threatened, you'll notice stress in his coat (fur will fluff), eyes (pupils will dilate or eyes will widen from an adrenaline surge), and body language (rigid body, tense muscles). Dogs can also feel stress from emotional strains in the home or in his life—for instance, with separation anxiety or fighting between couples. Bear in mind that if a dog makes a big poop in a main room or marks your side of the bed when he's stressed, there's nothing vindictive about his actions. Experts say it's just his way of showing you that he's anxious.

One or more stress signs can signal illness, so be safe and ask your vet about your dog's behaviors if he seems anxious. DAP plug-ins, lavender candles, or sound machines may otherwise mend the problem. Active toys, exercise, a healthy diet, and confidence-building games can also help with stress.

TYPICAL CAUSES OF STRESS

Loneliness

Boredom

Separation anxiety

Family fights and problems

Change in the family structure: baby, death, divorce, moving

Too little exercise

Changes to the routine

TYPICAL SIGNS OF STRESS

Licking (self, floor, furniture, walls)

Excessive shedding

Tail down or between legs

Ears flat and back against the dog's head

Avoiding eye contact, acting "shy," appearing wide-eyed

Pacing or running along a fence

Biting, growling, snarling

Panting, lip licking, drooling

Refusing food and water or treats

Scratching his body

Stressful pooping or peeing (as in an owner's bed or in the middle of a room)

Vomiting, diarrhea, lethargy

An inability to settle down

Trembling

NOTE: To make sure your dog isn't stressed, do your best to meet his needs. Is your dog getting enough attention? Company? Exercise? Training? Always teach your dogs new tricks, words, and behaviors. He doesn't have the Internet or iPhone apps to keep him busy; he only has you.

Never Get Physical with Your Dog

Physically reprimanding a dog or challenging him with dominating body language is not an option for many reasons. First of all, it's cruel. But when dogs are treated physically, it also triggers their flight-or-fight instinct and can lead to aggression. Yelling, raising your hand, tapping your dog with a rolled-up newspaper, pushing his head into a bathroom accident, forcing him into a corner, and pulling him by the scruff of his neck or collar can cause him to act out. It's safe to say that scruffing, pulling, pushing, or pinning of any kind is unacceptable.

In some cases, a dog may even react against being hugged, scooped up, or patted on the head. The best solution: Use your hands only for praise.

"Correcting" Your Dog with Startling Noises and Actions

A number of trainers suggest shaking or throwing a can of loose change, or using other startling techniques, to teach your dog to behave. Others find this to be a stressful way to teach a dog new commands and rules. With the help of a reward-based trainer, try to assess what you're asking the dog to do and how positive words and body language can enforce your message more effectively than scaring him. Only if your dog defiantly disobeys you by, say, chasing a rabbit should you consider using loud noises—and even then only with the help of a pro who will teach you how to provide a positive reward as an alternative to negative behavior. Similarly, some experts feel that using a water bottle to spray your dog is effective when you're initially training him, though a number of opponents don't feel there are many issues that this spray technique can actually resolve. Katenna says dogs will learn to "not do that" when a person is holding a water bottle, but you can't always have a water bottle in hand, and furthermore, squirting a dog may only serve to make him fear you and weaken the trust bond. From her experience, it doesn't do much to encourage your dog to behave in a respectful way.

In short, consider using a startling technique to correct a rebellious act, not to teach a confused dog new rules or commands. As with any aversive technique, noise aversives must occur every time the behavior occurs, or a connection will never be made. Automatic sensors can also help, such as the Tattle Tale device, which emits a loud noise when vibration is sensed and automatically shuts off after a few seconds. This is a helpful tool for keeping dogs off furniture, counters, or beds. And remember that every dog is starting from a different place: Some are more stubborn by nature, and others have a history of bad habits to break before they willingly move on to new ones. If you compare dogs to children who need guidance, think about the good kids who simply need boundaries and the more challenging ones who may need military school, and in between these two groups is a very gray area of discipline requirements. The same can be said for dogs. Do know that research says that when dogs are stressed, their brains shut down the ability to clearly process incoming information and instead rely more on primary instincts of fight or flight. So stress, fear, and pain will simply leave them in a blank and uncomfortable state. Using positive reinforcement for motivation will do the opposite.

When to Hire a Trainer Versus a Behaviorist

A personal or group trainer will teach your dog basic manners and skills, including general commands and techniques to manage basic behavior problems, such as housetraining, puppy nipping, chewing, and jumping. But a behaviorist is needed for help with problems like aggression, phobias, anxiety, self-mutilation, and any behavior that a trainer has not been able to resolve. Misbehavior can stem from poor breeding, inadequate early socialization, inappropriate training, abuse, neglect, boredom, fear, anxiety, bad training, and/or poor communication.

For help finding a certified behaviorist, visit the website for the International Association of Animal Behavior Consultants at IAABC.org or the Animal Behavior Society at AnimalBehavior.org.

Ask Dr. Z!

What does it mean when my dog . . .

Q: *Whines at the door but doesn't want to go out?*

A: You may think he's being a tease about wanting to go potty, but a dog that does this may simply hear or smell something on the other side of the door that you are unable to detect.

When a Needy Dog Becomes a Problem

A dog that seems a little clingy is a problem only if you don't have time to give him the love he craves (in which case, talk to a trainer for behavior modification advice). But dogs with separation anxiety are another story. These dogs exhibit behavior problems in the absence of their owners, always within twenty to thirty minutes after they've left the house or room. Signs of separation anxiety include scratching and digging near a door or window, chewing door frames, barking, whining and howling, chewing or licking their own bodies, puddles of saliva, and stressful urination/defecation.

Since separation anxiety can manifest itself in many ways, talk to a behaviorist if you sense that your dog is experiencing it. An expert will help you resolve the specific issues that are at the heart of your dog's anxiety. In the meantime, you can minimize the likelihood of separation anxiety by helping your dog find a healthy balance between enjoying company and feeling independent by fostering self-assurance, building tolerance to staying alone, minimizing the drama of arrivals and returns home, giving your dog attention during designated times to reinforce expectations, and establishing verbal cues that help him feel safe. It goes without saying that you should never punish a dog for showing signs of separation anxiety. Instead, learn how to improve his behavior.

Exercising Your Dog

Learning how to exercise your dog is a key part of the training process, since experts say it conditions both your dog's body and his temperament. The amount of exercise your dog needs will often depend on his breed, age, health, and size. A few facts and guidelines to keep in mind:

▶ Short potty walks are not exercise. They're maintenance.

▶ Consider using doggie day care, a dog walker, or a private caretaker service to provide daily exercise if you're not able to.

▶ Try to incorporate your dog's exercise into your daily routine. He can always fetch toys while you watch TV. It's when you designate an exercise time that you often find a reason to skip it.

▶ Remember that exercise has psychological benefits for your dog. Its calming and mood-stabilizing effects may come from an endorphin and serotonin release, similar to what humans experience after a great workout.

▶ Lack of exercise can lead to barking, anxiety, hostility, hyperactivity, weight gain, and destructive tendencies.

▶ Exercise can be physical or mental gymnastics, both indoors and out. Walking, running, swimming, or even errand-running with your dog can provide him with the stimulation he needs.

▶ Quality overrides quantity. Ball-chasing down a long hall is better than a slow, lumbering walk on your usual route; unlike on the walk, the dog is thinking and moving quickly in the hall.

▶ If it rains, play hide-and-seek with treats indoors, or bounce the ball from your perch on the sofa for your dog to retrieve.

▶ Breed and age dictate activity need. Circling the block can be a marathon to a small or older dog.

▶ Puppies need more exercise than adults, and dogs older than five need less than younger dogs.

▶ Puppies should not do extensive exercise until they're about two years old, including running on hard surfaces, which can put strain on their joints and skeletal system.

▶ If your dog limps or falls behind, see your vet about possible hip, arthritis, or joint issues.

▶ Overweight dogs are more prone to orthopedic problems, since extra pudge puts stress on joints and backs. If you notice that your dog is putting on the pounds, ask your vet about diet changes, vitamin supplements, and a new exercise regime. Swimming is a great fitness idea for obese dogs, since it puts less stress on their already taxed joints. Just be sure your breed of dog can swim (most bulldogs can't).

Ask Dr. Z!

What does it mean when my dog . . .

Q: *Scratches at doors to be let into a room, when he can just as easily push them open?*

A: Sorry, he's not being polite by knocking first! If you've opened the door in the past when he's scratched, he'll keep you working. Dogs repeatedly respond to behaviors that you reward. So if good things happen when this dog scratches—i.e., he scratches, and a door to another room opens—he'll keep doing it until you adjust his behavior with alternative means of positive reinforcement.

EXERCISE NEEDS FOR DIFFERENT BREEDS

I once heard that in a perfect world, your dog would get two hours of physical and mental exercise every day. But to make the most of the time you can realistically spend with your dog, Dr. Dodman suggests breaking down exercise requirements by breed, based on what your dog was originally bred to do. This is a great way to establish expectations for both your dog's stamina and your schedule. (As you can imagine, a dog bred to run will need a different amount of exercise than a lap dog.)

I've organized Dr. Dodman's points into a chart to determine some dogs' aerobic activity needs. As always, consult a vet before starting any exercise program, since your dog's health and age will also influence his routine.

ACTIVITY LEVEL: HIGH

Exercise: **More than 20 to 30 minutes of aerobic activity**

Breed Type: *Working breeds*

Examples: *Siberian Husky, Alaskan Malamute, Portuguese Water Dog*

Breed Type: *Sporting breeds*

Examples: *Weimaraner, Pointer, Setter, English Springer Spaniel, Lab, Golden Retriever*

Breed Type: *Non-sporting breeds*

Example: *Dalmatian*

Breed Type: *Herding breeds*

Examples: *Australian Shepherd, Australian Cattle Dog, Border Collie*

Breed Type: *Terrier breeds*

Examples: *Parson Russell Terrier, Miniature Schnauzer, Bull Terrier*

Breed Type: *Hounds*

Examples: *Foxhound, Saluki*

Breed Type: *Toy Breeds*

Examples: *Chinese Crested, Pomeranian, Schipperke*

ACTIVITY LEVEL: MODERATE

Exercise: About 20 to 30 minutes of aerobic activity

Breed Type: *Working breeds*

Examples: *Boxer, Rottweiler, Mastiff, Doberman Pinscher, Great Dane, Saint Bernard*

Breed Type: *Sporting breeds*

Example: *Cocker Spaniel*

Breed Type: *Non-sporting breeds*

Examples: *Chow Chow*

Breed Type: *Herding breeds*

Examples: *Old English Sheepdog, Briard, German Shepherd*

Breed Type: *Terrier breeds*

Examples: *Scottish Terrier, Soft-Coated Wheaten Terrier, Yorkshire Terrier*

Breed Type: *Hounds*

Examples: *Afghan Hound, Beagle, Greyhound*

Breed Type: *Toy breeds*

Examples: *Cavalier King Charles Spaniel, Toy Poodle*

ACTIVITY LEVEL: LOW

Exercise: A brisk walk around the block may suffice

Breed Type: *Working breeds*

Examples: *Bernese Mountain Dog, Newfoundland, Great Pyrenees, German Pinscher*

Breed Type: *Sporting breeds*

Examples: *Sussex Spaniel, Spinone Italiano*

Breed Type: *Non-sporting breeds*

Examples: *English and French Bulldogs, Lhasa Apso, Shiba Inu, Bichon Frise*

Breed Type: *Herding breeds*

Examples: *Shetland Sheepdog, Old English Sheepdog*

Breed Type: *Terrier breeds*

Examples: *Bedlington Terrier, Black Russian Terrier, Border Terrier*

Breed Type: *Hounds*

Examples: *Basset Hound, Scottish Deerhound, Dachshund*

Breed Type: *Toy Breeds*

Examples: *Chihuahua, Pekingese, Shih Tzu, Japanese Chin*

Dogs on a Treadmill

A number of behaviorists and trainers advocate treadmill workouts for dogs. Before doing this in your home, I suggest you ask a dog professional to guide you through specifics. Dr. Dodman says to start by getting on the treadmill with your leashed dog and walking together. Slowly increase the treadmill's speed until it reaches a trotting pace. Take off the dog's leash, and supervise him from a nearby chair. A dog should never, ever be tied to a treadmill, left unsupervised, or run until he collapses. Workout times are the same for dogs on a treadmill as they are off. So if your dog requires moderate exercise, a 20- to 30-minute trot should suffice.

As with any exercise program, your dog must work up to a *realistic* goal, which increases both distance and effort over time. Old age and medical conditions can slow progress, so be sure to customize your dog's routine with a professional. If your dog has health limits, talk to your vet about alternative workouts like play training or swimming classes, which are easier on his body.

Fun Exercise Ideas

Without the right amount of exercise, dogs can become aggressive, moody, fearful, and fat. Sustained activity for a dog requires exertion on his part and creativity and interest on yours. Just make sure that if you head for the water or an unleashed park, that your dog really knows his "come" command (you may want to practice for a while before you go out). To get things going, I've flexed my own thinking muscles to help generate a few fitness ideas for your pet; once you start moving with your dog, you'll be surprised at how many you'll think of on your own!

Signs That Your Dog Is Pooped

Slowing down

Dragging on leash

Losing interest

Stopping altogether

Lying on ground

Breathing with short, strained breaths

If your dog doesn't recover in ten minutes, call your vet and ask if you should bring him in for a checkup.

Swim class: Water therapy, or hydrotherapy, increases body awareness, balance, coordination, and muscle tone. It also benefits dogs with health concerns, including those related to geriatrics, injuries, arthritis, paralysis, dysplasia, and surgical rehab. To find a pool and swim specialist near you, visit the Association of Canine Water Therapy (ACWP) website at CanineWaterTherapy.com.

Play fetch in an empty tennis court: Run and chase balls in a caged area free of distraction. Just be sure to check for signs that say your dog is allowed in the space, and always remember to scoop any poops he might have.

Visit a dog beach: Great for long walks, family activities, or monitored swim time. A number of public beaches are also open to dogs and their owners after Labor Day. Make sure your dog is fully vaccinated, well mannered around other dogs, and comes when you call him.

Agility training: During a class or with a private trainer, you'll help your dog through an obstacle course in a race for time and accuracy. Several national organizations, including the United States Dog Agility Association (USDAA) and the AKC can fill you in on programs, tournaments, rules, and performance standards for fun or competition. Visit USDAA.org or AKC.org for more information.

Hide-and-seek (with treats!): Hide snacks in the house or under multiple bowls for your dog to suss out with his nose— and taste buds.

Frisbee: Great for picnics and at the beach. Use a dog-friendly disk so your dog doesn't risk chewing off a small piece of plastic. If he's a natural, join a Frisbee dog club near you.

Teach your dog a unique skill: Have you seen the dogs that surf and skateboard? Enough said!

Ask Dr. Z!

What does it mean when my dog . . .

Q: *Chases leaves in the wind?*

A: Dogs are predators. They're wired to chase moving objects. Leaves that move through the air present a particular challenge—they're hard to pin down!

Working Out with Your Dog

I love to run in the park, but Bianca never joins me. Her legs are so short that anything more than a walk around the block makes her stop and lie flat on the sidewalk like a frog. For active owners and their canine training partners, take Katenna's exercise advice on the road:

- ▶ Work up to your fitness goal. It's a lot to ask your dog to walk six miles the first time you try a long-distance excursion.

- ▶ Don't wear headphones while you exercise together. Keep an ear open for approaching distractions such as cars, strollers, children, and other dogs.

- ▶ Make sure your dog has good leash skills. Pulling, jerking, or darting can hurt the dog and you.

- ▶ Try a hands-free leash, which usually wraps around your waist and connects to your dog's harness or collar. This takes training to use but it is such a comfortable payoff. Make sure your dog stays at your side, not ahead of or behind you, so you don't lose track of each other. This works for running, walking, and hiking activities.

- ▶ Rollerblading, skateboarding, and biking require highly advanced loose-leash skills. Biking can be very dangerous for you and the dog; if he's too close to the bike, he can get caught in the chain or tires.

- ▶ Walking, hiking, or mountain biking require great recall if you don't use a leash, and long-leash skills if you decide to walk your dog on a long line.

"Want to Go for a Walk?"

Bianca and I take the best walks together. On a good day, we stop by the local dry cleaner for her daily liver treat and end at my favorite clothing store, where Bianca likes to visit customers in their dressing rooms. And on weekends, nothing beats her daily beach walks. However, we've learned many lessons during our blissful strolls. Here are a few tips I've gleaned:

▶ Dogs of any age can be trained to walk on a leash, but puppies are most amenable to learning. Familiarize your puppy with a collar and leash in the house when he first comes home, and don't expose him to other dogs until he's had all his shots.

▶ Stacy from Who's Walking Who says that male dogs and tracking dogs like Beagles love to sniff and mark their territory. At most, allow two pee stops per block or you won't get anywhere.

▶ Use a six-foot adjustable leash made of leather, cotton, or nylon during all walks. Pair it with a collar that's also made one of these materials. Stay away from retractable leashes, which pull and snap. Ask your trainer about a front-attaching harness, especially if your dog is prone to trachea and neck issues, which seem to be more common in small breeds.

▶ Don't gab on your phone while walking your dog. He deserves your full attention, so you can praise him when he does something good and make a mental note when he doesn't. The minute Bianca sees me pull the phone from my pocket, she refuses to continue walking until I'm done talking.

▶ Choose a quiet time to walk your dog at least once a day. I like to walk Bianca early in the morning, after Howard leaves for work, since the streets are so serene at that hour.

▶ Never rush your dog during his walks. This is his time.

Ask Dr. Z!

What does it mean when my dog . . .

Q: *Prefers to pee in the grass or on leaves rather than on the pavement?*

A: This behavior can be a result of early experience. Dogs that have been scolded for going on sidewalks or driveways when they were puppies may continue to avoid other hard surfaces. It also seems that dogs prefer to pee on a surface where the urine soaks in and does not force them to stand in a puddle.

WEATHER WARNINGS

In Hot Weather

▶ Limit the amount of time you walk your dog during hot and humid weather.

▶ Limit outdoor games to early-morning or night hours to avoid heatstroke (hyperthermia).

▶ Never walk your dog after a meal on a warm day.

▶ Unlike humans with pores, your dog can release heat only through his nose, through panting, and through the pads of his feet. Check the temperature of pavement, stones, and asphalt with your bare hand, and keep him off hot surfaces, since they cause blisters, burns, and cuts. Consider booties and prescription foot creams for protection and soothing treatment.

▶ Offer cool, fresh water to your dog throughout the day, instead of one long drink after a workout. Pack a gallon of water to pour into a small bowl every few hours if you're on the road or away from home.

▶ Older, overweight, and snub-nosed dogs like Bulldogs, Pugs, and Shih Tzus should be kept in cool or air-conditioned rooms as much as possible. Ditto for dogs with heart or lung disease, since they're already in a vulnerable state.

▶ Do not use sunscreen or insect repellent that isn't made for dogs. Human brands can be toxic to them. For sun protection, buy a dog-specific product for short-haired or pink-nosed dogs.

▶ Watch for signs of overheating. These include glassy eyes, frantic panting, weakness, vomiting, diarrhea, and confusion. If your dog develops heat stress, wet him down to cool off his body and call the vet immediately. For emergency treatment of heatstroke, see "Heat stroke (Hyperthermia) and Heat Exhaustion" on page 462.

▶ Don't leave your dog in a parked car on a hot day, not even in the shade or with the windows open. Heatstroke can be fatal.

▶ When sitting outside on a sunny day, choose a shady spot to relax so your dog escapes the heat. All that fur is hot, especially if your dog is a dark color!

▶ Provide a cool, dry indoor respite for your dog.

In Cold Weather

▶ Ask your vet about arthritis or osteoarthritis if you think your dog might be suffering from these conditions. Cold weather can worsen them in pets.

▶ Smaller breeds and breeds with short coats always benefit from warm clothes like sweaters and jackets. I don't suggest that you force a dog to wear clothes, but he can really benefit from pieces that keep him warm during frigid months.

▶ Buy booties for your dog's paws, for when he's walking near chemicals and salt used to melt ice. If your dog won't wear booties, try using Paw Wax by Shaws. This prevents him from slipping and getting hurt on gravel, asphalt, ice, snow, salt, and other hard surfaces. Apply the wax before he leaves the house, and wash his paws off with soap and water when he gets in.

▶ Check his paws for small cuts and cracks, and call a vet about solutions to these problems.

▶ Try using Bag Balm, a gentle salve, on chapped and superficially irritated skin.

▶ Ask your neighbors to use dog-friendly humane salts that won't hurt your pets—or consider providing them yourself, since they can cost twice as much as regular salts. Giving de-icer to neighbors will encourage them to use it!

▶ Immediately clean antifreeze spills, which can be lethal to dogs if ingested, even in small amounts. Consider using animal-friendly antifreeze if you live in an area that requires using this product regularly.

▶ If your dog is wet when you come inside, always dry him off.

▶ When you bathe your dog, dry his coat thoroughly before he goes outside.

▶ Trim the hair around your dog's paw pads. Less hair keeps paws free of ice and snow.

▶ Clean your dog's paws after every walk to remove snow and snow-removal chemicals. Some dogs lick their paws after they've walked through areas that have been salted, and the residue can be toxic.

▶ Shorten exercise walks for short-haired breeds, puppies, sick, and old dogs, since they get cold easily.

▶ Keep dogs away from bodies of water that are frozen or appear to be frozen.

▶ Check your dog's ears, tail, and feet for frostbitten skin, which may appear red or gray. If you think your dog has frostbite, wrap his feet in a warm blanket or towel and call the vet. For emergency treatment of frostbite and hypothermia, see pages 461 and 465.

▶ During cold weather, give your dog lots of water to hydrate and combat dry winter air.

▶ Don't leave your dog alone in a cold car. When the engine's off, a sealed car holds the cold in.

▶ Provide a warm, dry indoor respite for your dog to look forward to.

Yards Aren't an Exercise-Free Pass

A dog doesn't need a yard, though for many owners, it makes life easier. What a dog needs is exercise or he'll become depressed, overweight, and/or destructive. After letting your dog use the bathroom in the yard, meet him out back for a game so he gets the exercise he needs. No dog will exercise alone in a yard for any length of time unless he's acting out of frustration.

There's No Such Thing as an Outdoor Dog

Dogs should always live indoors and should remain under your supervision when they're outside. If you leave your dog outside, chained, leashed, or even contained inside a pen for any extensive and unsupervised amount of time, it can become very dangerous for the dog—not to mention extremely inhumane and, in some states, illegal.

Dog Park Tips

Dog parks or dog runs are a great way to exercise and socialize a dog in urban, suburban, and country settings. Generally large, fenced-in areas, dog runs are designed to accommodate unleashed dogs that are monitored by their owners. If you have a smaller toy breed or puppy, it is safest to stick to parks that offer separate areas for small dogs and large dogs. Most dog parks post rules on the fence or make rule flyers accessible; local governments may mandate provisions (you can usually find these listed online). Always read and follow the rules of the dog run, but also keep the following etiquette tips in mind, too. Here are a few typical rules that I've gathered from various dog parks in the nation. They're pretty universal.

▶ Before taking a dog into a dog park, have a good idea about whether he's well behaved around other dogs. Try a one-on-one introduction with another dog outside the park instead of starting him off in a group setting. If your dog needs time to acclimate, introduce him to the park for gradually increasing amounts of time. This will deter a stressful reaction to parks in the future.

▶ Enter the dog park only if your dog is friendly. No aggressive, fearful, or reactive dogs allowed.

▶ Open and close one safety gate at a time.

▶ Unleash your dog within the safety gates before you enter the park.

▶ Supervise your dog's play.

▶ Curb your dog if he harasses another dog or barks incessantly.

▶ Don't discipline another person's dog or tell another owner what he's doing wrong with his dog—unless he asks for your opinion.

▶ Don't offer treats to another person's dog without asking his owner first.

▶ Watch your dog and always look for signs of aggression from other dogs.

▶ If a fight occurs, all involved dog owners must help break it up.

▶ No sick, injured dogs or dogs in heat in the park.

- No rawhides, glass containers, or toys (especially small balls that can get caught in dogs' throats).

- No pronged, spiked, or chained collars in the park.

- Scoop your dog's poop inside and outside the park.

- Playing dogs should know basic manners, plus commands like "come" and "off."

- Honor the park's posted hours.

Ask Dr. Z!

What does it mean when my dog . . .

Q: *Bites my second dog after another dog lunges at him? Is he confused or turning against his friend? Or does he see an opportunity for play?*

A: This may be redirected aggression as a result of being aroused by the other dog. The dogs are so wound up that they need to do something, so they bite the first thing in reach. This is similar to a person punching a wall when he's angry and frustrated.

Doggie Day Care

If you're not home during the day, consider enrolling your dog in a day-care program for play, exercise, and socialization. Private and commercial facilities let him socialize with other dogs while you're busy or traveling. A number of these facilities also offer dog walking options. Research a center that's right for you, your budget, and your dog. Here are a few tips to keep in mind as you look into the perfect "home away from home" for your pet:

How to Break Up a Dog Fight

I hope that you never witness a dog fight, but if your pet is in the middle of a scuffle, Mike Malloy, manager of the pet behavior department at NSALA, says that you need to make some attempt to break it up. This doesn't include sticking your hands or other body parts between two fighting dogs, since they have no concept when they're fighting that they might bite you. Instead, try one of these methods:

▶ If your dog isn't already on a leash, keep him on a three-foot "tab leash" in situations when a fight could occur—like when he's at the dog park. This allows you to pull him away quickly if necessary. You can make a tab leash by cutting a canvas leash to size.

▶ If a fight happens near or inside your home, clash two metal bowls together and combine the bang with a loud voice correction. Should the two dogs continue their brawl (most won't), toss a bucket of water toward their faces. Be careful not to get too close to the animals during any point of this interaction, since dog fights are very dangerous. If this doesn't work, chances are the dogs really mean business and it's best to stay out of it.

▶ If you fear that your dog may encounter an aggressive dog (on walks, in the park, in unfamiliar locations), carry a small party horn that can fit in your pocket. The moment you notice a fight, use the shrill sound of the horn with a voice correction to distract the dogs long enough for you to separate yours from the situation by pulling on his tab leash. This technique also works with Direct Stop citronella spray.

▶ Ask your vet, neighbors, or local humane society for references.

▶ Private day cares, often run in people's homes, can be less expensive than commercial facilities. They may also care for fewer dogs, which can offer your dog more canine-human attention. Be sure that caretakers are licensed by the state to ensure that all safety and health laws are being observed and followed.

▶ Commercial day cares house more dogs and offer organized activities in updated facilities.

▶ Look for a low dog-to-staff ratio.

▶ Staff should be knowledgeable, friendly, helpful, and trained to deal with aggression.

▶ Make sure the day care has a standing agreement with a local vet in case of an emergency.

▶ Tour options before enrolling your dog. The dogs should be well supervised, and the center should be clean and odor-free. The facility should also use a pet-safe cleaner, since bleach is toxic to dogs.

▶ Inspect eating, grooming, bathing, and boarding facilities, even if you don't plan to use them. They can be very telling of a staff's priorities, and you may need to use them in a pinch.

▶ Learn about planned activities for the dogs each day. Are they stimulating, safe, and supervised?

▶ Learn about webcams, special events, and perks like rubberized floors and air-filtration systems.

▶ Ask about round-trip transportation for your pet, if needed.

▶ Ensure that your dog is healthy, free of parasites, vaccinated, and spayed/neutered before enrolling. Quality facilities require health records, so have a copy of your dog's on hand.

▶ Prices can range from $10 a day to an annual fee that's upward of $200. Costs depend on the provider, where the facility is located, and whether the day care is commercial or private.

Training Your Dog to Be Around a New Baby

Prior to her work with the AHA, Katenna Jones cocreated Baby-Ready Pets, a popular program that coaches parents on how to introduce their new child to an existing dog. After all, bringing a newborn or adopted child into your home can be disorienting for everyone, especially the dog who's always been the "baby" of the family. And because parenthood is so demanding, new moms and dads have less time and attention to devote to their dog; all the while, the child's unfamiliar noises, smells, and routines may confuse and stress a pet without proper training.

Sadly, each year, thousands of animals are sent to shelters by expectant parents who are concerned about whether their dog may affect their child's health or safety. Careful training can deter a dog from viewing the new child as competition or a new toy. I've listed some tips on the following page. For more on how to promote a relationship between your child and dog, visit AmericanHumane.org.

TEND TO THE DOG BEFORE THE CHILD COMES HOME

▶ Gradually decrease the quantity of attention you give your dog, and increase the quality of attention he receives. For example, a ten-minute walk can now replace forty-five minutes in front of the TV. Make changes before the baby comes, so the dog won't associate them with the child, which could encourage negative feelings. After all, dog owners lavish their pets with attention, and once there's a new recipient of that love, the dog can develop a negative association with the child who snatched it away.

▶ Encourage good manners. If your dog jumps on the counter now, he'll do it when you have a child, and the results could be more serious. Watch for problems and fix training issues before you bring a child home. Lax assumptions like "Oh, we'll work it out" lead to frustration.

▶ To your dog, a child's high-pitched cries and whines will sound a lot like a wounded animal. For months before your child comes home, download CDs of crying baby noises for your pet. He'll become familiar with crying, cooing, and gurgling before the child even arrives. (This is similar to playing animal noises or city sounds while initially training your puppy or dog.)

Ask Dr. Z!

What does it mean when my dog . . .

Q: *Stares at babies the same way he does birds and squirrels?*

A: Babies provide a panoply of sights, sounds, and smells. They are new and different. Babies have herky-jerky movements, make high-pitched sounds, and have yet to be inhibited of sharing bodily smells in public. Imagine how fascinating this is to a dog!

▶ Get your dog a checkup to make sure he's healthy. Parasites and zoonotic diseases can harm pregnant moms, young immune systems, and infants who put everything in their mouths. Existing injuries and sore joints should be treated now, since kids are known to poke, nudge, tug, ride, and prod pets.

DESIGNATE A HELPER TO ACCLIMATE THE DOG WHILE YOU'RE AWAY

▶ Ask a friend or family member to take care of your dog while you're in the hospital or finalizing an adoption. Your dog should feel comfortable with this person, and he/she should become familiar with your dog's routine while you're away. Their preliminary bond will help with introductions on the day the child arrives home.

▶ In your absence, ask your helper to bring home something that belongs to and smells like the child. This can be a blanket or another piece of the baby's clothing but should not be the cap that the baby wore after she was first born (it could still have blood residue and other overly stimulating triggers on it).

▶ Ask your helper to encourage plenty of sniffing but to never *give* the item or blanket to your dog.

▶ Tell your helper that if she scolds a dog that growls at the child's blanket or clothes, she's essentially reprimanding the dog's warning that he's uncomfortable with the child. If this is the case, he may skip the warning step and leap right to aggression when he meets the real child. Any aggressive, fearful, or questionable behavior should be addressed with a behaviorist right away. Don't give up on the dog yet! Oftentimes a few simple tips can make everything work out fine.

▶ Pay attention to your dog's noises and behavior around the child's objects. A growl is a warning that says, "I'm afraid of, or feel threatened by, the baby." Consult a trainer on how to address this.

GRADUALLY REUNITE WITH YOUR DOG

▶ Ask your helper to arrive at your home before the child does to exercise and exhaust your dog.

▶ Just before you enter the house, hand the child to a friend or family member while you're still outside the house, and have him hold the baby while you reacquaint with the dog indoors empty-handed. He will be so excited to see you!

▶ Once everything is calm and you've reunited, ask your helper to put the dog on a leash. Whoever has the baby should hand the child to you in front of the dog (make sure you wash your hands first). As the primary caregiver, you should not walk into the home while carrying the child.

▶ If you suspect growling, anxiety, or any negative or questionable behavior from the dog, keep the dog and the child apart and call a professional. In the meantime, gently correct the behavior, but don't punish it. Encourage good behavior with a treat or lots of affection. This way, your dog will think, "Wonderful things happen to me when I interact well with this child!"

Your Dog's Relationship with the New Child

▶ During initial interactions with a newborn, don't let your dog lick your child's hands, face, and head. If your dog is well behaved, it is fine to let him lick your child's feet. It's smart to take precautions for sanitary and bite-related reasons.

▶ Never leave your dog alone with your child, and never turn your back on a child who's sitting on the floor with a dog, regardless of size, temperament, or age. Your dog doesn't yet recognize the newborn as part of your family (or even human), since she smells, moves, and sounds different than you or your dog. He will treat the baby like a family member once she gains motor control and makes eye contact.

Ask Dr. Z!

What does it mean when my dog . . .

Q: *Presses his nose into the rug but isn't sniffing or chewing?*

A: Don't underestimate the power of your dog's nose. There may be smells buried deep in the carpet that you don't detect. They could come from another pet, another person, or even you—especially if you've sat in that location and left a "scent mark" from your body's natural smell.

Make No Training Assumptions

When you're training your dog, there is no room for generalizations or suppositions. For example, when Howard and I got Bianca, we just assumed that because she's a dog, she'd know how to doggie-paddle and that we didn't need to train her to do this. But sure enough, when Bianca fell into the deep end of a pool, I had to dive in—in sunglasses and Manolos, no less!—while Howard was busy untying his sneakers. Once I grabbed her, I swam to the side of the pool so Howard could reach over and pull her out.

Here are some other common training myths, according to APDT member trainers, based on assumptions made by past and current clients. (I left out the one about swimming.) Let's debunk these training fallacies once and for all.

MYTH: *A puppy has to be at least six months old to be trained.*

REALITY: A puppy starts learning the moment he's able to observe and relate to his environment, so start working with your puppy as soon as you can! Compared to an adult dog, a puppy may have a shorter attention span. This may require more patience on your part when teaching behaviors, but there's no reason your puppy can't start learning right away. The sooner you start, the sooner he'll learn!

MYTH: *If a dog won't learn a behavior, he must be dumb or stubborn.*

REALITY: Some dogs grasp behaviors quickly, while others require more time and guidance. If your dog has trouble learning a task, it's often because the trainer isn't communicating to the dog in a way he can understand. Other times dogs fail to learn a task because they're not properly cued as to when they've done it correctly and therefore have no way of knowing what the trainer wants. Always reward your dog for doing something right, and always be patient.

MYTH: *My dog knows when he did something wrong because he looks guilty.*

REALITY: Guilt is a human emotion and has no equivalent among animals. A recent study at Barnard College found that the "guilty" look people claim to see in their animals is entirely attributable to whether or not the person expected to see the look, regardless of whether or not a dog had actually done something to feel guilty about. Most often when a dog looks guilty, it's because he's reacting to a change in our body language that tells him something is wrong. What you see as guilt is more likely a look of worry and nervousness.

MYTH: *My dog pulls on a leash, lies on the sofa, or jumps on me because he's dominant.*

REALITY: The concept of dominance has been used to explain just about every inappropriate behavior in dogs that owners can possibly gripe about. The term "dominance," as used by many trainers and dog owners today, is misleading. Dominance describes a social relationship between two or more individuals. It is not a character trait. Dogs don't try to establish control over humans. If your dog pulls, lies, or jumps, it's because he hasn't learned that these are undesirable behaviors. Decide what you want your dog to do, then teach and reward him for doing these tasks correctly.

MYTH: *Using food in training is bribery.*

REALITY: When you're teaching an animal something new, there needs to be a motivation for getting it right and a signal that he's done so. In humans, this may be a paycheck, a bonus, or an A-plus from a teacher. All animals work for reinforcement, and dogs are no different. Trainers often use food because most dogs love food and find it worth working for, but they can also use toys, play, work, petting, happy talk, and a slew of other rewarding treats. A reward/reinforcement is part of a cause/effect scenario that's presented to an animal to show him he did something right. A bribe is what you give an animal to do something he already knows how to do.

MYTH: *Positive reinforcement training works only on small, happy, or even-tempered dogs, not tough, large, or obstinate dogs.*

REALITY: Using positive reinforcement to train animals is the norm among exotic animal and marine mammal trainers. If you can train monkeys and elephants by rewarding behaviors, there's no reason you can't do the same with your large-breed dog. As our knowledge of dog behavior is strengthened through research, the consensus is that using aversive training methods on fearful or aggressive dogs is more likely to lead to worse behaviors. Rewarding an animal and alleviating his fear and anxiety will lead to more well-adjusted dogs and stronger human-animal bonds.

MYTH: *Certain breeds, like American Pit Bull Terriers, Doberman Pinschers, and Rottweilers, are inherently vicious.*

REALITY: While there are certain genetic traits that predispose dogs toward reactivity with other animals, particularly in the Terrier breeds, no entire breed of dog is born "vicious." Dogs should be understood as individuals, and everyone who interacts with dogs should keep in mind that *any* dog can bite a person, regardless of breed. It's a dog's socialization history, environment, training, and a host of other factors that contribute to whether a dog will show aggressive behavior. Some of these factors relate to the owner and the way he cares for the dog.

MYTH: *Using head collars will cause neck and/or spinal injury.*

REALITY: This claim is all over the Internet. There are no documented cases of dogs getting either of these injuries from properly used head collars, which loop behind the dog's ears and around his snout to eliminate pressure on the throat that a traditional neck collar can cause. Proper use of a head collar should have no ill physical effects. Jerking or yanking a head collar is not the proper way to use it and can result in injury.

MYTH: *The only reason my dog listens to me is because he wants to please me.*

REALITY: Dogs do what they do because it works for *them.* Your dog loves you, but he's no sucker. As humans, we count ourselves incredibly lucky to have such creatures that appear to enjoy our company and share our lives. However, we need to understand that the relationship is mutual, and dogs benefit from their bonds with us through getting food, shelter, play, and affection, among other needs. When a dog makes us happy, we shouldn't jump to the assumption that he only wants to please us. A dog does things to make us happy because it gets him a treat, belly rub, or pleasant living environment. If you believe a dog should do things only to please you, and never be rewarded or reinforced for good behavior, your dog will become difficult to train because he'll have a hard time discerning when he's done something right.

4

Health

Your dog is a member of your family who deserves all the care and attentiveness you can offer. One of the most valuable ways to demonstrate your dedication and devotion to him is to be an advocate for his good health. Choosing a dependable vet is an integral part of this.

I never hesitate to call my veterinarian if I think there's a problem—and believe me, there have been a few false alarms and overreactions on my part. I'll never forget the time I trimmed one of Bianca's toenails too short, it began to bleed, and I assumed the absolute worst. Little did I know that this is a typical (and fixable) grooming scenario! But that's the beauty of having a vet you can trust. He's a reliable resource for information and care. A quick call to his office doesn't cost you a dime, and he'll give advice, schedule an appointment, or put your mind to rest if your dog seems fine. For your part, be sure to know what's "normal" for your dog, both in hard facts (temperature, breathing rate, heart rate, mucous membrane color) and more subjective ones (behavior, energy, attitude, appearance). If gut instinct prompts a concern, that's okay, too. It's not your job to diagnose and treat your dog's potential medical conditions, which brings me to my next point . . .

In no way should this chapter ever replace veterinary care. In fact, you'll notice the refrain "Ask your vet . . ." used throughout this section, since canine health should be managed and evaluated only by a qualified veterinarian. Use the information in this chapter to prompt a discussion with a professional vet who's equipped to make health-related decisions. Educated guesses and delayed treatment on your part, without expert guidance, could cause serious harm to your dog.

A lot of people ask me about the difference between integrative (or "holistic") and conventional veterinary care, so I've explored these subjects as well. In my mind, choosing a vet that values your dog's health in a responsible, progressive, and thorough way is most important. We live in a time when veterinary medicine is undergoing a great deal of change for the better, with noticeable influence from the integrative-care community. However, it would be irresponsible of me to suggest that there's one gold standard to treating your dog—frankly, there isn't. If you're interested in learning more about integrative veterinary medicine, I suggest you dive into a book devoted entirely to this topic. A few good ones include: *Dr. Pitcairn's New Complete Guide to Natural Health for Dogs and Cats* by Richard H. Pitcairn, DVM, and Susan Hubble Pitcairn; *The Goldsteins' Wellness and Longevity Program* by Robert S. Goldstein, VMD, and Susan J. Goldstein; *The Natural Health Bible for Dogs & Cats* by Shawn Messonnier, DVM; and *The Nature of Animal Healing* by Martin Goldstein, DVM.

Wishing you many healthy years together.

UNDERSTANDING THE LETTERS
AFTER A VET'S NAME

The letters following a vet's name can be confusing if you don't know how to decode them. The following key will help you begin to understand credentials so that you can work with an experienced, diligent vet who's put in the time and effort it takes to care for your dog. It will also foster a newfound respect for how hard these experts work for their titles!

To start, every vet should have a degree from a veterinary program and therefore have the letters DVM (doctor of veterinary medicine) or VMD (veterinary medical doctor) after his name, regardless of whether he practices traditional or integrative medicine.

Vets may also have the words "a special interest in" (or similar phrasing) to indicate additional training in a specialty—or a series of letters beginning with a "D" to qualify additional board certifications. The former does not recognize certification, while the latter does (the "D" stands for "diplomate"). For instance, if a vet's name is followed by the letters VMD, DACVECC, this means that the vet (VMD) is board-certified in emergency and critical care (DACVECC).

The exceptions to the "D" credibility rule are vets certified in alternative specialties, like those who work with chiropractic or acupuncture treatments. Such vets will have the letters DVM or VMD after their names—plus the licenses, certifications, courses, institutions, and/or associations that relate to their experience. Each of these can have acronyms of his own.

Here are some of the more common professional abbreviations:

DVM: Doctor of veterinary medicine. This degree is a four-year program at a college of veterinary medicine, usually preceded by an undergrad degree.

VMD: Veterinary medical doctor. This requires the same training as a DVM but is given by the University of Pennsylvania.

AHVMA: American Holistic Veterinary Medical Association. Explores and supports alternative and complementary approaches to vet care.

AVCA: American Veterinary Chiropractic Association. Provides certification for licensed doctors of chiropractic and veterinary medicine.

CAC: Certified in animal chiropractic

CVA: Certified veterinary acupuncturist

CVH: Certified veterinary homeopath

CAAB: Certified applied animal behaviorist. There are fewer than fifty applied animal behaviorists in the country, since the standards for certification are very rigorous.

BVMS: Bachelor of veterinary medicine and surgery. This is a five-year degree offered by universities in the UK and other countries outside the U.S.

BVSc, MBSc, DVSc: Bachelor, master, or doctor of veterinary science. This person is trained for research, not for clinical practice.

DACVB or Dipl., ACVB: Diplomate of the American College of Veterinary Behaviorists. This is one of the many specialty boards that will certify vets who receive a special education by meeting a strict set of requirements.

DACVECC: Diplomate, American College of Veterinary Emergency and Critical Care

CVT, RVT, LVT: Certified, registered, or licensed veterinary technician. This person passed a state or federal exam after graduation from an accredited veterinary technician program, but is qualified only to assist a vet at this stage in his career.

ACVS: American College of Veterinary Surgeons

AVDC: American Veterinary Dental College

"Has a special/strong interest in . . ." (or similar): The vet has additional training in the subject but did not pursue board certification (it may or may not be offered).

LOOK FOR YOUR VET'S LETTERS ONLINE

Before you meet with your vet, search online for a recent bio from a professional website. This way, you won't feel the need to prod him during a visit or scan his walls for diplomas.

Veterinary Care Vocabulary

FIVE IMPORTANT TERMS YOU MAY NOT ALREADY KNOW

Conventional (traditional) vet: A licensed veterinarian who treats symptoms one problem at a time and views the body as a series of parts. Uses Western medicine as a primary means of treatment and seldom focuses on the body's ability to heal itself.

Integrative-care vet: A veterinarian who employs both conventional and alternative treatments in his practice in order to get the "best of both worlds." Often has a strong focus on changing the dog's lifestyle habits to promote natural health and healing.

Holistic vet: Essentially the same as an integrative vet; he thinks of the body as being interconnected and uses natural treatments and remedies to help the body heal itself. For instance, if a dog has arthritis, the vet may explore whether it could be the result of a larger problem with the animal's liver—and not only treat his arthritis in and of itself.

Alternative therapies: Therapies that are not used by conventional practitioners. They include but are not limited to acupuncture, chiropractic, homeopathy, herbal medicine, nutrition, etc.

Therapies/modalities: Forms of treatment. For example, these may be conventional care, acupuncture, chiropractic, homeopathy, herbal medicine, nutritional medicine, etc.

Should I Choose an Integrative-
or Conventional-Care Vet?

Most traditional veterinary schools train doctors with a conventional perspective, though this is changing as integrative care (also commonly referred to as "holistic care") earns an increasing number of advocates based on its strong results. After all, veterinary science is constantly evolving. As a result, the meaning of integrative veterinary care seems to change, too, depending on who says it and the context in which it's said. Let's try to clear things up.

Integrative care uses the best of what alternative medicine has to offer while making the most of conventional (Western) medicine. What a great concept—the best of both worlds!—and it's not so different from how a lot of us view human health care. Integrative care combines conventional teaching with alternative methods to figure out what's wrong with your dog and find ways to make him better. When leaning on natural therapies, it attempts to help the body heal itself whenever possible. So an integrative vet treats the dog's body as one working unit, rather than a series of disconnected and separately functioning systems.

If you work with an integrative-care vet, I strongly suggest that you find out what this term means to him. After all, some integrative-care vets lean more heavily on alternative therapies like acupuncture, chiropractic, aromatherapy, herbal treatments, and homeopathy. Others tend to cherry-pick from both worlds a bit more, so they may choose a holistic approach to nutrition but prefer a more traditional route to treating fleas and ticks. Very few vets, even those in the conventional world, understand their field as a black-and-white arena.

Don't Assume That Natural Always Means Safe

When taking a holistic approach, don't forget to ask your vet about possible side effects of treatment. And always rely on him to lead the way! Even if some natural therapies are accessible to you, they should not be purchased or administered without medical supervision.

Take herbs and supplements, for example. While some dog owners might think these are harmless because they're natural and readily accessible, they can either have their own side effects or increase the chance of side effects when mixed with conventional medicines. Herbs and supplements can also interfere with a medication's effectiveness. And if herbs aren't purchased from a reputable manufacturer that's suggested by your vet, they can become contaminated during processing. (With all this said, it should be noted that holistic vets insist that natural remedies have fewer side effects than conventional remedies do.)

You wouldn't administer a prescription drug to your dog without a vet's approval, and the same care should be taken with natural therapies.

By combining the best and most appropriate therapies from all disciplines, I feel that a good vet, like a good doctor, will focus on preventative care to treat sick dogs more quickly and effectively. I think it's also worth noting that "alternative" topics like nutrition and minimal vaccines were once considered exceptionally holistic interests to traditional veterinarians, who ignored these subjects to a fault. Cut to today, and a healthy canine diet and fewer vaccines are becoming part of a mainstream conversation about how to simply provide solid veterinary care to your pet.

If you're hesitant about fully committing to integrative care, you may want to consider alternative therapies as a supplement to traditional vet care, just as you might in your own life. How many people do you know who see traditional doctors but also eat organic food and receive acupuncture for allergies or joint pain? This type of regimen can be extended to your dog, and you may change your mind about integrative care as you become increasingly comfortable with alternative therapies. Some traditional vets are more open to combining modalities than others, so make decisions within your comfort zone.

If you go the integrative route, most of these vets are affiliated with the American Holistic Veterinary Medical Association (AHVMA), which supports and teaches natural and holistic medicines. To find an integrative-care vet near you, visit the AHVMA's referral site at Holisticvetlist.com. This site also lists the modalities or treatments that each doctor employs and information about what each term means.

Alternative Therapies

Integrative vets may ask you to consider one or more alternative methods when treating your dog if he becomes sick or feels generally unwell. Many of these can be used as stand-alone treatments or in conjunction with other therapies (modalities). Since it's easy to dismiss or feel skeptical about unfamiliar ideas, I asked Shawn Messonnier, DVM, of Paws and Claws Animal Hospital in Plano, Texas, and host of the award-winning Sirius XM Radio series *Dr. Shawn, the Natural Vet*, to explain some of the more common therapies from the AHVMA's referral site. As you might expect, each specialist undergoes intense training and testing to qualify his degree.

ALTERNATIVE THERAPIES MAY INCLUDE BUT AREN'T LIMITED TO

Nutrition: Integrative vets strongly believe in individualized nutrition plans. These may include customized diets, vitamin supplements, and eating schedules for your dog.

Acupuncture: Uses very thin, sterile needles placed in specific points on the body to promote health and alleviate pain.

Chiropractic: Uses manual therapy to manipulate the musculo-skeletal system, particularly the spine, joints, and soft tissue.

Homeopathy: Uses extremely diluted amounts of herbs, minerals, and natural substances that stimulate the body's own healing process. This traditionally uses only one herb, mineral, or natural substance at a time.

Homotoxicology: Similar to homeopathy but uses combination remedies rather than a single remedy to remove toxins from the patient and encourage healing.

Applied kinesiology: Uses muscle testing (gentle pressure) to evaluate the function, structure, and balance of your dog's body. It also determines whether energy is blocked.

Glandular therapy: Whole animal tissues or extracts of these tissues found in supplements that are used for health maintenance and therapy of mild problems involving the glands of the body. For example, liver extracts are thought to benefit the liver, thyroid extracts benefit the thyroid, and so on.

Massage: Helps with pain reduction, circulation, flexibility, stress, and the removal of toxins.

Herbs: Used either on a regular long-term basis or to treat a specific health problem. Herbal treatments may also be found in natural pet care supplies. All herbs given to your dog should be recommended, prescribed, and monitored by your vet.

What to Look for in a Veterinarian

Kenneth D. Fischer, DVM, of the Hillsdale Animal Hospital in Hillsdale, New Jersey, helped me pull together this list of tips to always keep in mind when interacting with a vet. As with your trainer or groomer, this relationship should be a team effort between the professional, the dog owner, and the dog. Ultimately, you have all the decision-making power as your pet's owner, but a vet should educate you about your choices so you feel equipped to make them. To that end, a good vet will:

Make you feel comfortable: He'll interact with you in a way that makes you and your dog feel at ease. This is a subjective experience, since some people prefer a touchy-feely approach and others appreciate a more clinical rapport. Bear in mind, if your dog doesn't like his vet, this is rarely the vet's fault. Dogs hate being poked and prodded, even if it is for their benefit.

Be accommodating: Choose a vet with office hours that meet your scheduling needs. Your dog should always seem like a priority at the office, no matter what the situation, whether it's at the hands of your vet or one of his partners. Your vet should also provide an emergency contact or a hospital referral for after-hours emergencies.

Has a supportive staff: It takes a veterinarian many years to build his practice and then take pride in knowing that his clients are treated well at all levels of service. A good vet is aware of how his staff interacts with his clients, since that impacts both the dog's family and the vet's practice.

Listen to and address your concerns: A number of vets keep to a fifteen-minute appointment schedule, which, for some, is less than ideal. Choose one who listens to your concerns and examines your dog according to those concerns, in addition to the routine checks he'll perform in the allotted time.

Know his limits: When your dog has a problem, a quality vet will know the answer, find the answer, or send you to someone who can help. He will always do his best to resolve a problem, but he'll also know when a situation is beyond his level of expertise and will refer you to a specialist—all for the welfare of your dog.

Be open to second opinions: Ideally, your vet will act as a GP who suggests and manages consultations with specialists and is involved in ongoing decisions about your dog's care. Reasons to seek a second opinion aren't so different in dogs than they are in humans. Should you want a second opinion, the vet should respect your decision and stay committed to providing the best care and treatment for your dog. You may want a second opinion if:

> *Your dog has a rare condition.*
>
> *Your dog has an illness that requires special expertise.*
>
> *Diagnosing your dog's condition has been challenging or confusing.*
>
> *You'd like further information on alternative tests, procedures, and medicines.*
>
> *You want a second opinion about a treatment plan and outcome.*
>
> *You don't like how your doctor is handling your dog's health problem.*

A Vet's Emergency Affiliation Is Important

When choosing a vet, be sure he has affiliations with an emergency veterinarian in case your dog has a problem outside your vet's regular work hours. Many veterinarians who have their own day practice will also have a vet on staff who sees after-hour emergencies. If this is the case, be sure to meet the doctor who covers for your vet to make sure you approve of his care and credentials. Your vet might also refer you to an emergency clinic. If that's the case, you may want to tour the hospital before you use it to make sure you're comfortable with the doctors and the facility.

Some vets advertise that they provide twenty-four-hour emergency care when what they really mean is that their answering machine refers you to an emergency facility if you call after hours. This isn't a problem for some clients, but you'll want to ask for full disclosure when you first consider a vet so there are no surprises if you're in a desperate situation during off-hours.

It is entirely your decision about whether you choose a vet whose own facility can help with after-hours emergencies or one who refers you to another practice. Your ultimate decision will depend on costs, credentials, a vet's reputation, your animal's special needs, and so on.

Be sure to include the name of your emergency vet and the address of his affiliated practice or hospital on all emergency contact lists.

Ask Dr. Z!

What does it mean when my dog . . .

Q: *Would rather drink fresh rainwater in a puddle than purified tap water from his clean bowl?*

A: Your dog is not ungrateful for the fresh water you provide! Rainwater may have better flavor and a range of natural minerals that are removed by purification.

If you decide to get another opinion, don't keep your appointment a secret. Since the new doctor will need the dog's records, have a conversation with your primary doctor to avoid any awkwardness and the need for repeating any tests. Realize, too, that telling your vet you'll be seeking a second opinion doesn't need to be an insulting exchange. Simply say, "I don't intend to transfer my care, but I'd like another doctor to have a look at my dog." You're an adult, and your vet is a professional. Owners who want what's best for their pets won't let the prospect of hurt feelings get in the way. People get second opinions all the time. You're not cheating on your vet; you're helping your dog.

The Three Dynamics of a Good Vet Relationship

Like any good relationship, the one you share with your vet is comprised of important dynamics that cause it to function well. According to Dr. Fischer, these three are a must.

1. **Communication:** You and your vet should be able to speak openly about your vet's philosophies, any concerns you might have, and the general health of your pet. He should provide you with adequate information about your pet's condition, treatment and diagnostic options, and an explanation of why these are important to your dog's health.

2. **Balance:** Your vet should be able to help you strike a balance between worrying too much and worrying too little. He will help you navigate through any health predicament and provide education about the best ways to care for your dog in the context of his illness and explain how it can affect the health of other dogs and humans.

3. **Trust:** Your vet is only human, but you shouldn't spend much
   time second-guessing his opinion. A vet's job is a challenging one,
   since dogs can't speak for themselves, and they're covered in fur
   that can mask illnesses. But if you find yourself doubting your
   vet more often than you're trusting his opinion, it may be time to
   look for another vet.

DO YOU NEED A VET WHO MAKES HOUSE CALLS?

If either you or your dog is in a position to require a house call from a certified
vet, contact the American Association of Housecall Veterinarians (AAHV) at
HouseCallVets.com for a referral. Some small-town or high-end urban vets
who aren't affiliated with the AAHV may also come to your home if necessary,
as an extension of a practice. A house-call vet will examine your dog in his
own environment, which is especially beneficial to very young or very old
pets. These veterinarians have the added benefit of providing convenience to
you, personalized care for your dog in a familiar environment, and protection
from the types of sicknesses one might find in a vet's office (for you or your
dog). Plus, a house-call vet can save a dog owner time and provide greater
freedom when scheduling appointments. Evaluate the extent to which you
might need or desire this service, and choose a scenario that's right for you.

Should you opt for a house-call vet, be sure to ask about days and hours
of availability, specific services provided, clinic affiliations for blood work
and other diagnostic services, how emergency situations are handled, what
paperwork you'll need to send or have with you during the exam, the vet's
follow-up protocol, and appointment fees and payment policies. Some
house-call vets, though not all, can be expensive. Be sure to ask about the
costs for service, plus possible payment plans.

How to Set a Positive Example for Your Dog

How you act at the vet's office can influence your dog's behavior. If you're
relaxed and positive, it's easier to instill an upbeat attitude in your dog
about the trip. Dogs absorb our energy, whether we're coaxing them to

potty in the rain or taking them to the doctor. Here are a few ways to set an example for your dog during his trips to the DVM, courtesy of Dr. Fischer:

Keep your cool: Use a tender, reassuring voice when you're in the waiting room, and keep your nerves to yourself, even if you're upset about your dog's health. The more you fret, the more anxious your dog (and other waiting room owners and pets) will become. Long, comforting strokes along the back or a gentle massage behind the ears will put your dog at ease and give you something to do while you wait. Remember that dogs pay attention to changes in body language and tone of voice, so be sure that yours communicate a confident headspace.

Keep your dog on a leash: Your vet's waiting room isn't a dog park. Leash your dog to keep him under control and out of harm's way when he's among other ill dogs. If he's eager to sniff a fellow pup, ask the owner first if it's okay. Sick dogs can be anxious, aggressive, and/or contagious. If your puppy hasn't had all of his vaccinations, don't let him commune with other dogs at the vet. That said, you don't need to keep him from touching the floor, as some suggest. The floor of a vet's office should be clean.

Follow your vet's lead: Don't expect your dog to sit, stay, or obey any other training commands when he's at the doctor's office; this isn't the time to reinforce those lessons. If your dog is anxious, tossing these words out may aggravate a problem. Once you're in the examining room with a vet and vet tech, let them take the lead unless they ask for your assistance. Acting as an onlooker can make you feel vulnerable, but the best way to help is to let the vet do his job. You can also say, "If there's anything I can do to help you, let me know," before calmly stepping aside. If your vet doesn't mind, position yourself within your dog's line of vision. I always maintain eye contact with Bianca during a vet exam so that she feels safe. (If you're a wreck, the vet may take the dog to another room without you.)

Reward your dog after the visit: There are treats at the reception desk for a reason! If your dog doesn't have digestive issues or other health concerns linked to food, create a positive association between the reward and the vet visit. Remember how the pediatrician gave you a lollipop after each exam as a child? Same deal here.

Why Health Insurance Is Important

I highly recommend that you get pet insurance for your dog—and long before he really needs it. Your dog may seem spritely now, but any pet's health is unpredictable. Some experts say that one in three pets will need emergency treatment in a year, and two out of every three pets will experience a significant health problem during their lifetime.

Pet insurance helps owners manage the unknown costs associated with a dog's health care, via a monthly or annual payment. Most plans offer coverage for the diagnoses and treatment of accidents, illnesses, and some hereditary conditions. Blood work, dental cleanings, vaccinations, MRIs, hospitalization, and even chemotherapy are covered by good health care plans—and most work with traditional vets, specialists, alternative therapists, and chiropractic vets, too. Some even cover prescription food and kennel fees and provide discounts for multiple-pet households.

A multitude of plans are available, so shop around for one that accommodates your dog's age, treatment needs, and any preexisting conditions. Once you find a vet you like, ask which insurance plans he recommends and why. Most offices have pamphlets available for the taking, but talking to the vet who cares for your dog will be most helpful. You

---

Ask Dr. Z!

What does it mean when my dog . . .

Q: *Chases cars and other items with wheels (strollers, bikes, skateboards)?*

A: Many dogs are highly predatory and are stimulated to chase moving objects. The tires of a car are right at a dog's eye level and can be especially tempting to curious canines. Wheel-chasing is almost a hardwired behavior, but should be discouraged. Even dogs that have been run over by cars will start chasing them again as soon as they've recovered from injuries!

should also do research online and with friends who've had sick dogs in the past. When you decide on a plan, learn about its coverage options and cancellation policies, should you move or want to change vets in your dog's lifetime. As with human health insurance, there can be tricky loopholes, coverage and reimbursement rules, and claim deadlines that must be followed to always get your money's worth. These rules are seldom bendable, so if you're going to invest in health insurance, learn all you can about the policy before you sign on. The ASPCA claims that the costs of veterinary care have more than doubled over the past ten years, while specific treatments like surgery and chemotherapy have risen even faster. Reimbursement fees vary, and some even come with a money-back guarantee, but whatever plan you go with will be money well spent.

The Importance of Preventative Care

Vaccines, spaying and neutering, and parasite control are just three ways to prevent future illness in your dog. So is nutrition, which we'll cover in Chapter 5. I've found that integrative veterinary care focuses on the general topic of preventative care more than traditional vets do—and for a solid, logical reason. Why wait until your dog's really sick to help him when you can take smart steps now to deter future illnesses? Talk to your vet about preventative care measures that he thinks are appropriate for your pet.

Vaccinating Your Dog

The rationale behind immunization for dogs isn't so different than it is for humans: After administering a small amount of a disease-causing agent, the vaccine stimulates the dog's body to produce antibodies that then battle it (the injected substance has been modified so it doesn't actually cause the disease). So if a dog is exposed to a disease later, he'll already have the antibodies to fight it off. Some vaccines are given via injection with a syringe and needle; others are administered through the dog's nose with drops.

Vaccines have proved to be helpful in the past, but they're also a relatively controversial subject. Some integrative vets believe that the fewer vaccines your dog gets, the better—and that vets should tailor vaccine programs to the unique needs of a client and his dog. This has become the recent opinion of many traditional vets, too, though it wasn't always the case.

Not all pets should be vaccinated with all available vaccines. "Core" vaccines are recommended for most pets, and "noncore" vaccines are reserved for specific dogs based on their geography and lifestyle (exposure to kennels, classes, dog parks, etc.). Trust your vet to consider your pet's risk of exposure to preventable diseases, and to customize a vaccination program that's right for you. As with most aspects of health, one vaccination schedule will not work for all pets.

KNOW THE DIFFERENCE BETWEEN CORE AND NONCORE VACCINES

Core vaccines are vaccines that are recommended for most dogs. Noncore vaccines are administered to dogs that find themselves in specific situations (like kennel boarding or training class) or in certain geographic locations (places where diseases are more endemic) that require additional vaccinations. A vet will determine a vaccination schedule that is suitable for your pet based on your dog and his lifestyle. Here's a breakdown of common vaccines:

Core vaccinations: Distemper, Parvovirus, Adenovirus 2*, and Rabies

Noncore vaccinations: Leptospirosis, Bordetella, Parainfluenza, Lyme disease, Coronavirus

Not suggested: Giardia, Adenovirus 1

*These first three are what vets collectively refer to as a distemper vaccine; Dr. Fischer says that referring to all three diseases as the "distemper vaccine" is simply how vets shorten the name (it's like calling your train the White Plains train when it actually makes several stops on the way to White Plains). Some distempers also contain a vaccine against Parainfluenza virus and Leptospirosis, though not all vets recommend it. The distemper virus itself is highly contagious among puppies and some older dogs, with symptoms that include bronchitis, pneumonia, intestinal inflammation, poor appetite, fever, and congested head. If a puppy gets distemper, the death rate is exceptionally high, and if he doesn't die, then he can become permanently impaired. Hence the importance of this core vaccine.

Determine a Vaccination Schedule with Your Vet

Though we know that vaccinations have been administered too frequently in the past (the AVMA once suggested annual boosters, but now recommends boosters every three years), they have contributed to a great reduction in infectious diseases like rabies, hepatitis, and parvovirus that used to kill dogs and harm people. These diseases are now rare in many areas. Efforts to reduce vaccines to the fewest possible are well-intentioned, but there may be a danger in advocating an entire population of totally unvaccinated dogs.

During your first visit to the vet, make sure you really understand your dog's vaccination schedule and why your vet is suggesting it. You may want to consider not vaccinating your dog if he's sick, injured, or old—or if he has a chronic health problem, has a family history of drug or vaccine sensitivity, and/or comes from a breed that's predisposed to autoimmune diseases. You may also want to ask your vet if he thinks it's smart to perform a vaccine antibody titer test to assess your dog's level of protective immunity from previous vaccinations. A titer test is a blood test that shows the presence and concentration of your dog's immunological response (his body's ability to fight a disease, because of either vaccination or natural exposure). If your dog has satisfactory levels of vaccine titers, he may not need further vaccination against a disease.

What's a Typical Vaccine Program?

The topic of vaccine schedules can be a confusing one, so Dr. Fischer offers the following suggestions as a starting point. Like most integrative care vets, he recommends only core vaccines: Rabies, Parvo, Distemper, and Adenovirus 2.

In general, puppy vaccines should be given at six weeks of age or older, with at least two doses administered four weeks apart. A puppy should be at least fourteen weeks old at the final vaccine. Originally, distemper vaccines were given every year. While some vets still do this, most find this rule archaic; many integrative-care vets feel these vaccines are good for longer than three years. Adult dogs are boostered with a core vaccine at one year of age and every three years thereafter. Some vaccines are labeled for administration to puppies as described above and then every three years.

Dr. Fischer likes to wait until six months of age to give the rabies vaccine; this allows the puppy's immune system to mature, though it can be given anytime after twelve weeks of age. Adult dogs are boostered for rabies at one year of age and every three years after that (unless mandated more frequently, which may be done by individual states, counties, sections of counties, or municipalities). Your vet should remind you about booster shots when you see him during biannual visits. He may also send out reminder cards, like your dentist does for cleanings.

Ask Dr. Z!

What does it mean when my dog . . .

Q: *Snores like an old man?*

A: This is most common in dogs with short faces, such as English Bulldogs or Boston Terriers, due to the shape of their nasal passages. This may also happen if the dog is congested.

The Bordetella (Kennel Cough) Vaccine

If your dog is vaccinated for Bordetella, it should be done annually (although some kennels may require it more frequently). Please keep in mind that studies have found that the Bordetella vaccine is not entirely effective against kennel cough and can also cause the illness. This vaccine is often required if your dog is boarded or participates in training classes, since kennel cough is a highly communicable upper-respiratory disease that can be transmitted by a dog that coughs, sniffs, or even breathes near another. Experts say that Bordetella is an airborne infection and difficult to prevent, as dogs don't show symptoms right away. The illness can also turn from an innocuous cold to a lower-respiratory disease like pneumonia—and in severe cases, lead to death (although fortunately, this is rare). The most common symptom is a wet cough that can be followed by retching. A nasal discharge (watery or thick) may also be present. In mild cases, the dog may continue to eat and be alert and active. In more severe cases, symptoms may progress to fatigue, fever, and lack of appetite. The majority of severe cases occur in animals with compromised immune systems or in puppies that have yet to be vaccinated (or have yet to develop more capable immune systems).

Look for Possible Reactions to Vaccines

The worst reaction a dog can get is anaphylaxis, a sudden—and potentially fatal—shock that the body experiences from the vaccine; it happens within minutes of the vaccine being administered. It requires emergency treatment to prevent a fatal reaction. Fortunately, anaphylaxis is pretty rare, depending on the vaccine. It is much more common, for instance, with Leptospirosis vaccine than with distemper or rabies vaccine. Dogs that have experienced anaphylactic reactions in the past are seldom advised to receive future vaccinations, though you should discuss this subject with your vet to determine the best approach if it applies to your dog.

Other, less dangerous adverse vaccine reactions include lethargy, vomiting, and diarrhea. I suggest waiting fifteen minutes before leaving the vet after your dog is vaccinated, just to make sure he doesn't have an adverse reaction you can't treat at home. Normal vaccine reactions occur within twenty-four hours, during which time your dog might seem a bit sluggish and develop a low-grade fever.

Some dogs can have a negative reaction to the rabies vaccine, but it is required by law. Bad reactions include localized hair loss at the site of vaccination, thickened and scaly skin, or a lump that can form at the injection site and resolve on its own. Such reactions can occur as late as a few weeks after the vaccine.

In much rarer incidences, dogs can develop seizure disorders and significant behavior disorders from some vaccinations. Again, these are few and far between.

Spaying and Neutering

I strongly feel that unless you're a professional or hobby breeder, you should spay or neuter your dog to help control the pet population, minimize health risks, and reduce dog-to-dog aggression. During your first appointment, ask your vet when you should have the procedure done (most vets spay or neuter a dog at six months of age).

If you adopt a puppy or adult dog from a shelter, be sure to bring all paperwork to your first vet appointment. Not every shelter will explore the dog's medical history, but as an adopter, you should know if the dog has had vaccinations or been spayed/neutered. In some states, like New York, it's the law that a dog must be spayed/neutered before he leaves a shelter.

Spaying

What it means: Spaying involves sterilizing a female dog by removing her entire reproductive system (uterus, fallopian tubes, and ovaries). It's like a total hysterectomy for canines, and it makes her unable to have babies. Most dogs recover from the surgery within two days; the vet may use stitches that absorb into her skin or those that need to be removed in a few weeks.

When to do it: Before she's six months old (this will lower her risk of mammary cancer). If you miss this window before her first heat, spay her when she's finished her first cycle. In this case, schedule the spaying for at least six weeks after she starts spotting.

How a dog's body changes: Early spaying helps eliminate mammary cancer and cancers of the reproductive system (since you're removing all the organs), including uterine and ovarian cancer. Spaying before a dog's first heat is best, but spaying before the second or third heat can also reduce mammary tumor risk. After the fourth heat, there is less protection against these forming.

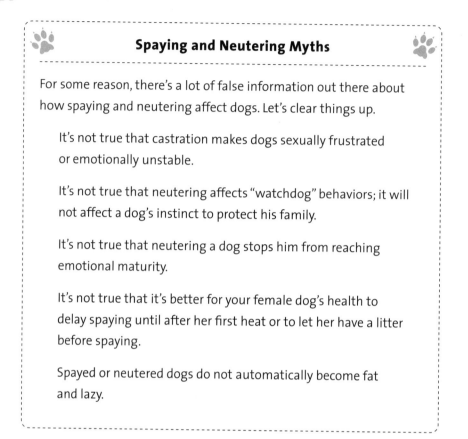

Spaying and Neutering Myths

For some reason, there's a lot of false information out there about how spaying and neutering affect dogs. Let's clear things up.

It's not true that castration makes dogs sexually frustrated or emotionally unstable.

It's not true that neutering affects "watchdog" behaviors; it will not affect a dog's instinct to protect his family.

It's not true that neutering a dog stops him from reaching emotional maturity.

It's not true that it's better for your female dog's health to delay spaying until after her first heat or to let her have a litter before spaying.

Spayed or neutered dogs do not automatically become fat and lazy.

Neutering

What it means: The words "neutering" and "castration" are used interchangeably. The procedure removes the dog's testicles from its scrotum through an incision (the loose skin eventually shrinks up and disappears).

When to do it: If a young male dog shows signs of aggression, you may want to neuter him earlier rather than later. Ask your vet about the best time for your dog's castration, since opinions on early neutering vary.

How a dog's behavior changes: Neutering may improve a dog's behavior—depending on the specific canine—and it is especially helpful for those with aggression or other behavioral problems. Neutered dogs may display and solicit less aggression toward other dogs and are less confrontational, less likely to mount other dogs or people, less likely to urine-mark in the house, less inclined to roam or run away, less likely to bite, and unable to get testicular cancer. Neutering also may decrease the risk of prostate disease.

Why Do Spayed and Neutered Dogs Still Mount Each Other?

Though testosterone encourages dogs to mount, hold on, and thrust against other dogs, this isn't always a sexual act. Katenna Jones, the humane educator and animal behaviorist with the American Humane Association (AHA) mentioned earlier, says that more often than not, humping is about establishing dominance with another dog and signaling seniority among dogs of the same sex. Dogs may also mount each other if they've been separated for a while—for some dogs, mounting is simply a form of bonding (it's also a very embarrassing behavior, so you may want to discourage your dog from doing it).

As for why dogs mount people or furniture, the jury is still out. Katenna says that some dogs mount from sheer excitement (they just get all riled up, and it manifests as mounting), while others do it as part of the maturation process (juvenile dogs can be more prone to mounting). But on the whole, it seems that dogs mount because it feels good. Somehow I think we can all relate.

Parasite Control

Integrative and traditional veterinarians can have very different opinions about how to handle parasites like fleas, ticks, and worms. Most integrative-care veterinarians don't advocate the use of pesticide chemicals on your lawn *or* on your dog, since they feel that the same chemicals that are designed to protect your dog against parasites can also make him very sick. Before you begin any parasite program, speak to your vet about his prevention and treatment preferences and really educate yourself about what is in each of these products and how your dogs may be affected by the formula. These change and update on a regular basis, so once you choose a parasite-control plan, keep your vet apprised of its effectiveness as your dog gets older.

Holistic vets tend to lean toward natural remedies for both external (flea, tick) and internal (worms) parasites. (In a similar vein, some groomers like to add natural tea tree, lemon, or lavender oils to shampoos to prevent external parasites, though this treatment is seldom sufficient on its own. See "Grooming Products" on page 353 for recipes.) These vets advocate diet, homeopathy, and herbal remedies to keep all parasites at bay, but they strongly feel that all must be administered by an expert, since large doses of any treatment, whether it's a conventional drug, herb, or nutrient, can have side effects. Holistic preferences for worms include Parasite Formula by Quantum Herbal Products, but they should always be administered by your veterinarian.

I like to defer to veterinarians with an open mind for parasite-control guidance, since so much of your dog's risk depends on where he lives. For instance, I suspect that leaning more heavily on a natural oil-enhanced shampoo, and less on a chemical treatment, may be more appropriate in locales with a lower incidence of flea and tick cases.

After Bianca almost died from Lyme disease, I came to prefer conventional prevention and treatment for parasites, especially via products by Frontline and Revolution. Frontline kills fleas, ticks, and chewing lice, and you can buy it through your vet, pet store, or an online vendor. On the other hand, Revolution requires a prescription in the U.S.; it prevents fleas, ticks, chewing lice, and heartworm. These are topical treatments applied once a month to the area between a dog's shoulders. Read the product's directions and notes on frequency of application to avoid harm to you, your dog, or children.

While I follow a conventional regimen, natural remedies can also provide excellent solutions; I just haven't been exposed to them firsthand, as I have with products like Frontline. I do think that flea baths, chemical or electronic flea collars, and flea bombs/sprays/foggers are a terrible idea because they're either ineffective, toxic to your dog, or both. (They're also toxic to children.)

Know your parasites and speak to your vet about how to keep your dog and home safe from infestation. Check for fleas, ticks, and bites while grooming your dog, and always take a good look at his poop to make sure it's free of obvious intestinal parasites. However, a laboratory microscopic evaluation of a stool sample is critical to detect the presence of these parasites in most cases.

Fleas

Adult and immature fleas can appear on your pet *or* around your home, since immature flea stages (eggs, larvae, and pupae) thrive in carpets, bedding, and cracks in the floor. Be vigilant! They reproduce indoors year-round, though a monthly use of preventative products can kill them hours after they've infested your pet.

All dogs will scratch and lick themselves from flea bites, but those that are allergic to fleas will experience more intense itching that's accompanied by hair loss and skin irritation. When a flea bites an allergic dog, it injects a small amount of saliva into his skin and causes a severe allergy. But fleas spend only a small part of their time feeding on dogs, since their main focus is laying eggs in the house and yard that will hatch into more fleas.

Regardless of how you treat fleas, never use multiple flea products at once, and always read the manufacturer's warnings very carefully. Note that places where dogs congregate most, like dog parks and beaches, have higher flea counts, especially in warmer months when fleas multiply more readily.

Ticks

Ticks attach themselves to fur and insert their pincherlike mouths into a dog's skin. These mouths lock in place, feed on blood, and can be dislodged at any time, although they will fall off by themselves only when they are full. To learn how to remove a tick from your dog, see "How to Fix a Grooming Disaster" on page 367.

Experts say that there are many types of ticks (brown ticks, American dog ticks, lone star ticks, deer ticks), and many of them breed in the same geographic areas, each spreading a number of terrible illnesses—among these are Rocky Mountain spotted fever, Lyme disease, and ehrlichiosis. All of the tick-borne diseases share similar symptoms, which include sudden fatigue and fever and, in the case of Lyme disease, sudden and severe lameness and possible vomiting. Call your vet if you find a tick on your dog, and ask if he'd like you to bring it to the dog's appointment. Pulling a tick off yourself also warrants an immediate call to your doctor.

Heartworms

Heartworm is a potentially fatal disease that's most prevalent in areas where mosquitoes breed. Here, an infected mosquito feeds on a healthy dog and passes on the infectious disease. The heartworm larvae, which are injected into the dog during a mosquito bite, mature into adult heartworms as they gradually travel to the dog's heart and blood vessels near the heart, where they can cause significant damage (including heart failure). Signs of heartworm disease are lethargy, appetite loss, difficulty breathing, and coughing. In areas where heartworm disease is more prevalent (warmer and more humid climates), sudden death may be the first symptom.

Ask your vet about dog-specific mosquito repellents; never use those made for people on your dog. If you don't use Revolution for flea, tick, and heartworm prevention (it takes care of all three), ask your vet about giving him a monthly heartworm pill, like I do for Bianca.

TRAVEL NOTE

After traveling with your dog, always have him tested for internal and external parasites like heartworm, roundworm, hookworm, fleas, and ticks. You never know what he might contract.

Worms and Other Intestinal Parasites

Internal parasites like tapeworms, roundworms, coccidia, giardia, hookworms, and whipworms can cause serious harm to dogs. If your dog experiences nausea, vomiting, diarrhea, and anemia, intestinal parasites may be to blame. Call your vet if you see any of these symptoms, though experts say that in many cases, there are no symptoms associated with parasitism.

Sand Flies!

Biting sand flies are an upsetting and itchy pest for dogs that visit or live near the beach. Come August in the Hamptons, they swarm Bianca and bite her back and legs. Since neither Frontline nor Revolution protects against sand flies, some experts say it may help to spritz your dog with Avon's Skin So Soft and/or burn citronella candles when you're both outside. Give yourself a good SSS spritz, too, since biting sand flies can hop from humans to dogs and vice versa. If your dog is visibly bitten, call your vet; he may ask you to treat the area with a triple antibiotic ointment.

For DIY mixologists, celebrity dog groomer and NSALA volunteer Jorge Bendersky suggests filling an empty spray bottle with one teaspoon of tea tree oil to one cup of water and misting your dog each time you leave the house. You can also mix four drops of tea tree oil to one ounce of shampoo to provide a soothing bath. Tea tree oil is a natural antiseptic, with anti-inflammatory and antifungal properties. It will keep insects away and soothe dogs that have been bitten.

While some worms are visible to the naked eye, not all of them are, so it's important to bring a fresh stool sample to your vet if your dog shows signs of parasite infection. The vet will run fecal tests to confirm the type of parasite in a dog's body and will issue a treatment for the concern.

Puppies are especially prone to intestinal worms, and believe it or not, most are born with roundworms; pups can also become infected from nursing if roundworms are present in their mothers. Puppies pick up hookworms and whipworms from their environment as well. If your puppy is being treated for any worms when you get him, there's no need to worry about his health or whether the breeder was neglectful, so long as the dog is properly treated. All puppies are routinely and repeatedly given deworming medication during their first few weeks of age.

Ask Dr. Z!

What does it mean when my dog . . .

Q: *Gets rough patches on his belly?*

A: This can result from a dog rubbing his belly on rough surfaces, experiencing dry skin, eating a poor diet, or being exposed to dry air. Licking a rough patch can make the condition worse, so call your vet right away for a soothing treatment.

Dog First Aid Kit

If you own a dog, you need a first aid kit. It's that simple. This kit will be your go-to resource for common problems and dire emergencies. If your dog has special medical conditions, ask a vet which items need to be added. Be sure to refresh expired medicine and used supplies on a regular basis.

I suggest storing your first aid items in a large tackle box or plastic storage crate; you may also want to make a second, smaller version for the car or travel. Keep all kits away from children, since they contain items that could be harmful if they're ingested or tampered with.

I asked Dr. Messonnier to help assemble a list of items that you should always have in your kit, and I've added a few of my own as well. The following first aid items are not intended to replace veterinary care, nor should you ever attempt medical intervention without a call to your vet *first*. A vet will talk you through an emergency on the phone, so you only need a basic understanding of how to use each item. For more on the most common emergencies that require immediate first aid from you, see Chapter 8.

WHAT YOU'LL NEED

☐ Copy of your emergency contact list, including phone numbers for your vet, emergency clinic (if applicable), and the ASPCA poison-control center

☐ An updated copy of your pet's medical records

☐ American Red Cross's *Dog First Aid* book and DVD

☐ Muzzle: Either a cage muzzle (a wire basket that fits around the dog's snout) or a soft muzzle (made from nylon or another durable fabric) will work, depending on your dog, though a soft muzzle may be easier for you to carry because it collapses. You can also make one from rolled gauze. Even the gentlest dogs bite and snap when they're in pain!

- [ ] Disposable, non-latex, powder-free gloves
- [ ] Pediatric digital rectal thermometer (non-mercury/non-glass)
- [ ] Petroleum jelly (to lubricate the thermometer)
- [ ] Small scissors with a blunt, rounded end and/or grooming clippers (for trimming hair around wounds, abrasions, and hot spots)
- [ ] Triple antibiotic ointment (to treat wounds and tick bites)
- [ ] Gauze sponges (to act as absorbent compresses)
- [ ] Non-adhesive gauze pads in assorted sizes (for wounds)
- [ ] Three rolls of rolled gauze (for bandaging, stabilizing joints, and makeshift muzzles)
- [ ] Hypoallergenic adhesive first aid tape (to hold bandages in place)
- [ ] Hydrogen peroxide (to wash out wounds and induce vomiting)
- [ ] Empty baby-dose syringe (to administer hydrogen peroxide)
- [ ] Benadryl (or generic) antihistamine (for insect bites, allergic reactions, and itching)
- [ ] Rubbing alcohol (to clean the area around wounds)
- [ ] Tweezers (for removing ticks and splinters)
- [ ] Sterile eye lubricant and eyewash from a pet store (for eye emergencies)
- [ ] Dog grooming clippers (for toenail emergencies)
- [ ] Kwik Stop powder or cornstarch (to stop bleeding on broken nails)

☐ Clean cloth and towel (to clean wounds and immobilize small dogs)

☐ Blanket (find one large enough to immobilize your dog)

☐ Nylon leash (for transport)

☐ Milk of magnesia (to potentially absorb poison)

☐ Epsom salt (mix one teaspoon in two cups warm water to draw out infection and soothe itchy skin)

☐ Baking soda (for skin irritations)

☐ Needle-nose pliers (to remove foreign objects)

☐ Expired credit card (to scrape away bee stingers)

Recognizing and Suppressing Pain

Call a vet if you suspect that your dog is experiencing pain of any kind. Signs of pain include:

Flinching, biting, snapping, or yelping when a specific area is touched

Increased heart rate and temperature

Constant barking or whining

Panting, rapid breathing

Licking, chewing, or scratching a specific area

Lying awkwardly, with frequent position changes

Sleeplessness

Limping

Trembling

Never, ever give human pain medications—Tylenol, Advil, a prescription, or otherwise—to your dog without your vet's permission first. Dogs with arthritis, post-op pain, luxating patellas, or other joint pain might require a pain prescription from the vet. Glucosamine and chondroitin products are widely used on dogs with joint or hip pain.

On a related note: Some dog treats and dog foods contain various amounts of glucosamine and chondroitin, but before you consider giving your dog either of these, talk to your vet first about a treatment plan. Bianca started to limp due to achy joints, but her problem went away when I began giving her a daily Glyco-Flex supplement (available as a pill or treat). She still takes them and hasn't had a problem since. Ask your vet about using these in addition to (or even instead of) medical treatments.

Tending to Tears, Strains, and Sprains

Never diagnose or treat a muscle, joint, or ligament problem on your own (though you may feel tempted to treat and bandage your dog the minute you notice a problem). Call the vet immediately, and even if it turns out that your dog is hobbling from a simple sprain, follow the vet's advice before providing any care. Once your vet is on the phone, ask for his permission to:

1. Apply a gel freezer pack wrapped in a dishcloth or paper towel, or even a bag of frozen vegetables, to the injured area. Use it for fifteen minutes, then wait an hour, then repeat. This process reduces pain and swelling during the first twenty-four hours after an injury.

2. Restrict activity, and minimize his leash walks both during, and shortly after, he's healed.

3. Use a heating pad to increase circulation and reduce stiffness twenty-four hours after the injury. Hold a warm (not hot!) pad on the injured area, but don't leave a dog unsupervised with the electrical cord. You can also heat a wet towel in the microwave to accomplish the same goal or use a commercial first aid heat pack.

How to Give Your Dog Medication

Bianca has taken so many medicines in her life (albeit, for benign health issues) that I feel like an expert on how to administer them! But because I'm not, I turned to Dr. Messonnier and the Red Cross.

Each time you're given a new medicine by the vet, ask how to give it, especially if you'll be giving your dog shots. I won't even suggest how to give a dog a shot, because your vet needs to show you. Also ask about any tricks you can use to make the process easier, and whether an oral medication can be combined with food. Bianca can't resist a pill coated in peanut butter or wrapped in cheese! Here are a few tips from the experts:

Eye Meds

1. Rest the side of your hand that you'll use to give the medicine on the bone above your dog's upper eyelid.

2. Slightly tilt his head back with the palm of your other hand, and pull down on the lower eyelid with your thumb.

3. Holding the dispenser far enough away to make sure the tip of the dispenser doesn't touch the eye, place drops or ointment directly into the eye.

EAR MEDS

1. Position yourself on the same side as the ear you'll be treating. Try to approach your dog laterally; you may intimidate him if you hover above him with medicine in your hand.

2. If your dog has floppy ears, lift an ear and turn it over to expose the inside of the ear.

3. Place the drops or ointment in the middle of the ear opening. Even in small dogs, the ear canals are long enough to allow you to place the entire bottle nozzle into the dog's ear. The tip is designed for this purpose, so don't push it any deeper than need be.

4. Rub or massage the base of the ear where it meets the head. (It's easy to find this area, because the cartilage feels thicker here.) This helps the drop go deep into the canal.

NOTE: You can also soak a cotton ball with the right amount of fluid and squeeze it into the ear (though this may not work with thicker medicines).

ORAL LIQUID MEDS

1. Place the end of a plastic syringe (from your vet) on one side of your dog's mouth, just behind the canines, where the teeth are shortest and flattest.

2. Position the dropper above the lower teeth, or in the pouch between the cheek and teeth.

3. Slowly squeeze the syringe, dispensing the medicine no faster than your dog can swallow.

NOTE: Most liquids are flavored so that a pet will like the taste.

Elizabethan Collars, aka "E-collars" or "The Cone"

When you see a dog with a plastic funnel around his head, he's wearing what vets call an E-collar and what I like to call "The Cone." It is intended to keep a dog from aggravating a wound and/or biting stitches, and it may also be helpful in keeping him from licking off ointments and creams. Not surprisingly, most dogs don't like E-collars, since they can cause dogs to bump into walls and corners (they cut off a dog's peripheral vision). You can get E-collars from your vet or the pet store, but you should use one only with your vet's approval. To make a collared dog feel more comfortable, you may want to make him a soft bed from pillows or a blanket on the floor in front of the TV where he'll feel comfortable and relaxed.

ORAL PILLS AND CAPSULES

1. With one hand, hold your dog's upper jaw toward the ceiling by taking hold of his snout and pointing it upward. With your other hand, gently pull down the front of his lower jaw.

2. Place the tablet in the center of the tongue, as far back as you safely can.

3. Hold your dog's mouth closed until he swallows or licks his nose. Gently blowing on the nose or rubbing the throat will cause him to swallow.

NOTE: Tucking a pill inside a treat is much easier! Foolproof tricks include tucking it inside a piece of meat or cheese or coating it in peanut butter or cream cheese.

TOPICAL CREAMS AND OINTMENTS

1. Apply a thin layer of medicine to the affected skin.

2. Ask your vet whether your dog should wear an E-collar to prevent him from licking the medication.

Everyday Dog Dangers

Every home is filled with ingestible dog dangers, far beyond those that new dog owners nix when puppy-proofing their homes. And while I could fill a whole book with stuff that can cause your dog some form of harm, I asked Susan LaCroix Hamil, a certified vet tech and renowned Bloodhound breeder, for her take on the most frequent culprits that she and her peers have witnessed during their professional tenure. Here's her thorough list, with a few of my own potential hazards sprinkled throughout.

Alcohol (drunk dogs aren't cute—this is very dangerous)

Antifreeze (if you live in a cold climate, purchase dog-safe antifreeze for your car or truck)

Avocados

Batteries

Bones (if mishandled, some bones can cause choking, get stuck in the esophagus or stomach, puncture internal organs, or cause intestinal blockage)

Caffeine (from coffee/coffee grounds, tea, soda, chocolate, or other source)

Candy

Cat food or litter

Chocolate and cocoa

Children's toys (small plastic ones, especially)

Christmas tree and its water

Cigarettes

Cleaning products

Cocoa bean mulch

Corn cobs

Dish detergent

Disinfectants

Fabric softener sheets

Fat trimmings

Feminine hygiene products

Fertilizer products, especially those that contain bone meal or blood meal

Fly strips

Fruit stems, leaves, seeds, and pits

Garlic, but only in very high doses (it's common and safe to find it in some OTC flea and tick prevention medicines, usually combined with brewer's yeast)

Grapes

Grass that has been recently treated with chemicals

Hair ties, barrettes, or rubber bands

Hops (found in beer)

Macadamia nuts

Marijuana and other illegal drugs

Moldy or spoiled food

Mothballs

Onions, onion powder

Over-the-counter and prescription meds for humans, including antidepressants, painkillers, diet pills, and cold medicines

Persimmons

Plants and flowers like azaleas, amaryllis blooms and the bulb, English ivy, Japanese yew, mistletoe, eucalyptus, tomato plants, daffodil bulbs, rhododendron, and poinsettias. (The ASPCA counts 380 toxic plants and flowers in its database; visit ASPCA.org for a complete list.)

Plastic wrap

Popsicle sticks (wooden)

Potpourri

Potato, rhubarb, or tomato leaves; potato and tomato stems

Prescription medicines

Psoriasis cream

Raisins

Raw fish in large amounts

Snail, roach, and rodent bait

Snow globes (the liquid inside these can be a form of antifreeze)

Soap-based cleaners

Sponges

String, rope, or ribbon

Sugary foods

Tobacco products

Tylenol or other acetaminophen-based medicine

Underwear, socks, and nylons

Vitamin supplements for humans (especially those with iron),
unless suggested by your vet

Walnuts

Wild mushrooms

Xylitol (sweetener found in sugar-free candy and chewing gum)

Yeast dough

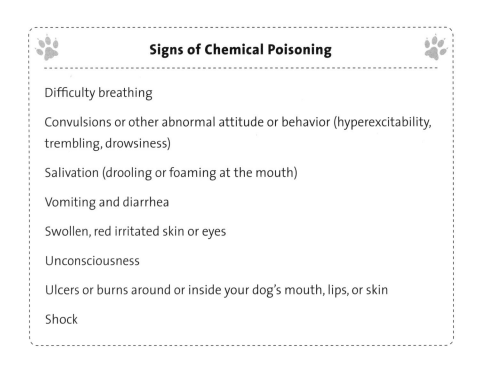

Signs of Chemical Poisoning

Difficulty breathing

Convulsions or other abnormal attitude or behavior (hyperexcitability,
trembling, drowsiness)

Salivation (drooling or foaming at the mouth)

Vomiting and diarrhea

Swollen, red irritated skin or eyes

Unconsciousness

Ulcers or burns around or inside your dog's mouth, lips, or skin

Shock

POISON CONTROL

If you have even the slightest hunch that your dog was exposed to some form of poison, call an emergency animal hospital or the ASPCA Animal Poison Control Center immediately. The toll-free hotline is open twenty-four hours a day, 365 days a year. A consultation costs $60, but it is money well spent to save a dog's life (it can be applied to your credit card).

Step 1: Contact your emergency animal hospital or the ASPCA Animal Poison Control Center at 888-426-4435 to learn how to stop poison from entering your dog's system.

Step 2: Do not take any action on your own. You must wait until a vet or the poison-control hotline counselor tells you what to do next. Different scenarios command different actions.

Step 3: The vet or hotline counselor will want to know the exact name of the poison, how much the animal ate or was exposed to, the time of ingestion, the dog's vital signs, and his weight. Also have your first aid kit, with hydrogen peroxide and a clean baby syringe, at the ready in case you need to induce vomiting. Never do this without prompting from an expert.

Ask Dr. Z!

What does it mean when my dog . . .

Q: *Gnaws on his front legs?*

A: This could be the result of anxiety, stress, or a medical problem. Consult a veterinarian.

Know What Is "Normal" for Your Dog

Deborah C. Mandell, VMD, DACVECC, an emergency and critical-care specialist at the Matthew J. Ryan Veterinary Hospital of the University of Pennsylvania in Philadelphia, and pet care adviser for the American Red Cross, says that a great starting point for assessing whether your dog needs medical attention of any kind is to know whether he's acting at all abnormal. But in order to do that, you need to first know what is *normal* for your dog.

Here's how: Always keep an eye on your dog and make mental notes about how he breathes, eats, drinks, walks, sleeps, urinates, and defecates so you'll be sensitive to changes that might signal a problem. What does your dog's panting sound like when he's anxious? What is the usual color and consistency of his poop? How lethargic is your dog on an average day? Being familiar with all of your dog's functions and behaviors is key to detecting a problem.

Next, keep the following list of what's normal for a dog—*and for your dog*—in your first aid kit. Fill in the blanks below so you know your dog's level of "normal" (as with humans, this can vary by small increments). That way the information is accessible in case something is amiss.

Normal Dog Temperature

How to take a dog's temperature: Ask someone else to hold your dog's head and scratch him behind the ears to distract him from the process. Use the pediatric digital thermometer (rectal) from your first aid kit and lubricate the tip. Insert the tip into the dog's rectum, just beneath his tail. Leave the thermometer inserted until it beeps. Remove and read the temperature.

What's normal: 100 to 102.5 F. A temperature lower than 99.5 F or greater than 103.5 F may be an emergency. Call your vet immediately.

My dog's temperature is ___.

Normal Breathing Rates

How to check breathing rates: When your dog is either standing or lying down, watch his chest as he breathes. Count the number of times it rises and falls in one minute. To check whether your pet is breathing during an emergency: If you cannot see his chest rise and fall, hold a mirror in front of his nostrils to look for condensation, or a tissue in front of his nostrils to see if it moves.

What's normal: 10 to 30 breaths per minute. Up to 200 pants per minute (breathing with his mouth open and tongue out) is also normal.

My dog breathes at approximately ___ breaths per minute.

What Does the Nose Know?

I've heard a number of times that when a dog has a dry nose, it means that he's feeling under the weather. But when I asked Dr. Messonnier about this, he said the nose trick is a myth!

Only if your dog's nose is always dry could it be a problem (it may indicate inactivity or dehydration). If your dog's nose is too hot, Dr. Messonnier says your dog may have a fever—but the best way to detect this is with a pediatric digital thermometer (rectal).

Normal Heart and Pulse Rates*

How to feel your dog's heartbeat: Lie your dog on his right side. Bend the left front leg at the elbow and bring it back to where it touches the chest. In this groove, place your hand over the area to feel and count his heartbeats.

How to take his pulse: You can take your dog's pulse in three ways while he's lying down on either side. 1) With your index and third finger high on his upper inside thigh where it meets the body, feel for a recess in the middle of the leg, halfway between the front and back. You should feel his pulse here. 2) You can also feel for a pulse below the dog's wrist, just above the middle pad on the underside of either front paw. 3) Find the area just below his ankle on the top side of either hind paw, and place your middle and index fingers at this point. In all places, count the beats for fifteen seconds and multiply by four (which equals 60 seconds).

What's normal: Puppy (less than a year old): 120–160 beats per minute. Small, miniature, or toy breed (30 pounds or less): 100–140 beats per minute. Medium to large breed (greater than 30 pounds): 60–100 beats per minute.

My dog's heart and pulse rate is ___ beats per minute.

*Note: Heart rate and pulse rate should be the same number in an animal, if he is not having a problem like a cardiac arrhythmia. In fact, the way that vets diagnose an arrhythmia is by noticing if the heart rate is different (usually much faster) than the pulse rate. So while your dog's healthy heart and pulse rate are the same number, a difference between the two indicates a problem.

Normal Gum and Inner-Eyelid Colors
(Or Mucous Membrane Color)

Detect the color of your dog's mucous membranes: Observing the normal color of your dog's gums and inner eyelids can help you recognize whether enough oxygen and blood are flowing to his tissues. To check this, lift your dog's upper or lower lip and notice the color of his gums or inner lip above the teeth. If he has black or pigmented mucous membranes, so that you cannot detect the color in his mouth, place your thumb on the skin just under the lower eyelid and gently pull down to observe the inner-eyelid membrane color instead.

What's normal: Your dog's mucous membranes should be pink, which means the tissues are receiving enough oxygen. *If your dog's mucous membranes are pale, blue/yellow, cherry red, white, brick red, or brown, this is an emergency. Call a vet immediately.*

My dog's mucous membranes are ___.

Normal Capillary Refill Time

How to check your dog's capillary refill time: After checking his mucous membrane color, press lightly on your dog's gums or inner lip. Noticing how soon his gums or inner lips return to their normal pink color after pressing on them can tell you if your dog's blood circulation is normal.

What's normal: Your dog's gums or inner lip should turn from pink to white to pink again. The pink color should return after one to two seconds. If the pink color returns in less than one second or more than three seconds, call your vet immediately. This is an emergency.

My dog's capillary refill time is ___ seconds.

Frequent Warning Signs of Illness

After you've evaluated the degree to which your dog's temperature, breathing, pulse, and mucous membrane color are normal, you may want to keep an eye out for future developments. You should *always* notice changes in your dog's attitude, energy, and behavior. To that end, Dr. Messonnier passed on some of the more common warning signs of general illness, categorized below by body system. Don't use this info to play doctor yourself, but if you notice that one or more of these symptoms are making your dog seem abnormal, initiate a call to your vet.

If a *puppy* has any of the below behaviors, call the vet immediately, since a puppy's immune system isn't as strong as an adult dog's, and his situation could worsen quickly.

INDICATES PAIN CONCERNS

Reluctance to move

Abnormally heavy panting

Labored breathing

Withdrawn

Loss of appetite

Increased body temperature

Lethargy or restlessness

INDICATES DIGESTIVE CONCERNS

Vomiting (with or without blood or pain)

Loose stool (without blood, bad odor, or dark color)

Weight loss

Diarrhea

Drooling

Depression

Excessive water intake

No desire to eat or drink for twenty-four hours while not acting well (i.e., bright and alert)

INDICATES RESPIRATORY CONCERNS

Heavy panting

Rapid or noisy breathing

Reluctance to move

Bluish or purplish mucous membrane color

Significant coughing with or without nasal discharge

Labored breathing indicated by increased respiratory effort; often the abdomen will heave or move in and out heavily as the dog is trying to take in or expel air

INDICATES SKIN CONCERNS

Red, scaled, greasy, crusty, or scabby area on the skin, nose, or foot

Skin odor

Painful, red, hot, crusty, and/or oozing bumps

Rash

Abnormally heavy shedding

Hair loss

Scratching, chewing at spots

Bruising or red dots on skin

External nosebleed without trauma

INDICATES NEUROLOGICAL CONCERNS

Paralysis

Dragging a limb or limping for more than twenty-four hours

Seizures

Depression

Pain when touched

Refusing to play or walk

Lethargy

Changes to vision

Shallow breathing without exertion

Weakness in limbs

Walking hunched over

Walking "knuckled over" (dog's paws do not flip back up into position when walking)

INDICATES URINARY TRACT CONCERNS

Inability to urinate

Urinating less frequently or more often than usual

Blood in urine

Straining to urinate

Crying while trying to urinate

Swollen testicles or scrotum

INDICATES JOINT CONCERNS

Reluctance to move

Seems pained when moving

Difficulty walking, getting up, or lying down

Wobbly joints

Swollen joints

Limping

INDICATES EAR CONCERNS

Odor

Redness

Pain to the touch

Discharge from the ear

Difficulty hearing

Shaking the head

Scratching at the ears

Rubbing the ears on the ground

Bleeding from the ears

A puffy swelling of the ear flap (it looks like a pillow)

Shying away from having the ears scratched or being petted around the ears

Indicates Eye Concerns

Yellow or green discharge (whitish-gray color is usually normal)

Cloudy eyes

Red or bloodshot eyes

Inability to open lids

Blindness

Shying away from being touched around the face, especially near the eyes

Difference in pupil size from one eye to the other

Sensitivity to light

Increased blinking

Pawing at the eyes and/or rubbing the face on the ground

Indicates Cognitive Concerns

Staring into space

Vocalizing at the wall or door

Decreased hearing

Inability to recognize owner

Increased sleep, especially during times when the dog is normally awake

Waking up at night

Inappropriate urinating in the house

Forgetting where the food and water bowls are

Forgetting that he just had a meal and seeming to want more than usual

Restlessness

INDICATES ANAL PROBLEMS

Scooting, dragging his bum on the floor

Blood in stool

Change in poop consistency and color

Pain or reluctance to be touched near the tail

Frequent licking of the anal area

Swelling on either side of the anal area (inside or outside)

Dog jumps to check his bum, as if he's been bitten or stung

Ask Dr. Z!

What does it mean when my dog . . .

Q: *Sleeps standing up?*

A: There are some types of seizures that will result in dogs standing still and/or staring into space. They may appear to be sleeping, but they're not. This dog may also be narcoleptic. Narcolepsy can affect Doberman Pinschers, Dachshunds, and Labrador Retrievers. A narcoleptic dog can fall asleep on his feet and enter a REM-like state. Food and excitement may trigger the narcoleptic behavior, and medical treatment is necessary.

Twenty-one Most Common Medical Conditions and Diseases

I strongly believe in leaving vet care to the experts, and I feel that providing too much detail about severe illnesses in this book will either serve to fuel your neurosis or provide you with an oversimplified explanation of a condition that's better discussed with your vet. After all, your vet should always be your primary source for education, diagnoses, and treatment. I did, however, ask Dr. Messonnier to help me describe the most common health problems he's seen in dogs, from bacterial infections to cancer (God forbid). We fleshed out each one here to provide you with a baseline understanding of the illness, its symptoms, and some treatment options. And since Dr. Messonnier is an integrative-care veterinarian, he added that there are many natural remedies that can be used as treatments for these conditions, too. Natural remedies are very individualized treatments, much more so than those found in conventional medicine, so you'll need to work with an integrative-care vet to find a formula that works for your dog.

As with any health problem, symptoms and treatments vary from dog to dog. Trust your vet to provide guidance, and if you have doubts about his methods, seek a second opinion.

Allergies

Allergies are one of the most common conditions that affect dogs. (Some vets attribute them to environmental toxins, mass-produced conventional dog food with unhealthy ingredients, overvaccination, and stress on the immune system.) A dog is exposed to foreign substances (allergens or antigens), which cause his immune system to rebel and trigger one, two, or all three of the following reactions: 1) itchy skin that's either localized (in one area) or generalized (all over the dog's body); 2) impact on the respiratory system, which causes sneezing, coughing, and/or wheezing, or nasal or eye discharge; and 3) digestive problems like vomiting or diarrhea. Dogs that scratch, chew, or lick their hair—especially on their paws—may have allergies. Treatments include antihistamines, allergy shots, antibiotics, monitored diets, anti-itch shampoos, and steroids. Experts claim that 50 percent of dogs that undergo allergy treatment get relief, though allergies take longer to resolve in some dogs than in others. There are five known types of allergies in dogs:

▶ **Inhalant allergies (atopy):** This is the most typical dog allergy, in which a dog reacts to tree pollens, grass pollens, weed pollens, molds, mildew, and/or dust mites. Inhalant allergies can occur either seasonally or year-round. Symptoms include severe and generalized itching.

▶ **Flea bite allergies:** Normal dogs experience only minor irritation in response to flea bites, but flea-allergic dogs have a severe itch-producing reaction to a flea's saliva on their skin. This can cause extreme scratching and biting that may lead to hair loss. Open sores and scabs on the skin, which might lead to bacterial infections, are also signs. Flea allergy symptoms often manifest themselves above a dog's behind.

▶ **Food allergies:** Food allergies account for 10 percent of all allergies in dogs, and after inhalant and flea bite allergies, they are the most common. They also account for 20 percent of itching and scratching in dogs, and most dogs with food allergies also have inhalant or contact allergies. The main symptom of food allergies is itchy skin around the face, feet, ears, forelegs, armpits, and anus. Signs also include respiratory and GI distress, chronic or recurrent ear infections, hair loss, excessive scratching, hot spots, and skin infections that respond to antibiotics but recur after the drugs are discontinued. Food trials and elimination diets, under the supervision of a vet or specialist, are extremely necessary.

▶ **Bacterial allergy:** When staphylococcus (staph) bacteria lives on an allergic dog's skin, he can develop round areas of hair loss that resemble ringworm, measuring one half to two inches in diameter. Staph-allergic dogs are often treated with antibiotics, though infection typically recurs after you've stopped using the medication.

▶ **Contact allergies:** These occur when a dog's skin reacts to a specific catalyst like a flea collar or wool. They are the least common type of allergy. The reactions are often localized.

Anal Sac Problems

Anal sac disease is a frequent problem when the dog's anal glands become infected, impacted, and/or abscessed. General signs of anal gland problems include licking the anal area, scooting along the floor, or problems with pooping. Impacted anal sacs are an extremely common problem for dogs, especially in smaller breeds. They seldom affect your dog's overall health, though you can schedule mini-appointments with vets and groomers to help express (or clean) them; you can also do this at home, but you'll need a veterinarian to show you how. If anal sacs are exposed to bacteria, they can become infected and abscess. Abscesses may be lanced by a veterinarian, with antibiotics to follow. Warm compresses can also relieve pain and swelling. Scar tissue can damage nerves and muscles in this area, which may cause incontinence. Dogs with chronic anal sac problems may need their glands removed, though most dogs with recurrent impacts are often put on a high-fiber diet from a veterinarian.

Other anal problems include tapeworms, diarrhea, food allergies, rectal cancer, and items that become ingested, and then stuck, inside a dog's bowels. There are so many reasons for a dog's anal discomfort that it's best to rely on your vet to examine and test for possibilities. You may even want to keep a notebook of food intake and bodily functions if your dog is experiencing digestive issues. This way you can tell the vet exactly what is going on—particularly if you're rotating food for medical or dietary reasons.

Arthritis

Arthritis, also known as degenerative joint disease and osteoarthritis, is the term used to describe the loss of smooth cartilage that covers and protects the ends of bones in a movable joint. When the two ends of a bone in a joint touch each other, that causes pain and inflammation; small bony projections also form on the bone close to the joint, which adds to the pain. It worsens with time.

Dogs with existing joint problems, or injuries to a joint or knee ligament, are more likely to develop arthritis. It often occurs as a dog ages, or can result from another condition that affects the joint, such as hip or elbow dysplasia (this is called secondary degenerative joint disease). Symptoms vary, depending on the dog's age and the severity of the condition, but they can include an altered gait (walk), muscle atrophy, difficulty jumping, difficulty standing after lying down, and changes in appetite and behavior. Some dogs will even lick or bite an area that feels painful.

Arthritis is diagnosed through an exam, X-rays, and lab tests. It can be treated medically and surgically, including with joint replacement, to slow the disease and promote comfort.

Bacterial Skin Infections

A staphylococcal bacterial infection is the formal name for a staph infection. Widespread staph bacteria can cause mild to severe skin infections in dogs. Signs can range from crusty skin lesions on the belly in mild cases to draining lesions that cause severe itching. Some staph infections are linked to bacterial allergies (see "Allergies," on page 230). They can be secondary to another problem like parasitic infections, allergies, and hormonal problems. Oral antibiotics and medicated shampoos are common treatments, with steroids or injections for some staph allergies.

Bladder Problems

Urinary tract infections (UTIs) and bladder stones are regular urinary bladder problems in dogs. UTIs involve bacteria in the bladder, but other infections can affect the kidney, ureters, and/or urethra. Bacterial infections in the urinary bladder are also called bacterial cystitis. Bladder stones can be known as urinary calculi, or urolithiasis. These can be found in the kidneys, ureters, urethra, or bladder (most common).

UTIs are the result of bacteria in the urethra that travels to the bladder or into the kidneys. Diseases such as Cushing's disease, kidney failure, diabetes, and bladder cancer can predispose a dog to a UTI. Bladder stones can increase the risk of recurring UTIs.

Symptoms of UTIs include small, frequent amounts of urination, painful urination, blood in the urine, and accidents. Kidney infection can cause fever, pain, loss of appetite, and general lethargy. (Your vet should check for diseases that cause similar symptoms, like bladder stones, bladder cancer, and prostatitis.) Treatment includes antibiotics that the doctor might prescribe based on the results of a urine sample and exam.

Dogs with bladder stones may have blood in their urine and urinate frequently. Abdominal X-rays, lab work, and an exam can detect the presence of stones. Causes can be genetics, concentration of stone constituents, urine pH, and/or bacterial infection. Treatment is medical, dietary, or surgical.

Bloat (Gastric Dilation and Volvulvus, GDV)

Bloat occurs when a dog's stomach overextends after eating, as it fills with gas, secretions, and food—to the point that it twists back on itself and causes pressure, severe pain, and compression of other organs and the dog's diaphragm. Pressure on the diaphragm also makes it hard for the dog to breathe. GDV is an extremely serious situation and should be considered a life-threatening emergency when it occurs. Dogs can die from GDV within several hours, and even with treatment, experts say that 25 to 33 percent of dogs with bloat will die.

The breed and build of a dog has been directly linked to the likelihood of bloat. GDV is more likely to occur in large breeds with deep, narrow chests, while bloat rarely occurs in small dogs. A reputable and often-quoted Purdue University study compared the likelihood of certain breeds to develop the problem to the likelihood of a mixed breed suffering from it, and as it turns out, a purebred's risk is much higher than that of a mixed breed (for this reason, plus the fact that GDV is often genetic, you may not want to breed a dog with a first-degree relative who had bloat).

Here is Purdue's list of breeds that are most susceptible to bloat, ranked from highest to lowest risk potential.

Great Dane

Saint Bernard

Weimaraner

Irish Setter

Gordon Setter

Standard Poodle

Basset Hound

Doberman Pinscher

Old English Sheepdog

German Shorthaired Pointer

Newfoundland

German Shepherd

Airedale Terrier

Alaskan Malamute

Chesapeake Bay Retriever

Boxer

Collie

Labrador Retriever

English Springer Spaniel

Samoyed

Dachshund

Golden Retriever

Rottweiler

Mixed Breed Dog

Miniature Poodle

A few additional facts about bloat: Experts say that bloat primarily affects dogs over two years old—and dogs over seven are twice as likely to develop bloat than those that are two to four years old. Male dogs are twice as likely to develop bloat as females (neutering doesn't affect risk). Dogs fed once a day are twice as likely to develop GDV as those fed twice a day, and dogs that eat rapidly and exercise soon after a meal may be at increased risk. Nervous, anxious, or fearful dogs are especially susceptible, since their body isn't in an ideal relaxed state as it digests.

Signs of bloat include a swollen belly, nonproductive vomiting (nothing comes up), heavy drooling, and retching. Restlessness, abdominal pain, and rapid, shallow breathing are also signs. If a dog quickly deteriorates with GDV, there's a good chance that he'll go into shock—in which case, look for weakened pulse, pale gums, rapid heart rate, and eventual collapse.

At the animal hospital, GDV is assessed via blood samples and, if the animal is in shock, treated with IV fluids. Antibiotics and pain relievers may be administered. Once the dog is stabilized, abdominal surgery is performed, and the dog is monitored for several days for signs of infection, heart abnormalities, DIC (a bleeding disorder called disseminated intravascular coagulation), stomach ulceration and perforation, and damage to the pancreas or liver. Antibiotics and additional meds may need to be given.

Though there is no sure way to prevent GDV, owners of susceptible breeds should look for early signs and talk to their vets about medical management (a preventative stomach surgery called gastropexy might be recommended). Owners of large dogs should feed their pets two or three times a day (versus once a day) from an elevated bowl, and water should be available at all times but limited immediately after feeding. A calm environment will help slow a dog's eating pace. Avoid exercise, excitement, and stress one hour before and two hours after every meal. Realize that dogs that survive bloat are at an increased risk for future episodes.

Cancer

The topic of cancer is a painful one, and its symptoms and treatments are as vast as its potential outcomes. What we do know for sure is that cancer is on the rise, and it isn't a subject that should be taken lightly by dog owners or animal care professionals. J. J. Wen, DVM, of the Hampton Veterinary Hospital in Speonk, New York, has sustained the lives of many dogs with cancer, and he attributes rising cancer numbers to pesticides, poor diet, and increased inbreeding, among other factors.

If your dog has cancer, it needs to be explored in great detail with your veterinarian and potential specialists. Surgery, radiation, chemotherapy, and other medical and alternative treatments will depend upon your dog's health, your finances, and your personal views about animal empathy and discomfort. Your best treatment options are not something I can decide for you. However, I do think that this may be a scenario in which you should follow the treatment advice of an integrative-care vet, if your regular vet isn't as holistically inclined. With canine cancer, a holistic or integrative-care veterinarian will devote a lot of time to adjusting a sick dog's diet, exploring alternative therapies, and making his body as comfortable and free from environmental toxins as possible.

The most common types of cancer in dogs are osteosarcoma (bone cancer), mast-cell tumors (the most common skin cancer for dogs), melanocytoma skin cancers (canine melanoma), lymphoma (cancer of the lymph system), mammary cancer (breast cancer), thyroid cancer, pancreatic cancer, anal sac cancer, bladder cancer, kidney cancer, hemangiosarcoma (cancer of the blood vessels), and brain tumors (very rare). While some tumors are benign and treatable (for instance, some melanocytomas are benign), others are, sadly, more aggressive (bone cancer, hemangiosarcoma). Some tumors, like breast cancer, have a 50 percent malignancy rate—meaning that half are malignant, half are benign, and the malignant ones are those that have a tendency to spread. Some breeds are more at risk than others, depending on the cancer type.

Warning signs aren't so unlike those for humans: abnormal swelling, swollen glands, unusual lumps or masses, sores that don't heal, unexplained weight loss, loss of appetite, difficulty eating, loss of stamina, stiffness, and difficulty breathing/urinating/defecating. Other signs include bleeding or discharge from the nose or mouth and a bad odor from the mouth. Unlike people, dogs can't tell us when they feel under the weather, so it's up to a dog's owner to keep an eye out for unusual trends in a dog's health, behavior, and lifestyle habits.

The following websites provide relevant, detailed, and updated cancer information and may even link you to clinical trials that could help a cancer-stricken dog. These sites contain news on canine cancer, care options, specialists, and support information. Cancer information can be found on veterinary college websites for Cornell, University of Pennsylvania, and Tufts. Ask your vet about regional support groups in your area, though these sites are a good start:

The American Veterinary Medical Association: AVMA.org

The Veterinary Cancer Society: VetCancerSociety.org

National Canine Cancer Foundation: WeAreTheCure.org

Canine cancer support groups: CanineCancerAwareness.org, CanineCancerProject.com

Financial support organizations: IMOM.com, Uan.org/lifeline/index.html

Canine Cognitive Dysfunction (aka "Doggie Alzheimer's")

Recently, a growing number of older dogs have been diagnosed with canine cognitive dysfunction (CCD) or cognitive dysfunction syndrome (CDS). Studies show that many older dogs with geriatric behavior problems also have lesions on their brains, similar to those that human doctors see in Alzheimer's patients, hence the name "Doggie Alzheimer's." Symptoms include confusion or disorientation, pacing or staying awake all night (change in sleep patterns), loss of housetraining abilities, decreased activity, inability to recognize family and friends, and decreased attentiveness. Anxiety, increased vocalization, apathy, and decreased ability to respond to commands are other signs. To diagnose CCD, a veterinarian must first rule out medical or behavior problems that could prompt similar responses. In the hands of a competent vet, there are various medical, dietary, and exercise stimulation treatments that can alleviate CCD symptoms.

Coughing

Experts say that, unlike people who may clear their throats or have a nervous cough in a stressful situation, a healthy dog doesn't cough without a good reason. Coughing can be a sign of a significant disease, so call a vet about it right away. Do not try to treat it yourself. You can, however, help the vet diagnose a cough by taping it, noting the time of day in which coughs occur, and recognizing if the cough is soft, raspy, dry, honking, persistent, and so on. Tugging on a leash can worsen a cough, as can perfumes or cleaning solutions. Obesity and secondhand smoke can worsen coughs, too.

Conditions that can cause coughing include Bordetella (kennel cough), chronic bronchitis (inflammation of the bronchi), heart disease (deterioration of a heart valve, which enlarges the heart and puts pressure on the bronchi), collapsed trachea (cartilage rings in the trachea lose their shape), pneumonia (inflammation of the lungs), heartworm (internal parasite that lives in pulmonary arteries), lung cancer (rare as a primary site; secondary spreading is more common), congestive heart failure, tracheal collapse, and laryngeal paralysis (damaged nerves in the voice box).

Your vet may want to run diagnostic tests, including chest X-rays, complete blood count (CBC), blood chemistry profile, urinalysis, heartworm test, and a fecal exam. Treatment of a cough depends entirely on its cause, but all coughs are a cause for concern and should be addressed by a professional.

Cushing's Disease

Cushing's disease is a common hormonal disease that results from the chronic overproduction of glucocorticoids by the pituitary or adrenal gland. It's a very complex disease with an array of symptoms and causes. Cushing's affects middle-aged and older dogs, and the typical age of a dog suffering from the condition is six or seven (though it can strike between two and sixteen). It affects male and female dogs.

Symptoms of Cushing's disease include increased appetite, increased water consumption and urination, constant panting, restlessness, vomiting, diarrhea, insulin-resistant diabetes, seizures, hair loss and thin skin, abdominal enlargement, depression and apathy, lethargy, recurrent urinary tract infections, loss of reproductive ability, and motor irregularities (weakness in back legs, extreme stiffness). Cushing's can be either pituitary-dependent or adrenal-based.

As you can tell, Cushing's disease can present many symptoms, so a vet should include a complete blood count (CBC), blood chemistry panel, and urinalysis as part of his evaluation (these are just some of the many diagnostic tests he may wish to perform). Surgical and non-surgical treatments are available, depending on the severity of the dog's disease.

Dental Disease

See "Canine Dental Care" on page 358.

Diabetes

Diabetes is a common and serious disease of the pancreas gland, which produces a hormone called insulin. Insulin sends glucose (blood sugar) into the cells for nutrients. When a dog doesn't have enough insulin, glucose collects in the bloodstream and causes high blood sugar, or hyperglycemia. The cause for diabetes is unknown, though genetics, infection, insulin-antagonistic diseases and drugs, and long-term treatment with corticosteroids for other conditions may predispose a dog to become diabetic. Signs of diabetes include enormous thirst and appetite, frequent urination, weight loss, and weakness.

As with humans, diabetes in dogs requires careful management with insulin shots, a monitored diet, and mealtime regulation. As with diabetic humans, exercise is a must. The owner of a diabetic dog must monitor his glucose and insulin levels, especially during the first stages of his treatment. Regular blood sugar tests, urine cultures, and blood tests are part of a diabetic dog's treatment and medical management.

Breeds with a high rate of diabetes include Pugs, Cairn Terriers,

Dachshunds, Golden Retrievers, Miniature Pinschers, German Shepherds, Miniature Schnauzers, Beagles, and Poodles.

Ear Problems

Ear problems are frequent issues for all dog owners. The moist, tight corners of a dog's inner ears make them an ideal home for parasites (ear mites) and bacteria. Signs of an ear problem include odor, scratching of ears and head, ear discharge, pain around the ears, changes in behavior (depression, irritability), redness or swelling of the ear flap or canal, and head shaking or tilting to one side. Only a vet can resolve these issues, with plenty of follow-up on your part. The longer you wait to resolve an ear infection, the worse it will become and the harder it will be to treat.

Causes of ear problems include allergies, parasites, infections (bacteria, yeast), foreign bodies (plant matter), trauma, hormonal abnormalities (hypothyroidism), ear anatomy, excess moisture in the environment, hereditary or autoimmune conditions, and tumors. Treatment includes antibacterial, anti-fungal, and allergy treatments.

The best way to prevent ear infections is to clean your dog's ears at least once a week. Dogs with ears that hang down, dogs that have a history of ear infections, and dogs that are regularly exposed to water may need their ears cleaned up to three times a week. A groomer can also clip the hair around a dog's ears to allow for more airflow. To learn how to clean a dog's ears, see Chapter 6.

Eye Conditions

Cataracts and glaucoma are common eye conditions in dogs. While the first is a treatable disease, the second is considered an emergency.

Cataracts have a white or crushed-ice look that's found in the eye lens. The disease is caused by the breakdown of the normal arrangement of lens fibers or the lens capsule (the lens is encased in a capsule that is like a wrapper; usually, the cataract is due to the breakdown of this casing). The result of this breakdown is a loss in transparency and impaired vision. The age at which a dog gets cataracts is an important factor in determining the cause. Cataracts can be congenital (present at birth), developmental (early-onset), senile (gradually occurs later in life), or inherited. Dog breeds most prone to cataracts include the Afghan Hound, Boston Terrier, German Shepherd, American Cocker Spaniel, Chesapeake Bay Retriever, Golden Retriever, Labrador Retriever, Miniature Schnauzer, Standard Poodle, Old English Sheepdog, Siberian Husky, Welsh Springer Spaniel, Staffordshire Bull Terrier, and West Highland White Terrier. Diabetes and trauma can also cause cataracts. Treatment, when needed, involves surgical removal of the lens.

Glaucoma, on the other hand, occurs when the pressure inside a dog's eyeball becomes higher than normal, which can damage the eye's internal structures (especially the retina and optic nerve). In glaucoma, increased pressure of an eye fluid called aqueous humor cannot drain correctly from the eye, and as fluid builds, the eyeball's pressure crushes or displaces the eye's internal structures and renders it nonfunctional. Glaucoma can be primary (caused by physical or physiological traits) or secondary (caused by another condition). An eye wound, such as from a grooming accident, can cause glaucoma. Early signs include pain, dilated pupil, cloudy cornea, bloodshot eye, and one eye that appears larger or more protruding than the other. Most dogs display only one or two of these signs initially. You can tell your dog is in pain if he rubs his eye with his paw or rubs it against the carpet or your leg. He may also seem to flutter his lids or squint with one eye.

If treatment for glaucoma doesn't begin within a few hours of the pressure increase, a dog can lose his vision in the affected eye. Treatment includes medical and surgical remedies.

Epilepsy and Seizures

Epileptic dogs have recurring seizures, during which time the brain fires unexpected neurons that cause convulsions lasting from a few seconds to several minutes. Seizures can be caused by various conditions, including high or low blood glucose levels, anemia, kidney disorders, liver disorders, infections, low calcium in nursing females, tumors, fevers, brain damage, hyperthermia, certain medications, and primary, or idiopathic, epilepsy. A dog may experience partial or generalized seizures. A partial seizure affects a small part or one side of the body, whereas a generalized seizure affects the whole body. A seizure should not be confused with your dog experiencing a dream; a dog can be woken from a dream, but he cannot be stopped in mid-seizure.

Vets require a detailed history, a physical and neurological exam, a panel of lab tests, and X-rays to determine the cause of any seizure. If the cause can't be defined, the condition is then diagnosed as idiopathic, or primary, epilepsy. Epilepsy occurs in all breeds, including mixed breeds, but it can be a genetic trait when an epileptic disorder is passed down within one family. Beagles, Poodles, Cocker Spaniels, Collies, Pointers, Boxers, Irish Setters, German Shepherds, and Golden and Labrador Retrievers are among the breeds that have a high tendency to develop this disease. There is no cure for epilepsy, but it can be treated with diet adjustments and oral or IV medications to decrease the frequency, severity, and duration of the seizures. If your dog is put on anti-seizure medication, the meds do not cure the cause of the seizure; they simply help reduce the number and severity of episodes. Your dog will probably have future episodes and will require frequent checkups at the vet.

If you witness your dog seizing (see page 467 for signs your dog may be having a seizure), stay calm and move nearby furniture or sharp objects so that he doesn't get hurt. Dim the lights to reduce sensory input. Do not put your hand, or anything else, in the dog's mouth.

This will not help your dog (there's no risk of him swallowing his tongue), and you may be bitten, since your dog could become disoriented when he's coming out of the episode. Always record the date, time, and duration of any seizure. Also note what happened before, during, and after the episode so that you can immediately call the vet with details. Severe and long seizures—if a seizure lasts longer than twenty minutes or if your dog has two seizures in a row—are major causes for concern. Although length, recovery time, and frequency can warrant emergency treatment, you should always call your vet when your dog has seizure activity, and insist on an appointment.

Hair Loss (Alopecia)

A number of conditions and diseases can cause a dog's hair to fall out. Some reasons are absolutely normal, while others may indicate a serious illness (still others are behavioral). It may be difficult for your vet to diagnose the reasons behind hair loss, so be patient throughout the process. There may be some trial and error involved.

The most typical reasons for hair loss include allergic and irritant contact dermatitis, allergic inhalant dermatitis, Cushing's disease, food allergies, an infection of the hair follicles, hypothyroidism, ringworm, and sarcoptic mange (infection from the sarcoptes mite). Treatments vary greatly depending on the condition, but include steroids, vitamin supplements, hormone replacement therapies, shampoos, diet change, antibiotics, and behavior modification.

Heart Disease

Heart disease usually affects dogs later in life. The most common type of heart disease in dogs is called chronic valve disease (CVD), and it occurs when a dog's heart valves can no longer close properly, which causes abnormal blood flow throughout the body. The second is called hypertrophic cardiomyopathy, in which the muscle walls become thin and weak. Annual checkups should help prevent general heart disease, since your vet can detect early stages of the condition. Only when heart disease progresses to moderate heart failure do symptoms like coughing, lethargy, and difficulty breathing surface. Severe heart failure presents with symptoms like difficulty breathing (when resting), an unwillingness to exercise, fainting, weight loss, and loss of appetite. A heart murmur is often the first sign of chronic valve disease, but again, only a vet can detect the leaky valve. A hacking, deep cough is the most obvious sign of heart trouble.

CVD progresses slowly and is the most frequent cause of congestive heart failure. A dog can live with CVD for years with the right treatment, including diet modification and medication. Breeds prone to CVD include Cavalier King Charles Spaniel, Cocker Spaniel, Dachshund, Llasa Apso, Miniature Poodle, Schnauzer, Shetland Sheepdog, and Yorkshire Terrier.

There is no cure for hypertrophic cardiomyopathy in dogs, but early detection of any cardiac disease can lead to helpful medicines, diets, diuretics, ACE inhibitors, and even pacemakers. You may want to consider a canine cardiologist and alternative modalities as part of your dog's treatment plan.

Intestinal Problems

Constipation, diarrhea, gas, and vomiting are as typical in dogs as they are in humans—and the causes are as widely varied. Many of the reasons for intestinal problems in normal dogs are linked to diet and exercise. As with people, intestinal issues need to be resolved on an individual basis, since vets, depending on their philosophies and modalities, seem to differ on what even qualifies as, and contributes to, a healthy poop.

A constipated dog that has difficult or infrequent poops may pass small or no feces, or may seem to be in pain when straining to go to the bathroom. Causes for constipation could be an indigestible item that causes blockage, lack of exercise, insufficient diet or fluid intake, a tumor in the rectal area, constipating medication, or a neurological disease that affects elimination. Any constipation is a real problem, and you should consult your vet about it right away.

A number of conditions can cause diarrhea, though the most common is the consumption of food that a dog can't properly digest. The common treatment for diarrhea is to withhold food for twenty-four hours, with small and frequent amounts of water followed by a bland food diet for one to two days. Call your vet if your dog's diarrhea doesn't resolve in forty-eight hours; if he has blood in the diarrhea or his stools are black or tarry; may have eaten something toxic or poisonous; has a fever or seems depressed; has yellow or pale gums; appears to be in pain; is also vomiting; is a puppy without all of his vaccinations. Seek your vet's guidance right away, since treatment for an upset stomach is very different than it is for worms, benign rectal polyps, viral infections, inflammatory bowel disease, or colitis.

Gas is common among dogs that swallow too much air with their food. Putting an object that's too large for him to ingest (like an overturned bowl) in the middle of your dog's food bowl will slow his eating, since he'll need to navigate around it. Elevated feeders, light walks after dinner, and fewer table scraps (not to be confused with healthy people food like organic chicken or green beans) may also diminish gas. Ask your vet whether he thinks you should change dog foods or add probiotics or enzymes to your dog's meals to help with digestion.

A Recipe for Upset Tummies

Steamed (or boiled) chicken (without skin and drained of fat) and white rice is a tried-and-true remedy for upset stomachs. I like to think of it as the soothing equivalent of hot tea and toast for humans. This is often called the Bland Diet, since you shouldn't add anything except water to the chicken and rice concoction to whet a dog's appetite, and even then only if your dog hesitates to eat it (a little water will create a broth). Variations on the recipe work for dogs with vomiting or diarrhea.

Dr. Fischer says you can use hamburger in place of chicken, but as with the chicken, the fat should be drained from the meat.

The Bland Diet

Mix half a cup of steamed chicken or cooked ground beef, plus white rice (it's binding), for every twenty pounds of a dog's body weight every day. This portion should be divided into two to four meals.

For diarrhea: Give the dog only water for twenty-four hours, then follow the Bland Diet for one to two days. Gradually switch back to the dog's regular diet over the next day or so.

For vomiting: Fast the dog completely (food and water) for twelve hours after vomiting. Once there is no more vomiting, give the dog water for the next twelve hours and follow the Bland Diet, above.

Finally, it's very natural for dogs to vomit if they have an upset stomach. If this happens, withhold food and water for the first twelve hours. Slowly introduce water over the next twelve hours, and if the vomiting has ended by that time, introduce the same bland food diet you'd feed a dog with diarrhea. Sometimes a dog will expel food from his stomach, while other times his empty stomach will vomit a foamy yellow liquid (stomach bile). If your dog is alert and vomits only once, there's likely no need to call the vet. But if your dog appears sick or vomits more than once, call the vet and clean up the vomit immediately, so your dog doesn't eat it. When you speak to the vet, he'll want to know when the vomiting started, how many times the dog vomited, what it looks like, and if your dog seems uncomfortable. You should also call the vet if your dog has unproductive vomiting, has blood in his vomit, appears bloated or has a swollen stomach, may have eaten something toxic or poisonous, has a fever or is depressed, has pale or yellow gums, is in pain, has diarrhea, or is a puppy without all his vaccinations. Because vomiting is often indicative of another problem, rely on your vet to diagnose and treat this problem properly.

A HEALTHY POOP IS . . .

Formed but not too hard (when it drops on the ground, it should stay intact).

Any shade of brown, depending on your dog's diet (constipated poop is tarry and black).

Determined by quality, not quantity. Dogs on raw diets may have smaller poops than those on canned and kibble food diets. They can also have scent-free poops that break down into a powder.

Regular. Dogs should poop about once or twice a day, depending on the dog.

Is Your Dog Constipated?

If your dog's stool is very firm (though he's otherwise healthy), try adding a quarter teaspoon of fiber, such as bran or canned pumpkin, to your dog's diet. If adding fiber doesn't work, and he's straining to poop or seems at all ill, take him to the veterinarian for a checkup.

Kidney Disease

Kidney disease (also known as renal disease) is common among senior dogs. It can take the shape of acute renal failure (ARF), in which the signs occur suddenly and severely, or chronic renal failure (CRF), which has a slower progression with nonspecific signs ("He just doesn't seem right"). Causes of kidney disease include age, infection (viral, fungal, or bacterial), parasites, cancer, inflammation, autoimmune disease, trauma, and congenital and inherited disorders.

Dogs with kidney disease can show a variety of nonspecific signs, some of which may be seen in other diseases such as liver or pancreatic diseases or urinary tract problems that don't involve the kidney at all. Typical signs include increased water consumption, increased urination volume, decreased urination, peeing during the night (out of routine), blood in urine, decreased appetite, vomiting, weight loss, diarrhea, lethargy, and hunched posture. Your vet can best detect other symptoms such as irregular kidneys, mouth ulcers, and high blood pressure. To diagnose a dog with kidney disease, a vet will run several tests (including X-rays, a urinalysis, and blood work) to confirm the disease and learn what's causing it. Treatment for ARF includes antibiotics, fluid therapy, and a change in diet. For CRF, vets advise fluid therapy, a change in diet, vitamin supplements, and other treatments. Kidney transplants are also an option, though surgery is only considered for some dogs in the early stages of renal failure if there's a donor match.

Luxating Patella

A luxating patella seems to affect a dog suddenly and without warning: One minute he seems okay, and the next, he's either limping or wobbling about with one back knee (or both) popped out of the joint. It can be a mild to severe condition; some dogs aren't bothered by the occasional displacement, while others might hold their hind leg up for days to relieve the pain. A dog with this condition may also extend his leg away from his body and be unable to flex it back into a normal position. Dogs with a luxating patella on both hind legs may change their entire posture to suit their sore joints. Smaller and toy dog breeds are most affected by this condition, and genetics can play a role (for this reason, please don't breed dogs with luxating patellas). Most dogs with a luxating patella are middle-aged, with a history of irregular lameness in the rear leg/s. Without surgical correction, the dog will become worse. Arthritis will affect the joint and cause a permanently swollen knee with poor mobility. Surgery is not necessary for every dog with a luxating patella, though when a corrective procedure is performed, the previously lame dog usually recovers quickly, within thirty to sixty days.

Thyroid Disease (Hypothyroidism)

The thyroid gland regulates a dog's metabolism by producing thyroid hormones; therefore, a dog develops hypothyroidism when not enough thyroid hormones are produced. This can cause a variety of symptoms like weight gain, obesity, hair loss, and skin problems.

Hypothyroidism develops in dogs between the ages of four and ten years old. It affects mid- to large-size breeds and is rare in toy and miniature dogs. Golden Retrievers, Dachshunds, Cocker Spaniels, and Irish Setters seem to be predisposed to developing the condition, while German Shepherds and mixed breeds are at a reduced risk. Spayed females also appear to develop thyroid disease more often than females that haven't been spayed. Typical symptoms include lethargy, hair loss, weight gain, dry coat, anemia, and high blood cholesterol.

Hypothyroidism is easily detectible via blood tests that check your dog's levels of thyroid hormones. The disease is easily treated with a synthetic thyroid hormone. Once therapy begins, the dog will need to be on treatment for the rest of his life, though his symptoms will resolve.

Helpful Health-Related Websites

Because I can't possibly discuss every condition that may affect your dog in his lifetime (nor would you want me to; this would be such a sad chapter!), I've listed below some very helpful websites that log great articles and information about canine health. In many cases, these will help put your mind at ease and guide you toward a smart discussion with your vet. The following sites apply to both integrative- and conventional-care philosophies, so take from them what you wish. They also include valuable nutrition information, since health and nutrition are inextricably linked. Your own vet may have a great website with his own articles and discussion topics on them, too. I've left room for you to add these, and other findings, to the list.

AnimalArk.com

Aspca.com

DogAware.com

DogFoodProject.com

EarthAnimal.com

HealingCenterforAnimals.com

ILoveDogs.com

OnlyNaturalPet.com

PetCareNaturally.com

PetCenter.com

PetEducation.com

PetPlace.com

PetWellBeing.com

Whole-Dog-Journal.com

VetInfo.com

5

Nutrition

In my family, food is love, so I've devoted a lot of time to learning about the most sustaining foods to feed Bianca. Diet has such a huge impact on a dog's health. Good food contributes to a dog's high energy, good looks, happy disposition, and ability to fight disease. Studies show that dogs that don't eat a balanced diet increase their risk of GI issues, arthritis, diabetes, and obesity, among other conditions. And if that weren't reason enough to make sure my dog is well fed, most vets feel that feeding your dog a sub-par diet can supply growth to cancer cells and fuel allergies.

While there are still some veterinarians who treat nutrition as an afterthought, those who've kept up with their field understand how quality diets help dogs thrive. They also appreciate that there isn't one way to feed a dog, though most agree that dogs need a diet that's rich in protein, with whole grains and fresh vegetables added for balance. Canine diets also demand a well-rounded mix of vitamins and minerals, as well as essential fatty acids and digestive enzymes (some from foods, others from supplements). Above all, dogs require responsible feeding from their owners.

When it comes to finding a diet that benefits your dog, there are an endless number of options on the market right now. From raw diets to canned and kibble meals, we'll explore the advantages of each in this chapter. I'll talk about how to read a dog food label, plus the roles that fresh food, whole food, and variety play in your dog's well-being. While one dog might need more fiber as another requires more protein, we'll discuss why it's the source of each one that you need to be most vigilant about. I learned so much from all the vets and nutrition experts who helped with this section, and thanks to them, and now you, dogs will live healthier and longer lives.

Create a Dining Ritual for Your Dog

Dogs both rely on and look forward to routines, especially when they involve food! Below are some tips that will help you establish dining rituals to make mealtime a memorable experience for you and your dog.

1. Create a relaxed dining area. Establish a dog's eating space in a relatively calm environment, away from excess stimulation. A kitchen or mudroom may seem ideal because of the easy-to-clean floor, but these rooms can also be highly trafficked. Let your dog eat in peace for fifteen minutes, or at least move his dish a few feet from where you prepare food or rush in and out of the house.

2. Feed your dog in the same area every time. This will create positive associations with the space. If your dog is startled for any reason near his bowl, he may be hesitant to enter the dining area again. If this happens, slowly coax him into the room with food and praise him in a happy voice.

3. If you feed your dog healthy people food, don't do it from the table. Put the food in his bowl, so he knows that his dish is where his food comes from, and not at your side when he begs or jumps.

4. Invite your dog to eat dinner. Always use the same cue ("Bianca, do you want to eat?") so he knows what to expect when his bowl hits the ground. Teaching your dog to wait for an invitation, with you as the food source, is a great way to help establish yourself as "the leader."

5. Always give your dog fresh water and food. No leftovers from his previously uneaten meals!

6. Ask your trainer how much time you should allow for your dog to eat. Expert opinions range from fifteen minutes to an hour, depending on the dog and rules in your home. Establish an eating pattern when the dog is still young, or new to his home, so he knows when to expect chow.

7. Adult dogs should eat twice a day, based on a schedule that suits you. Some holistic vets suggest feeding times in the morning and late afternoon (versus at night) to allow your dog time to digest before he goes to bed, since you don't want him to have a digestive problem while you're asleep. Puppies will have different eating and drinking schedules that should be dictated by your trainer, though most pups need to be fed three times a day when they're young and will begin weaning to twice-a-day meals at nine to twelve months. Puppies should also be kept to a strict schedule when housetraining.

A Mealtime Alternative: Feed Your Dog at Unpredictable Times

Rather than keeping your dog on a strict food schedule, some experts prefer that you feed him at different times each day. The thinking goes that when you feed a dog at the same time every day, you'll create a canine that begs, usually an hour before his designated feeding time—and worse yet, experiences real anxiety if you're off schedule (due to staying late at work, running errands, sleeping in). However, a dog that's fed at unscheduled times won't anticipate meals and will understand feeding as just one more activity in his day. He also won't get upset or whine for food if he's missed mealtime.

Do Puppies Need Special Diets?

Contrary to what some dog food brands market, most integrative-care vets don't believe that puppies need to follow a different diet than an adult dog, good health permitting. Instead, all ages should become accustomed to a well-balanced meal early in life. Among dogs that still live in the wild, pups are nourished by their mothers' regurgitated food; there's no difference between what she ingests and what her little ones eat. Experts say that while you don't need to worry about transitioning your dog from puppy- to adult-formula dog foods at a vaguely defined life stage, serving size does matter. Consult your vet, breeder, or food label for portion guidelines for puppies, as well as small, medium, and large dogs.

Ask Dr. Z!

What does it mean when my dog . . .

Q: *Drinks from the toilet?*

A: It seems undrinkable to us, but toilet water is usually cold and reasonably fresh to a dog, since the toilet is flushed several times per day. You can't blame the dog, really, but you should discourage this behavior for obvious reasons related to health and good manners.

How to Set the Floor

Lay down a place mat to gather water and/or food that spills over the side of your dog's bowls.

Use stainless steel or porcelain bowls for your dog. He can chew plastic ones to pieces.

It's okay to keep both bowls on the floor at all times, one filled with fresh water and the other empty except at mealtime, but you can lift the food bowl if you prefer. The key is to remove uneaten food from the bowl when mealtime is over.

Dogs at risk for bloat or other intestinal disorders may benefit from an elevated bowl that sits off the ground (see "Twenty-One Most Common Medical Conditions and Diseases" on page 230 for more on bloat). This issue is bandied back and forth by experts, however, so ask your vet for his take.

Feeding Big Versus Small Dogs

Though we've learned to breed big dogs into small dogs, their physiology is the same. However, vets tell me that little dogs may need to eat more often than big dogs, since small-breed dogs have a higher metabolism but a smaller stomach than larger breeds. That means they need more energy packed into less food to thrive. Small dogs should also be fed a diet high in protein, with moderate carbohydrates and vegetables, and a good fat source that's high in omega-3s and omega-6s—unless they have health conditions that dictate otherwise. The label on your dog's food should provide a portion guideline according to a dog's weight, and it should suggest serving sizes either as the day's allotment (in which case, break the serving into at least two portions) or as a per-serving requirement. It's best to confirm your dog's diet with your vet if you suspect he's putting on pounds.

When it comes to large, deep-chested dogs, you may want to take precautions to deter bloat, which is most likely the result of numerous factors that have come together to cause a "perfect storm." Deep-chested dogs have a higher incidence of bloat than other dogs, and

---

Ask Dr. Z!

What does it mean when my dog . . .

Q: *Pushes his food bowl across the floor before eating his dinner?*

A: Wild dogs must engage in a wide range of search, chase, and capture behavior before they are able to enjoy a meal. Domestic dogs may exhibit elements of this by engaging in a range of ritual behavior before eating—one of which can be "chasing and capturing" his own food bowl.

since there is some evidence that large meals may be a factor in bloat, owners and breeders who deal with large, deep-chested dogs often recommend feeding smaller, more frequent meals as a precaution.

Set High Standards for Your Dog's Diet

It's as essential for you to know what types of ingredients are added to your dog's food as it is to know the sources and quality of those ingredients. With so many diet choices on the market, look for a balance between food that satisfies your dog's personal needs and tastes, plus a general health ideal based on what experts know about canine nutrition. Realize, though, that canine nutrition isn't a one-size-fits-all topic, so it may take some trial and error to figure out what works best for your pet. Experts say that a balanced diet of fresh protein, vegetables, and whole grains applies to all canines; how much you integrate of each category may be more individual.

Pet nutrition experts say that the best diet for dogs is similar to the best diet for people. It's full of real food that's rich in vitamins, minerals, enzymes, and supplements if necessary. These elements promote optimal health, as they work to prevent disease and address existing issues. Experts also agree that the best dog food is made from human-grade ingredients in the meat, vegetables and fruit, and whole-grain categories. Meat and grain by-products (leftovers from ingredients that have been slaughtered, milled, and processed for other uses) that figure prominently in a food source are less ideal, since they have fewer nutritional benefits.

Better-quality food results in a healthier coat, fewer digestive problems, and firmer stools. (Since your dog will absorb more nutrients from better-quality dog food, less will be passed as waste. This is one rea-son that you can't assume that big poops mean that your dog is eating healthy food.) Good food will also strengthen a dog's immune system and boost overall health. Here are some general standards to lay the groundwork of how to understand what should be in your dog's food.

- ▶ Fresher food is healthier food. The more "real" (unprocessed, whole, and complete) the food is, the better it is for your dog.

- ▶ Seek out food that features quality animal proteins at the beginning of an ingredient list. Look for whole meats with a named source like "chicken" or "lamb," versus "poultry meal" or "chicken by-products." A named, whole source of meat, fish, or poultry should figure as the first (or first few) ingredients in a food.

- ▶ Try to find foods that contain whole, unprocessed vegetables like peas, potatoes, and carrots.

- ▶ Look for foods with whole, unprocessed grains. Organic rice, brown rice, barley, and oatmeal are high-quality grains that provide roughage. Grain meals and by-products have lower nutritional value.

- ▶ The fat sources in your dog's food should be high in omega-3s and omega-6s, and not saturated fats.

- ▶ Do not buy commercial foods that contain poultry or grain by-products. These are leftovers from ingredients that have been slaughtered, milled, and processed for other uses. They are poor protein and fiber sources.

- ▶ Avoid foods with artificial colors, flavors, texture enhancers, sugar, or other sweeteners. If your food must have a preservative, it should be a natural one, like vitamin E or C.

What does it mean when my dog . . .

Q: *Licks inanimate objects—like the wall or even fabric—incessantly?*

A: The walls may have a texture or taste that attracts the dog. At one time you may have splashed champagne, a cat may have sprayed, or you may have leaned or left some sweat against this wall, which will be attractive to a dog. Obsessive-compulsive licking is another story. Here, the dog may be anxious and attempting to soothe himself with the repetitive motion.

How to Read a Dog Food Package

As you read through this chapter, it won't take long before you realize that a balanced meal is a healthy meal that includes fresh meats, vegetables and fruits, and whole grains. Unfortunately, some dog food manufacturers haven't made balanced eating a priority, since including whole meats and vegetables is more expensive than using empty carbohydrates like corn and brewer's rice.

Deciphering the language on a dog food label shouldn't feel too intimidating, since the best foods won't contain words that can confuse you. As when you read labels on your own food, if you don't recognize an ingredient or its source, it's probably not the healthiest thing to eat. You can apply the same rule to your dog. However, the words that pet food companies use to promote their products can be deceiving, so I've decoded the typical terms used on dog food packaging, from marketing-speak to ingredient sources:

Ultra Premium! Super Premium! Premium! Huh?

If you decide to feed your dog from a bag or a can, you should know the differences between ultra premium, super premium, premium, and grocery store and warehouse brands for canned and kibble food. These words often appear on the food's package, or are casually referenced on the brand's website. I'm told the formulas used for kibble and canned foods are the same, though canned will always be fresher, since so many nutrients and vitamins are lost in the processing of kibble.

Ultra premium: Food bearing this label is generally very low in carbohydrates, since it is primarily meat and usually grain-free. The meat used is human-grade. These brands don't use by-products or chemical preservatives. Some examples: Nature's Variety, Merrick, and Evanger's.

Super premium: These are similar to ultra premium foods but typically contain some grains, though meat protein should still be the first ingredient listed. Super premium foods also use good-quality meats and do not contain by-products. Some examples: Wellness, Innova, and Solid Gold.

Premium: Premium foods use much less meat than ultra or super categories. Grain and/or water is often the first ingredient (in ultra premium and super premium brands, meat is the first ingredient), they often use meat by-products, and they contain far more grain than meat. Some use chemical preservatives. Many times, if all the grains were added together, they would equal or exceed the amount of meat in the food. Some examples: Eukanuba, Nutro, Royal Canin.

Typical grocery store and warehouse brands: These foods contain very little meat, are made with substantial amounts of meat by-products, and primarily consist of grain and grain by-products. They often contain artificial colors, flavors, and chemical preservatives. Some examples: Alpo, Kibbles 'n Bits, and Ol' Roy.

What Is a Grain-free Diet?

A number of holistic vets champion grain-free diets that are high in meat, with some vegetables for balance. They are helpful for all animals but can be especially beneficial to dogs with obesity, allergies, diabetes, and anal gland problems, among many other conditions. Grain-free isn't for every dog, however, so talk to your vet. It is not recommended for dogs with kidney problems or some dogs with aggressive behavior.

AAFCO Nutritional Statement

AAFCO stands for the Association of American Feed Control Officials, and its nutritional statement means that your dog food is formulated to meet nutritional levels established by the AAFCO dog food nutrient profiles (this is printed on the food's label or package). Unlike the FDA, which is a government-regulated agency that ensures food and drug safety, the AAFCO is an independent corporation that aids industry and government representatives in setting standards for and supervising the entire animal feed industry, including dogs and cats. If a dog food manufacturer meets the AAFCO's basic protein, fat, moisture, and fiber requirements, it can be called a pet food. Unfortunately, the nutritional statement only estimates the percentage of protein, fat, moisture, and fiber found in the food, *without identifying the source of each ingredient,* which is why it's important that you're discerning about where these ingredients come from.

Guaranteed Analysis

At the very least, a pet food label must state guarantees for the minimum percentages of crude protein and crude fat, and the maximum percentages of crude fiber and moisture. "Crude" refers to how the protein and fiber are tested; it has nothing to do with the quality of nutrients. The guaranteed analysis compares protein to fat to fiber, but only in the package you're holding. If you want to compare one product to another, the two must have the same moisture content.

I suppose one could argue that a guaranteed analysis could help you shop around for pet food, but this requires sharp math skills and a lot of patience, since you cannot compare products by weight, cost, protein, fat, and fiber without converting the values for all products on an equal percentage. So you can't compare anything about wet and dry food on an apples-to-apples basis without first converting the wet food's guaranteed analysis numbers to that of the dry matter (if you're interested in doing this, ask your vet for the formula). Once you have the dry matter numbers, the guaranteed analysis can give you an accurate comparison of the foods, but it's a lot of work. (Any dry food can be compared to another dry food with the label information and without any math. Canned to canned is the same, too.)

My advice is to ignore the guaranteed analysis content altogether. A better way to analyze and compare dog foods is to examine the ingredients themselves. Look for the types of proteins, fats, and fibers in the food, not the percentage of each in a guaranteed analysis. After all, different sources of protein and fat vary in digestibility and the number of nutrients required for a dog to maintain good health. A chunk of lean meat and a handful of ground peanut shells are both sources of crude protein, but which would you rather feed your dog?

Feeding Guidelines

These guidelines are a rough estimate of how much to feed your dog according to his body weight, but ask your vet to confirm his daily feeding amount. Your dog's age, breed, environment, activity level, and body condition all impact how much he should eat at mealtime.

Ingredients

The first five or six ingredients that appear on a commercial label are the crux of the product's content, but it's your job to critique its protein source, amount of grain, presence of poor grains or poultry by-products (these are gross and have no nutritional value for your dog; see explanations below), and artificial ingredients like preservatives, colors, or flavors. The ingredients on a dog food label are listed in order of predominance by weight, as regulated by the AAFCO.

Ingredients are listed by weight, and some canned and kibble manufacturers use this to their advantage when disguising less desirable ingredients. One common method is to break one ingredient into several different, smaller ingredients and list them individually. Doing this pushes less desirable food ingredients farther down on an ingredient list. For example, a label might name chicken as its first ingredient, then follow with ground corn, corn gluten, ground wheat, corn bran, wheat flour, wheat middling, and so on. If you were to group all corn ingredients as one, they would likely outweigh the amount of pure chicken and wheat; come to think of it, if you group all grain and grain products together, you'd be feeding your dog a diet higher in grain than meat (which is not ideal, since dogs are carnivores)! If owners are trained to value the first five or six ingredients, assuming their weight is the crux of the food, many wouldn't look past wheat middling for even worse components. See how easy it is for companies to pull a fast one?

Finding meat meal, instead of meats, high on a kibble ingredient list can also be a bit misleading. While some say that having meat meal (meat with the water removed) is a fine indication of a high-protein dry food (since less water means more protein per bite), this ingredient has already been rendered, cooked, and perhaps sitting on shelves for months before it's even turned into dog food. It's much better to find fresh named meat high on an ingredient list than pre-rendered meat meal, since the food becomes further processed (and less healthy) when it is manufactured. The trickiest thing to educate yourself about is a food's excellence, if the pet food company skirts around quality standards. For instance, poorly sourced meat and meat by-products (yuck) can read within the first few ingredients of a dog food, but if these parts are from an animal deemed unfit for human consumption (yuck again), then they are of questionable quality and dubious value to your dog's health.

The easiest way to ensure that your dog's meat and meat by-products are from a conscientious and quality source is to read the company's website or their literature to see if they say that the meat ingredients are from USDA-inspected and -approved animals. Or look to see if they use the term "human-grade." Though there is no actual legal definition of that language, many companies use it to indicate that it is meat fit for human consumption. If you don't see any such wording, you can always contact the company and ask if they use only meat and meat by-products that are from animals fit for human consumption. Specifically, you can ask: "Do you use salvaged or condemned meat in your products? Do you use meat and meat by-products from uninspected and/or 'downer' animals?" (Downer animals are livestock that are unable to stand, often because of illness or injury, and are therefore ordered to be killed.) If the answer to either of those questions is yes—and you want the best health and nutrition for your dog—you'll want to avoid those foods. If they answer no, you might want to ask them to put it in writing.

I'm not saying that commercial dog food companies are run by bad people. It's just a stingy business model, and using inexpensive and low-quality ingredients leads to a robust bottom line. So if you value your dog's health, you'll need to police what he puts into his body, since nobody else will. A little extra attention and money will save you on vet bills down the road.

Learn to Read a Label So You Know What to Avoid

Since the ultimate mark of a high-quality dog food is the source of its ingredients, I'd like to alert you to some of the lower-quality terms on a dog food label. As with people food, the less you need to explain about an ingredient, the better. So if your dog food label looks like a recipe for healthy stew—weighted with whole meats, vegetables, and whole grains—it has a better chance of delivering whole nutrition than a label that reads like a box of processed cereal.

I've included some of the lower-quality ingredients in commercial dog foods and their definitions below. I want to familiarize you with the language used to describe what you don't want your dog to eat, so you can better understand later in the chapter what he should be digesting.

THE MEAT BY-PRODUCT MYTH

According to Melinda Miller, who has worked in executive capacities throughout the pet food industry and consults on holistic nutrition at Smith Ridge Veterinary Center, in South Salem, New York, there's a lot of confusion among dog owners about the safety of animal by-products. She says that while poultry by-products are nearly useless to your dog (there's no nutritional value in heads, necks, feet, and cleaned intestines of the birds, so they become a filler), contrary to what online myths report, there is nothing wrong with *meat* by-products if they're properly sourced. Livers and hearts are vital to canine health, and kidneys are good for them, too. Spleen, lungs—they're all animal tissue, so they're fine for a dog to eat. (In fact, kidneys, livers, and hearts are sold in grocery stores for humans to enjoy as well.)

So the problem with by-products is not the type of animal tissue (liver versus muscle meat) but the origin of the animal tissue. If the animal was 4D (dead, dying, down, diseased), then *every* part of it, both muscle meat and by-product (but, more accurately, organ meats) is bad. If the animal was inspected and approved, then all of its muscle meat and its by-products are nutritious for your dog— *though it's still better to have more named meat than by-products in your dog's food, especially as the first few ingredients.*

Ask Dr. Z!

What does it mean when my dog . . .

Q: *Will only eat off a porcelain or china dish? He is a snob about plastic plates.*

A: This is probably the result of early experience. There is some thought that plastics give off scents that are aversive, and therefore your dog may be turned off by the smell of his food on these dishes. Porcelain or china, on the other hand, does not retain smell.

Poultry by-products: These are parts of slaughtered poultry, including heads, necks, feet, and cleaned intestines, which have very little nutritional value to a dog. They are, in effect, poor-quality filler that drives up the protein percentage. Plus, the term "poultry" could describe any poultry animal (seagulls, chickens, geese, turkey). No, thanks!

Meat and bone meal: This ingredient is rendered from mammal tissues, including bone. The issue here is that meat meal has already been rendered, cooked, and sitting on shelves before it's turned into dog food. It's better to feed fresh and named meat, either alone or high in the ingredient list, than pre-rendered meal, since commercial food becomes further processed (and less healthy) when it is manufactured.

By-product meal: This refers to dry, ground, rendered, clean parts of the carcass of slaughtered animals. Chicken by-product meal, for instance, includes necks, feet, undeveloped eggs, and intestines.

Fish meal: This is clean ground tissue of undecomposed whole fish or fish cuttings, with or without the oil extracted. Labels don't indicate what type of fish, which can vary from one bag to the next. This means the fish that's used may not contain the fat-soluble vitamins and fatty acids that dogs need.

Poultry fat: The meat source isn't specifically named, which means this fat can come from any poultry animal (seagulls, chickens, geese, turkeys). It can also come from 4D sources (dead, dying, diseased, or down animals).

Vegetable fats: An animal fat source, like beef or chicken fat, is almost always better for, and more easily digested by, dogs than a vegetable fat. Fat is used to make food tastier.

Poor grain sources: Poor grains like corn and wheat are often among the first ingredients in low-quality kibble (if whole grains are one of the first few ingredients, listed after a named protein, this is fine for dogs who don't suffer from conditions linked to diet). Most manufacturers use them as a large source of the food's fiber—except for corn, which loosely qualifies as a protein—though these fiber and protein sources are not as easily digested and utilized by the body. Be on the lookout for by-products of milling and processing grains for other uses, and poor grain sources that include corn bran, cellulose, soybean mill run, and wheat mill run. Wheat products like wheat germ meal, wheat shorts, wheat middlings, and wheat flour are high allergens for dogs. Good grain sources are whole grains, like whole rice and barley.

Corn gluten meal: This is a by-product from the manufacture of corn syrup or starch. It's the dried residue after the removal of the bran, germ, and starch; corn gluten and corn gluten meal are binding agents.

Brewer's rice: This is made from small fragments of rice kernels that have been separated from larger kernels of milled rice. This processed rice product is missing many of the nutrients in whole ground rice and brown rice.

Peanut hulls: The outer shells of a peanut, used in some foods for fiber (and in some buildings as thermal insulation). The shells' texture lends itself to trapping and absorbing pesticides.

Powdered cellulose: Processed from the pulp of fibrous plant materials; this is essentially sawdust used to help bind food together and act as a cheap filler.

Beet pulp: This is promoted as fiber but used as sweetener. The sugar residue has little nutritional value.

Colorings and preservatives: Read to the end of a label to find these terms. BHA, BHT, and ethoxyquin are common preservatives under fire, so some companies are switching to natural options like vitamin C (ascorbate) and vitamin E (tocopherols), which are much safer.

Ask Dr. Z!

What does it mean when my dog . . .

Q: *Tears the skin off tennis balls?*

A: Normal eating behavior of wild dogs requires them to tear the hide off their prey. Tennis balls have a "skin" like a prey animal, and we all know how much dogs like to eat squirrels . . . That said, do not let your dog fully eat the ball or skin if he tries. This can cause choking or worse.

Fresh Food Is Central to Healthy Canine Diets

According to Martin Goldstein, DVM, of Smith Ridge Veterinary Center in South Salem, New York, and author of *The Nature of Animal Healing*, choosing a diet for your dog isn't a matter of right and wrong. Understanding what is most healthy, however, will help you move your dog toward his ideal nutrition options. And the more fresh food your dog eats, the more efficiently his body will work.

Fresh food comes in a wide mix of canine-friendly varieties, from raw food diets to kibble and canned diets that ultimately benefit from the addition of real food. (In "Dietary Options: From Most Fresh to Least Fresh" on page 279, I've broken down the best options for your pet and the benefits of each.) Experts say that fresh foods contain vitamins and nutrients that are at their most digestible and absorbable state—more so, even, than when the same vitamins and nutrients are added to processed foods via supplements. If your dog's food is fresh, the nutrients in meats, veggies, fruits, and whole grains are more likely to remain intact than in food that's been processed. (For this reason, raw food diets are at the high end of the freshness spectrum, and dry kibble is at the low.) Dry food is processed at very high temperatures, which can kill vital nutrients. Even all-natural, grain-free, and/or organic kibble is cooked at high temperatures, which destroys many of its vitamins, antioxidants, phytonutrients, and enzymes.

Storing Food to Maximize Freshness

Dry or wet food should be stored in a cool, dry place.

If you have an open can, refrigerate it between uses, and feed within two days.

Keep ingredients separate (meats separate from vegetables and oils).

If you prepare food in advance, refrigerating is better than freezing to retain nutrients.

A Quick Primer on Meats, Vegetables and Fruits, and Whole Grains

No matter which diet you choose to follow, there are three major categories of fresh food that should provide a foundation for a well-balanced meal: meat, veggies and fruits, and whole grains. Every meal should also have a well-rounded vitamin/mineral mix and essential fatty acids (see "The Role of Supplements in Every Diet," on page 295, for more on the topic).

Because every dog's metabolism, lifestyle, and health involve individual assessments, talk to your vet about whether your dog may need more or less meat, produce, or grains. Experts say that different dogs, especially those with health concerns, may require different food combinations; dogs with kidney disease, food allergies, and/or diabetes are just three types that may need tweaks. Since I plan to reference these three categories throughout the chapter, give yourself a quick primer first.

Meat (Preferably Organic)

Dogs are natural carnivores and need protein to thrive, which is why experts say that some form of named meat, poultry, or fish should be the first ingredient in a dog food, followed by healthy carbohydrate sources, including some vegetables. Lower-quality dog foods are seldom high in pure meat proteins, because those are the most expensive ingredient to add. Note that experts say meat by-products aren't bad for your dog if they're not made from waste parts that are unfit for human consumption; human-grade meats are ideal. You'll notice that some dogs that eat whole meats have fewer, harder, and less smelly poops. This is because they're absorbing more healthy food than their body feels the need to eliminate.

Some of the best-reviewed foods tend to have very high meat contents, like EVO's 95 percent meat varieties and Wellness's 95 percent meat varieties. I should add that these high-protein options aren't always the best option as an exclusive diet, especially if the dog has aggression issues or existing kidney problems (research shows that high-protein diets do not *cause* kidney problems, though misinformed sources say otherwise). Some dogs have trouble adjusting to these foods' high protein content but do well when they're used intermittently or for supplemental feeding. A recent study from Tufts University found that aggressive dogs may even benefit from low-protein diets, though it may depend on the type of protein the dog is fed. A dog's diet should always be based on the individual animal, not on the breed or size of the dog. All canines have different metabolisms, but for most, a meal with high protein content, best derived from meat, offers great nutrition. See the "Are Organic Foods Really Better?" on page 278 for more on organic ingredients.

Vegetables and Fruits (Preferably Organic)

Vegetables and fruits add flavor and nutrition to a dog's meal, often in place of refined salt and sugars. Blueberries, sweet potatoes, and carrots double as great flavor enhancers in homemade meals and quality dog foods. Fresh produce contains vitamins, antioxidants, and phytonutrients (chemical compounds like beta-carotene that occur naturally in plants and may affect health), which are essential to every dog's diet. For most dogs, a meal with no more than about 15 percent vegetables offers nutritional balance. All fruits should be fed in moderation, due to their typically high glycemic value. See "Are Organic Foods Really Better?" on page 278 for more on organic ingredients.

Whole Grains (Preferably Organic)

Canine diets can include whole grains like oats and barley, which still have their fiber and nutrients intact and benefit a dog's digestive system, though these shouldn't comprise more than 10 percent of a dog's diet. In fact, as far as grains go, oats are one of the better ones. They provide dietary bulk, which improves the digestive process and prevents constipation or eases it if the condition already exists. For optimum health, stay away from grain by-products such as brewer's rice, wheat middlings, corn fillers, and white or wheat flour, since these are loaded with simple sugars and have virtually no nutritional value; they may also cause stress to digestive organs. While some sources say that dogs can absorb almost all the nutrients from white rice, grains like wheat have almost no nutritional value for dogs—and corn products have little value. Experts add that glutens don't provide much nutritional value (they're primarily a binding agent) and are quick to remind dog owners of 2007's massive recall of pet food that was tainted by contaminated wheat and rice gluten from China. The amount of whole grains a dog requires may vary, depending on his tolerance. See "Are Organic Foods Really Better?" on page 278 for more on organic ingredients.

Are Organic Foods Really Better?

Definitely—but if these are too expensive for you, simply look for human-grade meats and ingredients. Feeding organic foods can reduce skin irritations and allergies; provide more energy, weight maintenance, fewer digestive disorders, and a healthier coat; and contribute to general longevity. Organic foods can be part of any canine diet, whether it's prepared at home or bought ready-made. But as with organic people food, the term can be loosely defined by the dog food industry. And while organic kibble is healthier than non-organic kibble, it is still cooked at high temperatures, which destroys many of its vitamins, antioxidants, phytonutrients, and enzymes. Here are a few ways to separate the organic wheat from the chaff.

Organic meats and produce don't contain pesticide residue or other toxins that increase susceptibility to various cancers and other chronic illnesses.

Rather than simply trust an "organic" sunburst on well-designed dog food packaging, examine the ingredient list, which should name organic items as "organic barley," "organic oats," etc.

Organic does not mean the same thing as "natural" or "all-natural." Though neither term is policed, the latter can have loose interpretations. Sawdust, for instance, comes from a natural source, as do peanut hulls—and both are common sources of poor protein in some dog foods.

Other positive buzzwords:

Hormone-free

Antibiotic-free

Pesticide-free

--- Ask Dr. Z!

What does it mean when my dog . . .

Q: *Breaks into cabinets for junk food like candy, cookies, and chips?*

A: Dogs are pretty smart, and they have many of the same tastes for junk food that humans do. If a dog has been successful at opening cabinets and gaining access to highly tasteful food, he will repeat the behavior. Amend this situation, since junk food may contain xylitol (a sugar substitute) or chocolate, both of which can be toxic to dogs.

Dietary Options: From Most Fresh to Least Fresh

Let's go through each of your dog's diet choices, listed in order of freshness. In the end, the diet you choose will depend on the time and interest you want to devote to preparing his meals, so review all options before hitting online resources or your local pet store. Your goal is to make your dog's food as fresh as it can be, which is why I've listed the types of foods available to feed your pet in order of most fresh to least. Don't forget: Every diet must also include a well-rounded mix of vitamins/minerals and essential fatty acids, as directed by your veterinarian.

Raw food diet (available in frozen and freeze-dried formulas; see page 281)

Premix diet (these include dehydrated foods; see page 285)

Canned food (see page 286)

Dry kibble (see page 287)

Variety Is Crucial to *Every* Diet

No matter what you choose to feed your dog—from home-prepared meals to premixes to variations on kibble and canned—your dog must have variety in his diet. Diverse foods provide balanced nutrition, which is helped along by rotating your dog's food on a regular basis. Rotating the brand and main protein source, within your dog's specific diet, will also increase his interest in food. The same meal, 365 days a year, becomes a yawn.

Every diet that I mention here lends itself to rotation. (See "Transitioning Your Dog from One Food to Another" on page 293 to learn how to mix things up so that your dog doesn't get sick from the change.) If you start your dog on a rotation diet while he's young, he'll transition easily throughout life. While most people don't feel they have the time or energy to do this, some vets say it can make a real difference in your dog's nutritional intake. Talk to your vet about your dog's diet and the extent to which rotation might be necessary. He will probably give you a timetable, specific to your pet, that details how often you should rotate his food so it's convenient and easy for you to understand and beneficial to the dog.

Ask Dr. Z!

What does it mean when my dog . . .

Q: *Eats poop—his own or another animal's?*

A: There is no real consensus on why dogs do this. Some conjecture relates to anxiety or possible dietary deficiencies. Keep in mind that the gustatory palate of the dog is quite different than ours. Objects that we would find objectionable may be quite the snack for him!

Raw Food Diets (BARF Diets)

Many holistic vets like raw food diets, since they're inspired by how dogs eat in the wild: hunting prey and eating the components of an animal's body, including organ meats, bones, and the intestinal tract. Raw food advocates feel that grain-based dry foods for dogs, though convenient, are unnatural and even unhealthy. While dogs can survive on them, raw feeders don't feel they necessarily thrive on them. From a raw feeder's point of view, raw diets represent a return to the whole, nutritious foods that dogs have always lived on and the way they would eat, even today, if left to their own instincts. (This may explain why some dogs can eat a backyard squirrel without so much as a burp, then suffer through GI issues from his canned and kibble dog food.)

Raw food diets are also known as BARF diets, though not for reasons that cynics might suspect. BARF is an acronym that stands for "biologically appropriate raw food," and the diet includes fresh raw meats, bones, and organ meats with very small amounts of fresh vegetables. These good protein sources are taken from animals that were healthy and properly slaughtered to ensure they contain vital and nourishing nutrients. Raw bones are also an integral part of raw food diets, since products like fresh, raw parts from chicken and turkey can help clean your dog's teeth, provide natural calcium and phosphorous, and add variety to a dog's diet. It is very important that all dogs have a source of calcium in their diet, so raw feeders must feed a dog bone in some form or the proper amount of a calcium supplement. Do not fall into the habit of regularly feeding your dog raw, boneless meat and organ meats without this important nutrient!

If you're interested in feeding a raw food diet, I encourage you to investigate it with a veterinarian who has a strong interest in canine nutrition. I've asked Melinda, who also acts as president of North

American Raw Petfood Association (NARPA), to provide a primer on how to feed a raw diet. You have two choices: either prepared or DIY. Here's a breakdown of each.

PREPARED RAW DIETS

Prepared raw diets come in a variety of forms, such as nuggets, patties, plastic tubs, and chubs (similar to a sausage tube). They are made of ground ingredients, including meat, bone, organ meats (such as heart and liver), and sometimes vegetables and fruit. Just a few of these diets include grain, but if you are searching for a grain-free diet, be sure to read the ingredient panel. The advantage of these diets is that they're convenient to use and typically contain everything a dog needs. Because the bone is ground, it's suitable for pets with dental issues like missing teeth, and there is no risk of injury from ground bone. Almost all of the prepared raw diets use USDA-inspected and -approved (human-grade) meats and bones, but you should check with the manufacturer if this isn't clearly stated in the company's literature. All of the major brands use sophisticated manufacturing techniques in order to eliminate or minimize the presence of bacteria, but do realize that these are raw products. While minimal bacteria does not pose a risk to the dogs, *you* should handle and store the foods just as you would handle and prepare raw meat for you and your family. Wash your hands after handling raw diets and foods, and wash the dishes, counters, and utensils that have come in contact with them. You don't need special cleaning solutions, just the same hot water and soap that you'd use when cleaning up after any type of raw meat handling.

Commercial raw diets are available in frozen or freeze-dried forms and are popular among the weak-stomached and time-crunched. They're sold in high-end independent pet stores and online. When you're ordering online, be aware that shipping frozen meat products is very expensive and adds significant cost.

Suggested Brands

Nature's Variety (available frozen or freeze-dried)

Bravo!

Primal

Stella and Chewy's (available frozen or freeze-dried)

Frozen Versus Freeze-Dried Foods

Prepared raw diets are available in fresh frozen and freeze-dried form. Both can stand alone or be used to enhance a meal, like those with a kibble base. Frozen raw diets arrive in either a mixed formula of raw meat, bone, and fresh vegetables, for total nutrition, or as pure raw meat. Store in the freezer and thaw before feeding.

Freeze-dried raw food from one brand is the same product as the company's unprocessed frozen siblings. For instance, Nature's Variety Instinct line of raw food comes in frozen nuggets/patties and in freeze-dried patties. The formula for both versions is the same. So the ingredients will vary by manufacturer and formula, but not by processing method. Freeze-dried raw is typically rehydrated by adding water to it, but it can be fed in its dry state as well. There is no reason to cook it. Freeze-dried foods can be used during meals or as a snack that provides nutrients, amino acids, and enzymes that processed foods lack. Since heat can destroy nutrients in food, freeze-drying is a better way to preserve the amino acids, natural enzymes, and probiotics of fresh foods. If your vet recommends a grain-free diet, freeze-dried foods can be part of your dog's rotation.

DIY Raw Diets

Many people use a wide variety of whole bone pieces and parts to formulate their own raw diet. This is cheaper than prepared diets, since you're not paying for the processing (grinding, mixing, and packaging), but since it is up to you to feed the right amount of bone versus meat, and supply the right amount of nutrients by including vitamin/amino acid–rich organ meats, Melinda encourages you to read books on raw feeding and/or to subscribe to one of the many Yahoo! Group e-mail discussion lists dedicated to raw diets before tackling a raw diet on your own.

If you choose to go this route, meat (chicken, beef, rabbit, lamb, pork, elk, venison, etc.) and whole bone pieces and parts can be obtained in a number of ways. Sources include grocery stores, meat wholesalers, ethnic markets, local farmers, raw diet feeding co-ops, hunters, and even Craiglist.com.

Is It Safe to Feed My Dog Natural Bones?

The topic of feeding natural bones to dogs can be a controversial one, depending on who you ask. Raw food advocates and some holistic vets say that raw bones will not harm your dog and that only cooked bones pose danger. Others err on the side of caution and suggest avoiding all natural bones. Realistically, choking, dental fractures, bowel impactions, and/or internal perforations can occur with raw *or* cooked bones, though cooked bones are more likely to splinter, which is the most common cause of problems. I've also heard that some breeds tolerate bones better than others, so please talk to your vet before giving your dog any type of bone. (The only type of bone that I allow Bianca to chew is her plastic Nylabone, since she tends to have digestive issues.)

If you decide to try raw bones on your dog, Melinda offers the following tips for feeding natural bones—either as a special treat or as part of a raw food diet:

Bigger bones cause fewer problems. When dogs need to work at a bone, they aren't able to gulp it down without sufficiently chewing it first.

Match the size of the bone to the size of the dog, so it's not too big or too small that it causes a problem. Turkey and chicken necks, for instance, can be exactly the right size to become lodged in a dog's throat if they are gulped.

To protect your dog's teeth from fracture, feed him softer bones like poultry bones. Wing bones, leg quarters, and breast bones are generally fine.

Meaty neck bones (pork, lamb, veal, and venison) are typically large and hard enough to provide a dental benefit (the soft abrasion naturally cleans the teeth) without causing tooth fractures.

Avoid beef marrow bones (the long leg shanks from cattle, sometimes called "soup bones"), which have no give, because they can cause tooth fractures. The marrow in these bones is also very fatty and can cause weight gain and/or digestion problems.

Note: See "Choking" on page 458 for first aid advice, in case a bone goes down the wrong pipe.

Premix Diet (Dehydrated Foods)

Premixes are great for those who want to feed homemade food but don't have the time or interest to prepare meals from scratch, since you can buy them online or in pet stores. Dehydrated foods arrive in a box or bag and simply require water to prepare; this may suspend enzyme activity until the food is rehydrated. You can also purchase vegetable and/or grain mixes designed to be added to raw or cooked meat; fish oils, flaxseed oils, and olive oils can be added as well.

A number of integrative-care vets, especially Robert S. Goldstein, DVM, of the Healing Center for Animals in Westport, Connecticut, and coauthor of *The Goldsteins' Wellness & Longevity Program,* name premixes as their top choice for clients whose dogs need healing with a nutritionally therapeutic approach. It's also quite easy to feed this way, since it's a modified home-cooking program. You can prepare a new premix every third day and store it in the fridge; just don't freeze it, since this can deplete nutrients. Be sure to separate the mix from its vegetables and supplements for maximum taste and preservation.

Suggested Brands

Sojos/Sojoiner Farms

Dr. Harvey's Canine Health

Honest Kitchen

Monzie's Organics Muesli

Canned Food

Canned foods are processed foods, so they contain a lot of water and aren't the freshest source of nutrients—but they are much healthier for your dog than kibble. Canned foods are also very useful for dog owners who want convenience, and they're great if you prefer to follow an easy grain-free diet (there are also grain-free kibbles on the market, should you choose to mix grain-free wet with grain-free dry). In fact, meat-based canned foods are close to ideal for some dogs, since too many carbs can cause obesity, cardiovascular disease, arthritis, and immune problems. If you'd like, you can upgrade the nutritional value of lower-quality canned food by adding real food to your dog's diet (see "How to Feed Table Scraps" on page 301 for more on this). You can buy good canned foods at select markets, independent pet stores, and online shops.

Dry Food (Kibble)

Commercially prepared kibble has become a diet staple for most dogs. It's inexpensive, convenient, and plentiful. But dry food is also much lower in quality protein than most dogs need for good health and easy digestion. A dog's digestive tract is much shorter, stronger, and efficient at breaking down protein than a human's is, but not as equipped to break down too many grains and carbohydrates, which a lot of kibble is made from. It's not true that the abrasive texture of kibble can help protect against dental disease, unless a special kibble is prescribed by your vet to do so, but if you offer your dog bones and other hard toys (with give), feed him raw vegetables, and brush his teeth, there's no real need for kibble in a dog's diet. If your dog is on a grain-free diet but really likes to crunch, look for grain-free kibbles to suit his palate and health.

A dog should never live on kibble alone, since it's cooked at very high temperatures, which depletes it of nutrients. Blending kibble with raw, cooked, freeze-dried, or dehydrated meats; fresh meat plus fruits and vegetables; or select table scraps will help restore nutrients to the otherwise empty meal. Just remember to use proportionately less kibble when adding these to the mix so that your dog doesn't gain weight, and if you haven't always rotated the food in his diet, transition him carefully. I should add that most integrative-care vets do not like any kibble diets and say that if you must feed your dog a processed diet, you should start with canned foods as your food base. You can buy suitable kibble at better grocery stores, pet food stores, and online.

What to Look for in Kibble

If you feed dry food to your dog as part of his diet, aim to give him the best-quality kibble you can find. Take this tip sheet with you when you hit the store.

▶ Look for the fat or oil in the food. The ingredients listed before the fat or oil source are the majority of the food (including the fat or oil). Those listed after are present in smaller amounts.

▶ One or more named sources of meat should appear as the first ingredients.

▶ The term "meal" means the ingredients have been cooked at high temperatures and pressure to remove moisture (and therefore are depleted of most nutrients). If a whole meat is listed, there should also be a meat meal to further enforce that the food's main protein source is from animals and not from grains.

▶ Grains should be whole grains, not grain by-products, like soy flour, brewer's rice, corn gluten meal, etc. Soy and corn are genetically modified and often grown with pesticides. If corn and soy are used, they should not appear as the first few ingredients—even then, organic is preferred.

▶ Dry foods always have a fat source, so make sure it's a named source like chicken fat, beef fat, sunflower oil, flaxseed oil, etc. Avoid foods with generic listings like vegetable oil, animal fat, and poultry fat.

▶ Fruits and veggies can provide additional nutrients, flavors, and minerals, but some are better for your dog than others. Fruits and vegetables like carrots, tomatoes, apples, and blueberries are preferred over more processed ingredients like beet pulp, tomato pumice, apple pumice, dried peas, and dried carrots.

- ▶ Avoid foods with artificial preservatives like BHA/BHT or ethoxyquin. High-quality foods use natural preservatives like mixed tocopherols; vitamin C sources like ascorbic acid, rosemary extract; and other herbs or antioxidants.

- ▶ Avoid foods with sucrose, fructose, corn syrup, sorbitol, glucose, and other sweeteners.

- ▶ Avoid foods with colors and dyes, especially numbered food dyes like Yellow 5 and 6 and Red 40.

CANNED AND KIBBLE RECOMMENDATIONS

Vets with a special interest in nutrition like to break down canned and kibble suggestions by grain and grain-free brands, since grain-free diets have become increasingly popular. While these diets are on the rise, I'd prefer that you didn't put your dog on one until you talk to your vet. All of the following formulas come in both canned and dry options, but the wet version is much healthier.

Grain-free Kibble and Canned Products

Instinct by Nature's Variety

EVO by Natura

Before Grain by Merrick

Core by Wellness

Taste of the Wild by Diamond

Barking at the Moon by Solid Gold

Wild and Natural by Timberwolf

Ocean Blue by Timberwolf

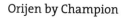
Orijen by Champion

Sweet Potato and Venison by Natural Balance

Sweet Potato and Salmon by Natural Balance

ALS Formula by Canidae

Salmon Meal Formula by Canidae

Better-quality Kibble and Canned Products That Contain Grain

Nature's Variety Prairie

Merrick

Evanger's

Solid Gold

Innova

California Natural

Wellness

Natural Balance

Canidae

Timberwolf

Dogswell

Halo Spot's Stew

What About Prescription Diets?

Traditional vets are split about the effectiveness of prescription diets, specifically formulated canned and kibble food thought to address certain health conditions, from companies like Hill's (which makes Science Diet) and Royal Canin, among others. While some swear by these, others insist that they may help certain symptoms by providing a change without addressing the underlying cause or problem. The diets are typically heavy on grains and can include chicken meal or chicken by-product meal, so if your vet does suggest a prescription diet to help what ails your dog, inspect labels carefully. Some diets even contain potentially harmful preservatives like BHA and BHT, which are common ingredients in floor cleaners and paint products.

Integrative vets feel that for many dogs with health issues, a change in diet to one that relies predominantly on real food (with minerals and nutrients intact) can make the biggest difference of all. If your dog is unwell, diet should always be part of a conversation with your vet.

How to Enhance a Processed Food Diet

If your dog exclusively eats a diet that involves any canned food, dried food, or both, you should enhance his meal in three ways to ensure that he has a balanced diet:

1. Rotate Brands and Main Protein Source

Melinda echoes the thoughts of most integrative-care vets when she explains the importance of rotation with any diet, especially commercial ones. As she puts it: If the only thing you ate was Kraft macaroni and cheese from a box for every meal, week after week, year after year, you might survive—but would you thrive? Or if a pediatrician handed a new mom a jar of pureed food and insisted she feed only this to her child until he left for college, with nothing fresh or whole in between, wouldn't you run from his exam room? Humans are told that to be healthy, we must eat a wide variety of foods to make sure we're getting the full spectrum of nutrients that we need. Studies show that our dogs are no different. Barring specific health issues that might require a special diet, dogs need a wide variety of food for optimal health, just like us.

Every commercial dog food is based on a formula, and the only ingredient that really changes in their products is the protein. Other than this, the nutrient profile for Brand X looks pretty much the same regardless of the variety you're feeding. Brand Y, formulated by a different person or with different ingredients, has a different nutrient profile. And Brand Z has yet another nutrient profile. By feeding all three brands (not just varieties within the same brand) on a weekly rotational basis, you will ensure that your dog is getting all the nutrients that his specific metabolism requires. He may need the extra amino acids in Brand Z and the lower mineral count in Brand X, while another dog requires exactly the opposite. It is the rotation of foods that provides him with health and longevity, since he's getting a full and varied spectrum of nutrients.

If you feed your dog real food with his kibble or canned food, you should also rotate the protein, plus produce, for the sake of variety and nutrition. However, you do not need to slowly transition your dog from one real food to another, since they are already a part of his regular diet (processed foods, by nature, are harder to digest). For more on how to mix people food with kibble or canned foods, see "Thumbs Up on Real Food" on page 300.

Transitioning Your Dog from One Food to Another

Melinda works with clients at Smith Ridge Veterinary Center to help them learn how to rotate their dog's food, and she says they rarely have a problem if they follow the schedule below. This timetable will help you transition your dog from one food to another. Some dogs can transition much faster, and a few need to go a little slower. The transition plan can be used when regularly rotating any diet (not just a processed diet) or if your vet prescribes a new food to your dog. If you begin rotation at an early age, your dog will have no problem with it throughout his life. The only time this transition isn't necessary is when you feed your dog an exclusively raw diet.

Days 1 thru 3: 25 percent new food, 75 percent old food; if all is well on day 3, then:

Days 4 thru 6: 50 percent new food, 50 percent old food; if all is well on day 6, then:

Days 7 thru 9: 75 percent new food, 25 percent old food; if all is well on day 9, then:

Day 10: 100 percent new food

2. **Add Digestive Enzymes**

Adding digestive enzymes back into every meal will not only improve digestion and the absorption of nutrients, it may also help protect your dog against allergies and immune disorders. Better digestion and more absorbed nutrients can also help to prevent and eliminate diet-related issues like body odor, excessive shedding, gas, and itchy skin. Natural pet stores or online sources sell digestive enzymes for dogs, but talk to your vet about which enzymes best suit your pet's needs.

🐾 Digestive Enzymes for Dogs with GI Problems 🐾

Digestive enzymes don't just help canned and kibble eaters! Dr. Goldstein says these supplements are great for dogs that experience digestive problems of any type. Ask your vet about digestive enzymes if your dog frequently experiences vomiting, diarrhea, burping, and flatulence. (A nutritional blood test can also help evaluate any nutritional digestive problems. See "Testing Your Dog's Blood for Metabolic Weakness" on page 296 for more on this.)

---

3. **Add Essential Fatty Acids (EFAs)**

Essential fatty acids (EFAs) are a must in every dog's diet, since a canine's body can't make them but requires them for normal growth, plus the function of muscles, nerves, and organs. EFAs also strengthen cardiovascular function, reduce inflammation, and nourish a dog's skin, coat, and digestive tract lining. EFA deficiencies have been linked to heart disease, cancer, and diabetes.

EFAs are divided into omega-3s and omega-6s, though most dog food diets are already high in omega-6s, which can stimulate the overproduction of prostaglandins (hormones involved in pain regulation; too much makes pain worse) if you don't balance them out with omega-3s. That said, focus on boosting your dog's omega-3 intake, since it has anti-inflammatory properties. Ask your vet whether he suggests a dietary supplement or natural oils from the original source. EFAs from fish oil are ideal, since they provide key nutrients called EPA and DHA in a form that the dog's body can utilize immediately. Excessive amounts of EFAs can be harmful, and in some cases toxic, so speak to your vet before you begin feeding supplements to determine the right ones for your dog's health, size, and established diet.

A final note: Don't be tricked by wet or dry food that advertises that they're high in omega-3 or omega-6 fatty acids, since they may be present but not in sufficient amounts or in the proper ratio for good health (either from the start, after processing, or both). Incorporating EFAs into a food is expensive in terms of ingredients and preservation, since omega-3s spoil quickly. (The AAFCO doesn't recognize EFAs as essential nutrients, though studies prove they are necessary to maintaining and improving your dog's health.)

Ask Dr. Z!

What does it mean when my dog . . .

Q: *Barks at overweight people?*

A: Large people may move in an awkward fashion that can attract and even bother dogs, especially if their guardians or other family unit members are not overweight.

The Role of Supplements in Every Diet

Regardless of your dog's diet, nutritional supplements will optimize his health with the right amount of vitamins, minerals, and other essential nutrients. Ask your vet which supplements your dog needs, depending on the diet you choose and his existing health. No pill should ever replace a well-balanced diet, but proper supplementation can make good nutrition even better, and a smart mix of vitamins, minerals, and essential fatty acids is a must.

Testing Your Dog's Blood for Metabolic Weakness

The gold standard for detecting your dog's health needs is a blood test called the Nutritional Blood Test, from Animal Nutrition Technologies. This test has been used for more than twenty-five years in dogs, cats, and horses. Your vet may not offer it as part of his exam, so you'll need to request it. Unlike standard blood tests that look for disease, the NBT is a metabolic analysis that can look deeper into the body at what is called the animal's core physiology. This reflects the health status of a body's immune system and can highlight areas of stress. The result of the analysis is a custom-made nutraceutical therapy (dietary supplements that act as medicine) that's formulated specifically for your dog to reduce inflammation, strengthen weakened organs, and metabolically support the core physiology of a dog by promoting healing and well-being at a cellular level.

Stay Current on Dog Food Information

The pet food recalls in 2007 doubled as a major wake-up call to a nation of pet owners, as well as some pet food makers, which consequently improved their formulas. Since then, owners have become more vigilant about how and where their dog's food is made, where the ingredients come from, and what kind of testing is done to improve them. I imagine you'll do the same.

New canned and kibble dog foods appear and fall off the market as regularly as any other food brand might, so stay current on the best dog foods out there. A good place to start is *Whole Dog Journal*

(Whole-Dog-Journal.com), which publishes updated subscriber-only lists of top-quality foods. Sites like AnimalArk.com, DogFoodProject .com, and PetFoodRatings.com also do a fine job investigating this topic. About.com has an extensive ingredient database but makes no judgment call.

Cooking for Your Dog

Cooking for your dog certainly has its benefits, the best of which is that you can control the source of your dog's food ingredients. Cooking will also provide him with a beautiful variety of meats, vegetables, and whole grains. It may seem time-consuming at first, but the long-term payoff is worth it, especially if your dog has allergies, GI problems, or autoimmune disorders. The only catch is that if you plan to cook entire meals for your canine, you must follow dog-specific recipes so his meals are balanced with vitamins and minerals necessary to a dog's health. *Dr. Pitcairn's New Complete Guide to Natural Health for Dogs and Cats* by Richard H. Pitcairn, DVM, and Susan Hubble Pitcairn provides great recipes for all dogs, including those with specific health problems. *The Goldsteins' Wellness & Longevity Program for Dogs and Cats* by Robert S. Goldstein, VMD, and Susan J. Goldstein also offers excellent recipes and nutritional guidelines.

Realize that cooking for your dog doesn't have to mean prepping full meals for him every day. Mixing fresh meats and vegetables into a variety of meal plans, from kibble to premix diets to raw diets, will make a difference, and meat and vegetable table scraps and leftovers are always good snacks.

Recipes from Rach!

My dear friend Rachael Ray, bestselling author, chef, TV personality, and proud mommy to a Pit Bull named Isaboo, sent me two delicious recipes for canine cooks. They're easy, yummy, and fun to nibble on yourself. Bianca's a huge fan of the burgers. Note: Always check with your vet about which foods are appropriate for you to share with your pet.

Beggin' Egg & Cheese Fried Rice

This rice dish, spiked with eggs, bacon, and cheese, will have your pup beggin' for more.

Serves 1 dog

> 2 slices turkey bacon
>
> 1 tablespoon vegetable oil
>
> ½ cup cooked brown rice
>
> 1 large egg, beaten
>
> ¼ cup shredded cheddar cheese
>
> Chopped flat-leaf parsley, for garnish

1. In a medium nonstick skillet, cook the bacon over medium-high heat until crisp, about 5 minutes. Drain on paper towels, then finely chop.

2. In the same skillet, heat the oil over high heat. Add the rice and cook, stirring often, until warmed through, about 4 minutes. Add the cooked bacon and toss. Push the rice mixture to the side of the pan; add the egg to the pan and cook, stirring, until set, then stir into the rice. Transfer to a bowl, top with the cheddar, and let cool. Sprinkle with the parsley.

Isaboo's Bacon-Cheese-Barley Burgers

Everyone loves bacon, including man's best friend.

Serves 4 (1 dog and 3 owners, 3 dogs and 1 owner, 2 dogs and 2 owners . . .)

½ cup pearl barley

2 cups fat-free chicken broth

2 slices lean bacon

1 large egg

½ cup dried bread crumbs

½ cup shredded cheddar or Monterey Jack cheese

1. In a medium saucepan, bring the barley and chicken broth to a boil over high heat; reduce the heat and simmer, uncovered, until the barley is tender, about 20 minutes. Drain off any excess liquid. Transfer to a medium bowl and let cool.

2. While the barley is cooking, in a large nonstick skillet, cook the bacon over medium-high heat until crisp, about 4 minutes. Reserve the fat from the bacon for cooking the burgers. Finely chop the bacon and add to the cooled barley. Mix in the egg, bread crumbs, and cheese. Combine thoroughly and score into 4 equal pieces. Wet your hands and form the pieces into patties.

3. Reheat the bacon fat and cook the burgers over medium heat for 4 minutes on each side.

HOME COOKING TIP FOR THE TIME-CRUNCHED

To help save time in the kitchen, you may want to cook enough food to last three days (six feedings). Delicious stews, for instance, are full of healthy meats, vegetables, and whole grains, and they're easy to make and serve. Always store prepared foods in the refrigerator, since freezing can deplete nutrients. Serve them alone or as a topping to kibble. Bon appétit!

Thumbs Up on Real Food

For years, dog food manufacturers told dog owners that feeding a dog people food was a terrible idea. But that's not necessarily true. Most of today's experts love the idea of feeding dogs people food—*if* the food you're eating is prepared in a healthy way. Real food should always fall under the whole meats, vegetables, and whole-grain categories. No dog should be fed pizza crust, potato chips, or other junk foods. High-fat, spicy, or potentially toxic foods are obviously out of the question. It's important to note that there is a big difference between cooking a healthy meal for yourself and portioning off an appropriate-size meal or topping for your dog and throwing him fat from your steak or a leftover roll. Just because your dog may eat the fat or the bread doesn't mean he should!

Much like how dog food manufacturers discourage owners from mixing brands because it cuts into their bottom line, they've taken a similar approach when dismissing natural foods. Your biggest concern with feeding dogs real food is that too much will create an unbalanced meal. So if real food is a supplement to your dog's diet, be sure to compensate proportionally.

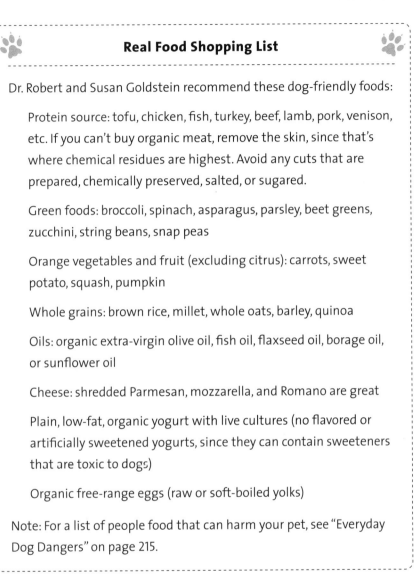

Real Food Shopping List

Dr. Robert and Susan Goldstein recommend these dog-friendly foods:

Protein source: tofu, chicken, fish, turkey, beef, lamb, pork, venison, etc. If you can't buy organic meat, remove the skin, since that's where chemical residues are highest. Avoid any cuts that are prepared, chemically preserved, salted, or sugared.

Green foods: broccoli, spinach, asparagus, parsley, beet greens, zucchini, string beans, snap peas

Orange vegetables and fruit (excluding citrus): carrots, sweet potato, squash, pumpkin

Whole grains: brown rice, millet, whole oats, barley, quinoa

Oils: organic extra-virgin olive oil, fish oil, flaxseed oil, borage oil, or sunflower oil

Cheese: shredded Parmesan, mozzarella, and Romano are great

Plain, low-fat, organic yogurt with live cultures (no flavored or artificially sweetened yogurts, since they can contain sweeteners that are toxic to dogs)

Organic free-range eggs (raw or soft-boiled yolks)

Note: For a list of people food that can harm your pet, see "Everyday Dog Dangers" on page 215.

How to Feed Table Scraps

Dr. Robert Goldstein and Susan Goldstein are longtime advocates of real food feeding. However, they suggest doling it out in tiny portions as a snack (like a thin slice of turkey) or as a supplement to a dog's base food: canned, kibble, or premix. The Goldsteins also suggest increasing the amount of people food in your dog's diet very gradually, especially if his body is used to commercial dog foods. Follow their formula below for happy bellies and satisfied taste buds.

1. Reduce your dog's base food by 25 to 35 percent.

2. Add back to the base food a 25 to 35 percent portion of your own protein (raw or slightly cooked), whole grain, and chopped or blended vegetable mix. Your table scrap ratio should be 65 percent protein, 20 percent grains, and 15 percent vegetables.

3. Add flax or salmon oil (one teaspoon for every twenty-five pounds) to this mix.

Food Sharing Suggestions

Experts suggest that when you're making food for your family, you set aside a batch to share with your dog before you add seasoning, gravies, or sauces. Though you can pull food from any meal, don't feed them to your dog more than twice a day unless your vet suggests otherwise. Fresh real foods are best, but you can reheat refrigerated leftovers if you have them to spare.

SHARE YOUR: *Breakfast eggs*

Why it's healthy: A poached, boiled, or scrambled egg made with a small amount of olive oil provides protein with essential fatty acids. Organic free-range eggs are preferable.

Leave out: Buttered toast. Extra fat and flour don't benefit your dog.

SHARE YOUR: *Midmorning yogurt*

Why it's healthy: A spoonful of plain low-fat or nonfat organic, live-culture yogurt aids digestion.

Leave out: Artificial fruit flavorings. They can contain sweeteners that are toxic to dogs.

SHARE YOUR: *Tofu and barley salad for lunch*

Why it's healthy: Tofu is a fine protein source. Whole grains provide daily roughage and fiber.

Leave out: Onions, since they can cause anemia in certain dogs. This is true for all forms of onion: raw, dehydrated, or cooked.

SHARE YOUR: *Green salad*

Why it's healthy: Pluck raw vegetables from the bowl before you add oils or dressing. Raw veggies are full of vitamins, healthy fiber, and nutrients—plus, they aid digestion. Grind or grate these into your dog's food (see "Feeding Fruits and Vegetables" on page 305 for which are best for him).

Leave out: Dressing or mixed oils. These are full of preservatives and spices. However, a drizzle of cold-pressed olive oil over a dog's food is great for his skin and coat. (Too much can loosen his stool, so don't overdo it.)

Ask Dr. Z!

What does it mean when my dog . . .

Q: *Eats grass?*

A: There is no clear consensus on why dogs do this and whether they are attempting to settle their stomachs, which is what we hear most often. What we know is that when most dogs eat grass, they end up vomiting. What we don't know is whether they vomit because they eat grass, or whether they eat grass to stimulate vomiting when they have some type of stomach trouble.

SHARE YOUR: *Steak, baked potato, and broccoli for dinner*

Why it's healthy: Steak is fresh protein! Broccoli is a great source of calcium and vitamin C (ascorbic acid). Cooked potatoes are full of complex carbohydrates, minerals like potassium, vitamin C, and fiber.

Leave out: Steak sauce, which adds preservatives and causes carpet stains galore. Gristle and fat should be trimmed off before feeding. Never serve potatoes raw.

SHARE YOUR: *Steamed vegetable broth*

Why it's healthy: The residue water from steamed vegetables is rich with vitamins, minerals, and nutrients. Add it to your dog's food so he can reap the benefits. All vegetables must be organic, or else pesticides leach into the water when cooking.

Leave out: Broth thickeners. These can contain flour and gluten, which are hard to digest.

NOTE: Although you're technically feeding your dog table scraps, always put people food in his bowl. This way, he doesn't expect his food to actually come from your table during meals.

VEGETABLE FACTS

Good source of fiber.

Stick to green and orange vegetables. Some dark red foods like tomatoes, peppers, and eggplant (okay, eggplants are purple, but that's in the red family) can trigger arthritis flare-ups.

Vegetables like peas and carrots are high-glycemic (high in sugar) vegetables, so you may want to temper these.

Fruit Facts

Peel first to reduce pesticide exposure.

Don't mix fresh fruit with other foods, since some sugary fruits cause an upset stomach when mixed with proteins.

Tropical fruits are also very high in glucose, so temper these as well.

Don't feed citrus fruits.

Avoid cherries, which are in the arthritis-triggering category.

Feeding Fruits and Vegetables

Feed your dog his fruits and vegetables either 1) lightly steamed, boiled, baked, grilled, or cooked, or 2) raw and finely ground. Melinda says dogs don't have the digestive enzymes to efficiently break down the cell walls of fruits and vegetables, but once this is done for them via cooking (which explodes the walls) or grinding (which shreds the walls), dogs can obtain their nutrients. This doesn't mean that giving your dog raw and unground vegetables is bad (all vitamins are good!), but he won't get as much from the foods as he would if they were cooked, or raw and finely ground. Vegetables and fruits should comprise only about 15 percent of your dog's diet. Again, feed your dog fruit in moderation because of its typically high glycemic values.

Don't Overcomplicate Your Dog's Diet

After discussing so many healthy feeding options, the best advice I can give is for you to follow one that's the least complicated for you while still nutritionally sound for your dog. Whether we're talking people diets or dog diets, the least complicated plans are always the easiest to follow. So if it's simpler for you to defrost a prepared and balanced meal, consider a frozen raw formula. If you like "just add water" solutions, premixes are best. Sometimes it's easier to set aside part of a healthy dinner and blend it with existing kibble. I like to cook, so steaming chicken or broiling a piece of fish for Bianca, then adding it to Wellness kibble with raw vegetables and supplements, is a no-brainer for me.

Choose a diet that works with your budget, schedule, and lifestyle, but make it part of your routine. Who knows? Your dog might just help you develop a healthier lifestyle, too.

Managing Your Dog's Weight

According to the Association for Pet Obesity Prevention, more than 44 percent of dogs in the U.S. are estimated to be overweight or obese. What's most upsetting is that various studies suggest obesity is the leading cause of preventable disease and death in dogs. Obese canines are at an increased risk for chronic but largely preventable conditions like diabetes, arthritis, and respiratory problems. They're at increased risk during surgery, more prone to injury, and have more stress on their heart, lungs, liver, kidneys, and joints. To put it in perspective, experts say that a few extra pounds on a dog are the equivalent of thirty to fifty extra pounds on a person!

Dogs gain weight for any number of reasons, but the wrong food and lack of exercise can quickly pack on the pounds. Every dog has a different metabolism, lifestyle, and caloric need, so see your vet about how to adjust your dog's portion size and exercise program if his weight starts to fluctuate. To gauge your dog's weight, check for fat deposits over his chest, back, tail base, and hind quarters. More specifically:

Feel for his ribs: Place your thumbs on your dog's backbone while he is standing, and let your fingers drape down either side of his body. You should be able to feel his ribs without pushing. If you have to push to feel them, he needs to lose weight. And if you can feel every rib with a deep indentation between each rib, he probably needs to gain a few pounds. Ideally, if you can feel just the rib with a slight padding of flesh, he is the perfect weight for his build. No fat should hang behind the dog's rib cage.

Squeeze his bottom and watch him walk: Extra fat around the base of his tail, and a waddle-like walk (note that this can also be indicative of a joint issue or similar ailment) are signs that it's time to monitor your dog's diet. You should be able to feel the two bumps of his pelvic bones, just above his tail, without pressing in.

Remember his birthday: Older dogs are more likely to be obese or overweight than young dogs. One 2008 study found that 52 percent of dogs over the age of seven were found to be overweight or obese.

Tips for Owners of Overweight Dogs

▶ Always see your dog's doctor about obesity, since it may be a symptom of a serious condition.

▶ Use a measuring cup for portion control, especially when feeding table scraps.

▶ Don't simply follow feeding charts on food bags; discuss a customized meal plan with your vet.

▶ Add natural fiber with vegetables to your dog's diet to fill him up sooner. Fresh or canned green beans are great, since they add volume without calories. (This is the dog version of you eating a salad to shed pounds!)

▶ Some veterinarians and local shelters offer obesity clinics to help you determine a customized meal plan. Ask your vet if there is an organization near you that can help.

▶ Provide longer walks, playtime, and training sessions to get your dog in shape and create a calorie deficit. A dog's time alone in a yard isn't sufficient. Romp, play, and run *together*. Note that very obese dogs can hurt their joints with too much exercise, so for these pudgy animals, try swimming or underwater treadmills to ease joint mobility.

▶ Don't blame weight gain on hormone changes related to neutering or spaying. Hormones, a lowered metabolism, and less exercise after surgery may contribute to a small temporary gain, but it's generally a myth.

▶ Extreme hot or cold weather can affect exercise habits. So can a personal injury or recent surgery. Adjust your dog's caloric intake to compensate for fitness differences.

▶ Some breeds have a head start on thick waistlines, like Labrador Retrievers, Beagles, Basset Hounds, Dachshunds, and Cocker Spaniels. If you own one of these breeds, be vigilant about your dog working off his daily ration so he doesn't gain too much weight.

▶ Don't let your dog bamboozle you into giving him too many cookies. We recently realized that Bianca tricks Howard into giving her a second treat every morning by first going potty for me and then pretending to go a second time for him (Howard lets her out through the doggie door, but he never watches to see if she actually potties—and she doesn't)!

Keep a Food Diary

Your vet is the best person to assess whether your dog has a weight issue and what to do about it. To help your dog stay slim, keep a food diary of his daily food intake, any intestinal reactions to a new diet, his daily exercise regime, and his weekly weight (you can use a bathroom scale to weigh your dog). Review your log with your vet at your next appointment.

And What if He Doesn't Eat *Enough*?

The average dog's appetite may fluctuate, just as a person's might. Some dogs enjoy consistent meals, while others eat less regularly but manage to maintain a healthy weight.

Shawn Messonnier, DVM, of Paws and Claws Animal Hospital in Plano, Texas, and host of the award-winning Sirius XM Radio series *Dr. Shawn, the Natural Vet,* says that appetite loss is the symptom of a larger problem if it persists longer than two days. If it happens a few times a month or is accompanied by lethargy, vomiting, or diarrhea, talk to your vet about a possible pattern and underlying issue. Uncertain circumstances like a new home or new baby can affect a dog's eating habits, too.

The point is, a dog with an ongoing lack of appetite is very different from a dog that's a fickle eater. I asked a handful of vets for their tips on how to perk up a dog's interest in food, in case your dog has a picky palate.

▶ Have patience. It may require repeated exposure to new foods before your dog really enjoys them.

▶ Increase exercise. Is he working up an appetite? If not, you may need to rev up his metabolism with a more active lifestyle. An extra walk or chase game that uses bursts of energy may make him hungry.

▶ Consider his past diet. If he's been weaned on the flavor enhancers, salts, sweeteners, and carbohydrates of many canned and dry foods, it may take your dog some time before he likes healthier options. When people eat diets full of processed foods, it can take two weeks for them to cleanse their systems, adjust, and appreciate better food. A dog that's used to poor-quality food is like a junk-food addict; his taste buds need time to adjust to new and natural flavors. This is seldom the case with meats, since most dogs love meat, but fruits, vegetables, and some grains can be a project!

▶ Create a feeding ritual. If your dog is reluctant to eat what you give him, he may be trying to teach *you* about what goes into his dish. Develop a feeding pattern so he knows what goes into his dish and when, plus how it's presented, so you can both establish expectations.

▶ Rotate food sources. Rotation will keep his "what's next?" interest piqued and his health in check.

▶ Enhance the food's flavor. A spoonful of canned food, a sprinkle of crushed treats, chicken broth, some low-fat plain yogurt, low-fat cottage cheese, or grated cheese, and one or two poached egg yolks are all good options.

Know Your Healthy Snacks

Every dog loves snacks. Here's a key to which are fattening and which are slimming:

SLIMMING SNACKS

Raw vegetables, like carrots and dark green vegetables (cooked or grated)

Sliced, skinless fruits—either cooked or grated. Do not feed citrus fruits because of the high sugar content (see "Everyday Dog Dangers" on page 215 for harmful fruits)

Air-popped popcorn or popcorn made with olive oil, but no butter or salt. Avoid microwave popcorn, which can be full of preservatives

Freeze-dried meat snacks like liver, salmon, cod, beef liver, and turkey hearts: these are dry, easy to handle, and full of protein

FATTENING SNACKS

Peanut butter in a Kong toy

Cheese chunks

Pigs' ears

Chips or other snacks that would make a human fat

Bread or other noncomplex carbohydrates

Tropical fruits (including bananas)

Make Eating Fun

Dogs that aren't excited by their food may need a little motivation. Trainer Greg Kleva suggests these scavenger games, which speak to a dog's natural predator instincts and can be used occasionally to sustain a dog's interest in meals even if he isn't especially finicky. Randomly timed games with immediate food rewards will help him constantly anticipate the delicious prize.

▶ Scatter some of the dog's food on the floor around his bowl. He may gobble it more readily if he has to sniff it out first.

▶ Stuff a meal's worth of rations into a few food toys (like a Kong) and spread them all over the house. This provides nourishment and mental stimulation with problem-solving techniques. This also appeals to a canine's natural instinct to forage for his food, especially with hunting dogs.

▶ Use your dog's meals as training motivation. Choose one new command to teach him, and divide your dog's food into portions and reward him with each one after he successfully responds to the cue.

Ask Dr. Z!

What does it mean when my dog . . .

Q: *Insists on sniffing, and sometimes eating, rocks?*

A: Dogs may do this for a variety of reasons. In some cases, it may be due to stress, anxiety, or boredom. A dog may initially like the taste or noise that rocks make against his teeth, but after repeat incidents, it can turn into a compulsive disorder. Even innocent rock chewing can be a problem, since it can wear down a dog's teeth. Swallowed rocks can cause intestinal problems and blockage. If your dog's health is at risk, see a vet about modifying your dog's behavior and environment. In some cases, you may even want to consider medication.

Puppies Are the Exception

When you first bring a puppy home, he may not seem anxious to clean his plate because he may need time to adjust to his new surroundings. If he seems apathetic about meals for an extended period, call the vet, since puppies can quickly become weak without regular sustenance and dehydrate from consequent illness. With the exception of some dogs that are being housetrained (trainers' rules about feeding and water during this time may vary), vets say that it's important to provide puppies with a regular supply of food and water at least three times a day. Reasons for a puppy to refuse food include:

Medical: He's experiencing diarrhea, vomiting, lethargy, and/or worms in his stool. A slender puppy with a distended belly could have parasites. Call the vet if your dog shows signs of any of these illnesses.

Stress: He's adjusting to a new home with a lot of stimulation. Try giving him a quiet feeding space of his own (see "Create a Dining Ritual for Your Dog" on page 256), and limit interaction during mealtimes.

Loneliness: On the other hand, your puppy may need you as his guardian to hang around while he eats, so that he feels comfortable feeding in a new place.

The weather: If it's too hot or too cold, a puppy's appetite could be affected the same way that yours might. Try to keep a comfortable temperature in your home to encourage regular eating.

Food brand: If he refuses to eat the food you've bought, talk to your vet about how long to wait before switching to another brand. You can also try adding a mild topping like organic chicken broth to entice him.

Depression and Weight Loss

Drastic weight and appetite loss are leading signs of dog depression. Others include lethargy, loss of interest in play and toys, neediness, atypical shedding, and anxious or aggressive behavior. Talk to your vet if your dog seems downright blue, in case depression is a symptom of a larger medical problem. If the vet feels that it's behavioral, ask him about ways to address the trigger that's causing the dog's glum attitude. Changes in weather, environment, and separation anxiety can trigger depression. Some vets may even prescribe an antidepressant like doggie Prozac, though this is not universally helpful for all dog behavior issues, and bear in mind that your vet is the best person to suggest this prescription-only drug (no, your dog can't just have some of yours). Very few dogs are so depressed that they can't be helped, and once your dog's love for life returns, so will his appetite.

Food Allergies

Allergies are one of the most common conditions that affect dogs, and a large number of veterinarians attribute itchy skin, respiratory problems, and allergy-related digestive problems to poor-quality diets. After all, food allergies account for at least 10 percent of all allergies in dogs, and they explain 20 percent of itching and scratching in dogs. Some dogs with food allergies also have inhalant or contact allergies. Typical offenders are beef, dairy, chicken, lamb, fish, chicken eggs, wheat, corn, and soy—though you can't possibly detect and nix the culprits on your own; food trials and elimination diets, under the supervision of a vet or veterinary dermatologist, are necessary for a proper diagnosis. Allergy solutions vary on a case-by-case basis, and most dogs find relief as a result of trial and error. Owners need to know where to start, though, so they should seek a nutritionally oriented vet and possibly a specialist who deals with allergies and dermatology.

FOOD ALLERGY SYMPTOMS (THESE ARE NOT EXCLUSIVE TO FOOD ALLERGIES BUT MAY INDICATE OTHER ALLERGIES)

Itchy skin around the face, feet, ears, forelegs, armpits, and anus

GI distress

Respiratory distress

Chronic or recurring ear infections

Hair loss

Skin infections that respond to antibiotics but recur after they're discontinued

Foods with a Purpose

Of course, all foods have a purpose. But these ingredients are especially helpful for . . .

A Shinier Coat

Fish, including salmon and herring

Sweet potatoes

Pumpkin

Fish oil or omega-3 supplements

Stronger Joints

Treats containing glucose and chrondroitin (Dogswell and Ark Naturals make great ones)

Sea cucumber as an ingredient in food or treats

Kelp as an ingredient in food or treats

Weight Issues

Low-grain and grain-free diets

Green beans

Whole meat

Fresh fruit and vegetables (see "Feeding Fruits and Vegetables" for prep tips on page 305)

NOTE: Always consult your vet before adding anything foreign to your dog's diet, and research safe preparation methods for the ingredients.

A Good Diet Isn't the Only Cause of Longevity

While diet is a fundamental factor in dictating a dog's life span, you'd be hard-pressed to find an expert who *solely* credits long life with a given diet. So remember the importance of a dog's lifestyle, plus personal and breed genetics, the next time someone tells you that her Golden Retriever ate a grocery store diet and lived to be fourteen. Exercise, a low-stress environment, clean water, and other factors contribute to longevity. Limited exposure to pesticides and chemicals like your neighbor's lawn spray and your own floor cleaner are influential, too. Holistic vets feel that overdrugging and overvaccinating a dog may impose risks. So as you can see, it takes a lot to influence a dog's life span. Plus, it shouldn't be enough that a dog lives a long life. You should want him to thrive! A healthy diet will help him do just that.

6

Grooming

Grooming your dog is about more than turning him into a gorgeous version of his shaggier self (though that's certainly part of it). Natural shampoos and conditioners, regular haircuts, and sparkling teeth are all important to your dog's beauty regime, but they're also a way to provide him with optimum health and wellness. Consider: Adding certain natural oils to your dog's shampoo will make him smell good *and* repel nasty fleas. Brushing his coat will add shine *and* provide an opportunity for you to check him for lumps, blemishes, infections, fleas, and ticks. Cleaning your dog's teeth will give him fresh breath *and* prevent dental disease that can lead to tooth loss, heart, liver, and kidney problems. Upkeep isn't the fluffy subject that some expect it to be!

Grooming isn't always a fun experience that comes naturally to most dogs, since it has the potential to hurt them. Experts say that in the wild, natural mud, grass, and water keep a dog sufficiently clean; but when humans domesticated dogs, we introduced health standards that rely on regular upkeep. My advice? Start grooming your dog when he's a puppy, so he can get accustomed to the touch and tools of the person who grooms him—whether it's you, a professional, or both.

Know, too, that using a professional groomer isn't taking the easy way out. Grooming is a team effort between a pro and a dog owner, and a groomer is essential unless you really know your brushes, tools, and techniques. I groom Bianca on my own these days, but it took years of practice and input from professionals to become good at it (she has a short coat, so I deal with fewer hair-related issues than a long-haired-dog owner might). My friends who take their dogs to groomers still do a lot of maintenance between visits. You'll need to do the same.

In this chapter, you'll find advice from skilled and stylish pros on how to prepare your dog for a groomer *and* care for him at home. All of the products and tools that I mention can be found at your local pet store, unless otherwise noted. Grooming can be a scary process without informed guidance, and like your vet, a good groomer can become an integral part of your dog's life. He'll develop an intimate and vested interest in your dog's well-being, far beyond whether he smells like lavender.

Hair Versus Fur

Experts say that the real difference between hair and fur is little more than a matter of length and texture, which is helpful to know when grooming your dog.

YOUR DOG HAS HAIR IF:

He experiences longer phases of new hair growth.

His hair seems to grow continuously.

His hair has a long, fine, wavy, or curly texture.

The curliness of his hair traps the shedding hair and dander, which makes it seem that the coat doesn't shed or produce allergens, which isn't necessarily true.

Experts often refer to him as a "long-haired dog."

YOUR DOG HAS FUR IF:

His hair experiences shorter phases of new hair growth.

He seems to shed continuously.

His hair is shorter and more densely textured.

He has a fine undercoat during colder months for warmth. Because shedding hair drops from fur-covered dogs, it only appears that the shedding is more profuse than that of finer-haired dogs.

Experts often refer to him as a "short-haired dog."

Choosing a Dog Groomer

Choose an experienced groomer who's anxious to learn about you and your dog. Be discerning, since you'll entrust your dog's care to this person on a regular and unsupervised basis. The reason I believe in the alliance between a professional groomer and a dog owner is twofold: First, a groomer will act as an extra pair of eyes that will spot curious marks, infections, or sensitivities; therefore, he should also have a working relationship with a local vet for regular queries and unexpected emergencies. And second, no matter how thorough you are, it's usually better to leave precise skills, like trimming the hair between a dog's paw pads, to an expert. I've spent years around dogs, and have learned grooming from the pros, and I realize that Bianca is an admittedly easy client. Not everyone is in the same situation I am!

While groomers may have certificates from special programs or schools, no government agency regulates or licenses professional groomers the way they do aestheticians for humans. Regional and national associations, like the National Dog Groomers Association of America (NDGAA), can help you find a dog groomer in your area, but there are no hard standards for excellence. I suggest visiting National DogGroomers.com for a referral, and asking friends and fellow dog owners for recommendations.

With all that in mind, Jorge Benderski, celebrity dog groomer and NSALA volunteer, helped me brainstorm seven tips to ease your search.

1. Look for the best-groomed dogs, preferably of the same breed, in your neighborhood and local dog park. Ask their owners who their groomers are, and if their dogs mind the grooming experience. Vets, trainers, and shelters can also make informed and seasoned suggestions (vets, for example, will remember the names of clumsy groomers who send injured dogs their way).

2. Keep in mind that not all groomers operate out of a storefront. Some work from home, while others visit their customers' apartments in mobile units for owner convenience. All three are potentially trustworthy scenarios, so don't discriminate based on grooming venue.

3. If you look online for referrals, try searching on review sites like GroomerReview.com, which direct you to facilities within your zip code. These sites also list local dog grooming academies that may groom your dog for *much* less money if he can be considered part of the learning process. Only students who've logged hours

of training are allowed to work with outside clients like your dog. (From what I understand, the only danger is aesthetic.)

4. After collecting referrals and numbers, check with the Better Business Bureau to find out if any complaints have been lodged against the facilities or individual groomers, just to be safe.

5. Call your prospects to request a tour of the shop, mobile unit, or home salon. Groomers who won't give tours probably can't be trusted. Ask about services, costs, and hours of operation.

6. Bring the checklist below to each grooming facility and rate which ones you like best. It's not a bad idea to hang out for an hour or so, to watch how the groomers work their magic on other pets.

7. A good groomer checks your dog's ears, teeth, paws, stomach, eyes, nose, anus, tail, skin, and nails. Some provide these services à la carte, depending on the groomer and how regularly your dog visits him, but most groomers consider this all-inclusive package to be standard practice. Ask to see a price list before making an appointment, so there are no financial surprises.

What to Look for When Touring a Grooming Facility

Bring this list of questions when meeting with groomers, and take (mental) notes during your tour. If your questions aren't answered by sight alone, speak up. When it comes to your dog's well-being and a stranger who wields electric clippers, this isn't the time to be shy.

☐ *Does the grooming facility look and smell clean?* Grooming facilities should smell fresh and look professionally maintained. Ask to see the groomer's tools and bathing tub, and evaluate their cleanliness. A reasonable amount of hair on the floor is fine, since groomers might not have time between clients to sweep up. Stains, however, are not okay, since they can point to blood, anal leakage, or other health problems from previous dog clients that can affect your pet.

☐ *What products do they use?* Ask to see which shampoos, conditioners, finishes, and other products are used on your dog. I prefer all-natural ingredients, but some dogs require products that are tailor-made for their skin and coat. If you suspect your dog will have a reaction to your groomer's products, tell him you'd like to bring your own shampoo and products (he shouldn't mind); based on experience, he may even have suggestions about how to calm problem areas.

☐ *Does the staff seem knowledgeable and caring?* Ask your groomer about his overall exposure to dogs, and ask to see a certificate that shows he's put in the hours to learn how to groom by the book. If he doesn't have formal training, ask about his background, and talk to at least one client in his salon as a reference. Ask all prospective groomers about their dog experiences: Has he worked as a vet tech? Did he ever breed dogs? Does he understand how dogs move and behave? Additional certifications, like one in dog first aid, are a plus. A genuine love and concern for dogs should always be apparent.

☐ *Does the staff handle pets gently?* Notice how your groomer and his peers handle each and every dog, and consider whether you'd like your pet to be handled this way.

- [ ] *What is the dog-to-staff ratio?* If there are too many dogs and too few groomers, you have reason to doubt how much attention and care is invested in each dog's service.

- [ ] *How long does it take the groomer to groom a dog?* Beware of groomers who promise a coiffed dog in two hours or fewer; on average, four hours is standard. Grooming is a meticulous process, and a rushed job only increases the dog's risk of injury. It also creates an anxious environment. And don't hurry a groomer based on your busy schedule. Over time, he'll get to know what your dog likes and doesn't, and he can only approximate the time it will take to groom your dog at the start.

- [ ] *Are the cages adequately sized? Do dogs have access to water?* Subpar groomers may use stackable plastic crates because they're less expensive than the larger wire crates that are more ventilated and can be washed down easily. Each dog should have his own wire crate, in which he can lounge comfortably, with access to water either in the crate or elsewhere in the facility.

- [ ] *Are dogs and cats kept in separate areas?* Though this seems obvious, you'd be surprised at how many smaller facilities cage these antagonists in one area. You'll want to avoid this setup.

- [ ] *Do all dogs seem content?* Most dogs, caged or otherwise, should seem generally relaxed and happy with the facilities and grooming process. Be wary of signs of general chaos, like excessive barking.

☐ *Are pets monitored to prevent overheating during a blow-dry?*
Some but not all facilities use blow-drying machines that look
like glass boxes and emit warm air from all directions. Make
sure these are monitored to ensure that dogs don't overheat
when they're inside.

☐ *Does the groomer keep updated records?* Groomers should keep
a history of services, medical problems, vaccination records, and
emergency contact information on all of their clients.

How to Prep Your Dog for the Groomer

Jorge says it's important to build trust with your groomer, since you'll
hope to use him for many years. But building this relationship with
you and your dog isn't the sole responsibility of your groomer. Jorge
notes that groomers aren't behaviorists (or magicians, for that matter).
Ultimately, your dog will look as good as he behaves, so help him get
used to the grooming process, which will, as Jorge says, "train your dog
for beauty." This includes desensitizing him to certain touches, tools,
and techniques. I took a quick survey of professional groomers, and
here's what the majority of them would like you to do before dropping
off your dog at their salons.

▶ Housetrain your dog, and teach him to walk loose on a leash.

▶ Practice maintenance on your dog between trips to the
groomer, who can do only so much for your dog; he shouldn't
be expected to fix two months of neglect in a period of four
hours. Maintenance also desensitizes your dog to water and
grooming tools.

▶ Learn how to desensitize your dog to human touch, from his nose to his tail. Your dog needs to feel that handling is normal, so he doesn't react against vets, groomers, and the like.

▶ Write down your dog's health conditions, and be prepared to discuss them with your groomer so he can handle your dog with proper care. Skin, ear, paw, eye, and joint issues like arthritis can be especially sensitive problems. If petting your dog in a certain place makes him calm, share this information, too.

▶ If you suspect that your dog will be difficult to handle or harmful to a groomer, ask your vet about administering a relaxation drug prior to appointments. A groomer should *never* sedate a dog.

A Word About Sedation

Tranquilizers should never be administered by a groomer. Make sure your groomer doesn't sedate dogs, and if you suspect that he does on the sly, confront him about it and move on to a new one. Experts say that dogs can die from adverse reactions to sedatives or ingesting too much of a drug. Your groomer is not a vet. He has no right to handle these meds.

What's more, many groomers have mixed feelings about working on sedated dogs. If you own a severely nervous, skittish, or frightened dog, discuss this problem with your vet to decide whether sedation is a smart grooming move. An anxious dog may need a mild sedative, administered by either a vet or his owner, before getting groomed; if you do plan to sedate your dog, be sure to receive specific instructions from your vet on how to administer the sedative. Then again, if your dog has major behavioral issues, most groomers prefer that you bypass the potential drama and take your dog to a vet that offers grooming services, or learn how to groom your own dog with a vet's guidance.

If your vet recommends a sedative, even one as mild as Benadryl, tell your groomer before the day of your appointment to see if he's okay with it, and on the day of your appointment, remind him. A sedated dog can slip in water or choke on his own saliva if his muscles are too relaxed. Since dogs don't understand sedation like we do, they can become scared, upset, or confused as they come out of an altered state. Humans might welcome an occasional muscle relaxer or sleeping pill, but we're aware of the effects after we swallow one down. Dogs, however, simply sense that they're losing control and don't know why. Because this can cause dogs stress, some groomers prefer to work on a non-sedated dog in stages, rather than a drugged dog that may become anxious as the sedative wears off (this doesn't work with all dogs, so it is a risk that some groomers will take). Ask your groomer what he thinks about your dog, so you can find an answer together.

Ask Dr. Z!

What does it mean when my dog . . .

Q: *Excessively licks his wrists or rear leg?*

A: Dogs can do this for a variety of reasons, ranging from anxiety to allergies to neurological problems. The condition may start when the dog has a wound or injury, then can continue long after he's healed. If it's a stress-related condition, larger breeds, especially mature dogs, are prone to compulsive behavior. Self-licking can lead to something called acral lick dermatitis (ALD), which strips the hair off the licked region, causing local baldness and affecting the skin. The condition should be examined and diagnosed by a veterinarian.

Desensitize Your Dog to Grooming with Positive Reinforcement

Cindy Ventura, head groomer at NSALA, suggests that you start desensitizing your dog to human hands and grooming tools as early as possible—preferably when he's a puppy, even if your dog has very little hair to groom at that point. The trick to making grooming a pleasurable experience for you and your dog is combining the learning situation with calm positive reinforcement in the form of delicious treats and well-deserved praise.

Before you break out the bubble bath and grooming tools, start by gently touching your dog in a relaxed atmosphere. Put him on your lap while watching TV or lie beside him on the floor, and then start by lightly massaging the areas around your dog's feet, tail, belly, ears, and mouth, using small circles, strokes, and very light pressure. Don't focus on one area for too long, and reinforce each body part with low-key praise in a happy tone ("Gooood Bianca") or a small treat.

The goal with the touching exercise is to massage your way to each of your dog's body parts that need grooming, hold that body part in a grooming position, and reward your dog for letting you do this. So if you're massaging your way toward your dog's paw, rub down his leg until you take his paw into your hand, in the position you'll need for trimming his nails. Hold his paw still, squeeze with light, pulsing pressure for a few seconds, and reward with a treat at the end of the exercise. When massaging your dog's ears, turn one ear over at a time to expose the ear glands, and hold the ear in the position you'll need to clean it. Reward with a treat once you complete the maneuver. Repeat these steps with your dog's tail, belly, face, and mouth. Catching on?

At a separate time, you'll need to introduce your dog to new grooming tools. Start by sitting on the floor with your dog in a relaxed environment.

> ### Don't Confuse Your Groomer with Your Vet
>
> Your groomer should act as a second pair of eyes when it comes to skin conditions your dog may be suffering from, like rashes, fleas, blemishes, and hot spots (a painful or itchy type of bacterial skin infection). A groomer can also alert you to unusual bumps or joint sensitivity. But while he may be a big help with the early detection of issues, you shouldn't rely on him to give you medical advice.
>
> Once your groomer makes you aware of a problem, take your dog to the vet for a proper diagnosis and treatment plan, and mention your groomer's observations. I don't suggest acting on a groomer's advice without a health consultation first—even if you just give your vet a quick phone call to discuss the situation.

Next, slowly let your dog sniff the brush, comb, or nail file with a calm presence, use reassuring tones ("Gooood Bianca"), and a treat just after he smells the tool. Touch him with the instrument before using it, and reward him again. Before applying pressure with any tool, brush or rub it against your own body first to make sure you don't inadvertently cause your dog pain. Continue to touch him gently on different parts of his body with the tool, and reward him, moving gradually into actual grooming positions that you've already practiced. Reward as you go. Regular "Gooood nails" and "Gooood brush" praise will settle him down while you're grooming. A few short desensitization sessions before grooming may be more effective than one long session that involves desensitizing *and* grooming. Each should always end with a treat.

The collective touch and tool experience should be pleasant and low-energy. Your dog may seem jumpy at first, but if you're persistent, it will pay off. Continue touch and tool techniques a few days a week, even after you've successfully groomed him. The more your dog accepts hands and tools on his body, the more he'll learn to accept the unexpected. This process also helps him react better to handling by strangers—vets, groomers, dog walkers, and new friends on the street.

Ask Dr. Z!

What does it mean when my dog . . .

Q: *Licks his own private parts?*

A: This is for both cleaning and self-soothing. Licking is how dogs groom, and a dog that does this may be cleaning up the equipment. At other times, licking may be a way to relieve anxiety. If the behavior seems at all excessive or out of the ordinary, check the area for hair mats or problematic skin conditions that he may be trying to relieve, and see a vet for treatment.

Did My Groomer Do a Good Job?

While your dog can't tell you himself, my friend Dana Cironi, a celebrity dog groomer in Englewood, New Jersey, says there are ways to tell if your groomer did a good job. Though services vary, most groomers will tend to your dog's coat, skin, ears, eyes, teeth, paws, and anal glands. He'll also check the nose and tail for any irregularities. Dana recommends that you examine your dog's nails, ears, paw pads, and genitals to gauge whether the groomer was thorough. For long-haired dogs, she also suggests running a grooming comb through the hair to see if it's free of knots. There will be some resistance, but ultimately, the comb should move through the hair without a real problem.

How to Tell if Your Dog
Had a Positive Experience

Overall, dogs can be excitable or downright exhausted when they return home from the groomer. It's a long and stimulating day for them!

Dana says the underlying factor in your dog's happiness with the groomer is time. It takes a while for a groomer and dog to establish a relationship. Once trust is established between the two, the dog relaxes a bit more, and the grooming session may continue with ease (and sometimes speed). Still, there are dogs that will never like grooming. Don't penalize your groomer for this.

Robert Tornello, owner of a grooming facility called Compassionate Grooming, says your dog's behavior will indicate whether he's had a positive grooming experience. Watch your dog as he enters the store and when he leaves. If he pulls on the leash as you approach the shop, or can't wait to leave when you pick him up, make a mental note. Differentiate, too, between melancholy and fatigue. Does your dog hold his head low or tuck his tail when he sees the groomer? Not a good sign. Or is he just a little tired from being groomed? Because some dogs don't like to be shaved, they can act sullen for a day. Having some of their hair removed can be an uncomfortable feeling, and their skin and body need time to adjust to a new equilibrium—since they're living with less weight—but the sullenness is not cause for alarm.

If your dog still drags and fights by your third trip to a groomer, try another who may be more in tune with your dog's demeanor. If your dog comes home with small burns or marks on his body, or incurs an injury beyond an innocent nick, you should seriously consider changing groomers.

Ask Dr. Z!

What does it mean when my dog . . .

Q: *Is afraid of my husband, even though he's only gentle with our puppy?*

A: Men may be larger and have deeper voices that can be somewhat threatening to puppies. The best thing for him to do is to sit on the floor with some treats and talk to the puppy in a soft voice.

Maintenance Between Grooming Visits

Your dog should see your groomer every six to eight weeks, depending on his needs and how adequate your maintenance is between visits. Your time, lifestyle, and budget are legitimate priorities. If you choose to *only* groom your dog at home, you must talk to a vet about how to handle your dog's body and meet any of his special needs. All DIY groomers should consider the following maintenance tips to be their general guidelines for grooming; it might also help to read breed-specific grooming books and magazines for niche product and styling advice. Bulldogs and Cocker Spaniels both have folds around their faces and necks that require daily maintenance, but their hair is entirely different. A general dog grooming book might talk about one or the other, but it won't piece together the process the way a breed-specific publication would. I've asked Jorge, Dana, and Artist Knox, Animal Planet's groomer of the year and star of the reality series *Beverly Hills Groomer,* to suggest their maintenance musts.

As you read through, you'll notice that I didn't include tips on how to express your dog's anal glands or how to trim your dog's body hair with an electric clipper. I strongly feel that both of these jobs are best handled by your vet and/or groomer. (Most vets provide less expensive mini-appointments for dogs that need their anal glands cleaned.) If you must do either at home, ask a professional to lead you through a very clear and precise training session, since it is risky business.

Facial Hair

WHAT YOU'LL NEED

Washcloth and warm water

Imagine how soiled your face would be if you walked through the world at a dog's height—and then further explored it with your nose. Exhaust, grass, dirt, dinner scraps, and more gather around a dog's mouth, so keep it tidy. Every few nights, use a warm washcloth to clean your dog's face and beard, but don't use soap, since it can strip essential oils. Jorge washes his dog's face and paws every night, since they share a bed and he doesn't want a day's worth of dirt to ruin his sheets!

Ask Dr. Z!

What does it mean when my dog . . .

Q: *Rubs his face against pillows, the back of the sofa, or across carpet after he's eaten a good meal?*

A: This is a tricky one. A dog that does this could be trying to clean his face and whiskers. After all, dogs can't hold a napkin in their paws. (Other facial rubbing could be a sign of allergies.)

Eyes

Dog eyewash solution (from your vet or pet store)

Saline (people version from the drugstore works well)

Gauze pads

Soft tissue

When your dog gets home from the groomer, he should not have any discharge or small hairs in his eyes; nor should his eyes appear red or bloodshot. If your groomer doesn't use a solution to clean your dog's eyes, he should at least remove the hair and discharge from the corners and outer edges. If a dog's eye discharge isn't regularly managed it can deter his natural tear flow and cause irritation or infection. To reduce irritation around the eyes in long-haired dogs, ask your groomer to trim the hair very short in this area. The normal color of eye discharge is a clearish gray. If it is darker and looks infected, call your vet.

How frequently you clean in and around your dog's eyes is determined by the breed and the dog's health. Some dogs require daily attention, while others can go for weeks without a problem. When cleaning a dog's eyes at home, use a soft tissue to remove excess discharge, and/or saline solution and a gauze pad to break up dried goop on your dog's face or around his eyes. (The saline trick is also helpful at the beach, when the wind kicks sand into your dog's face and between his paws.) Ask your vet about eyewash suggestions, especially to clean out dirt, suds, and hairs from inside the eye.

Ears

Alcohol-free ear solution for dogs (from your vet or pet store)

Premoistened pads (from Doctors Foster and Smith)

Cotton squares

Cotton balls (optional)

Groomers will clean your dog's ears and remove hair that becomes stuck in them. Between visits, however, you should clean your dog's ears at least once a week. Dogs with ears that hang down, dogs that have a history of ear infections, and dogs that are regularly exposed to water may need their ears cleaned up to three times a week. A groomer can also clip the hair around a dog's ears to allow for more airflow, which helps prevent infection in the long run.

Your vet and pet stores can recommend an alcohol-free astringent that's a gentle cleansing formula with odor control to use before, after, and between baths and grooming visits. This provides general cleansing of waxy, dirty, and/or inflamed ears. Experts say that floppy-ear breeds like Cocker Spaniels, Basset Hounds, and Bloodhounds are prone to these and other ear problems. Dogs with erect ears are less likely to have such issues (except for German Shepherds, which tend to have lots of ear problems). However, vets agree that infections with both yeast and bacteria are not uncommon for dogs with erect ears. They can also have mites. An ear wash from either your vet or pet store will keep things in order for all dogs.

To begin cleaning the ear, apply solution to a cotton square. From the tip of his ear, turn over the ear flap and use the cotton square to gently clean the exterior ear glands. Wrap the gauze around your finger to access each twist and turn. Don't use your gauzy finger to reach deep into the ear.

To clean inside the ear, tilt your dog's head with his ear flap held back so the inner ear is angled away from you. Fill the ear canal with as much solution as the bottle indicates to break up accumulated wax and crust. With many solutions, you don't need to worry about liberally flooding the ear, since it will spill out if you've used too much. Don't put the bottle's tip too deeply into the ear or squeeze with too much force, since the eardrum is delicate. Massage your dog's ears from top to tip, and take a second to work the pressure point just behind the ear canal where the ear flap meets your dog's head.

Bianca doesn't like liquid whooshing through her ears. (Can you blame her?) If your dog feels the same, cover his ear opening with a cotton ball that's been soaked in cleaning solution, then gently squeeze. Massage the fluid into the ear canal from the pressure point behind his ear—do this before your dog shakes the liquid free. The ear wash will surface the debris and wax that's deep within the ear, so you can wipe it at the opening. Never use cotton swabs like Q-tips on your dog, since you can hurt him by packing wax in his ear and/or rupturing his eardrum altogether.

Always check for yeast infections by smelling your dog's ears. Vets agree that a strong odor and/or discharge indicate that something is wrong. Baths, walks in the rain, dips in the pool, and swims in the ocean can cause infection, so clean your dog's ears after each of these activities. Other signs that your dog has an inner-ear infection are frequent ear scratching, a tilted head to show he's off balance, and a tendency to rub his ears against things in discomfort. As with any infection, treat inner-ear problems right away, since they can worsen very quickly.

Paws

WHAT YOU'LL NEED

Groomer

Dog wipes

Warm washcloth

Groomers should always trim the excess hair between, and the hair that overlaps, a dog's paw pads. (This area presents problems for long-haired dogs.) When this type of trimming is done during a typical grooming session, professionals use clippers and a special blade. A groomer will make sure hair doesn't grow over the dog's pads and cause traction issues, and if there is too much hair between the pads, a dog's skin can't breathe and bacteria can grow—especially when the area is moist.

Clipping between pads is not advised for the average dog owner. Experts insist that you avoid doing it at home, since the odds of nicking the area with a blade are very high. There is also very little room between each pad, and even the best dog will flinch for a novice with a blade and clipper in hand. If you have a short-haired dog, ask your vet if it's even necessary to trim this hair. Dogs with long hair, however, need to have this hair managed on a regular basis.

Groomers say that short-haired dogs may not need their paw pads tended as often as long-haired dogs. Trimming between and around the paw pads keeps them clean. It also keeps dirt and debris from becoming trapped between the pads. Every dog has a varied rate of hair growth between pads, and cutting should be judged accordingly. Even if your dog doesn't need a trim, a groomer should always check this area for embedded splinters, stones, and debris that can cause soreness.

Wipe your dog's paws at least every two days with dog wipes or a warm washcloth.

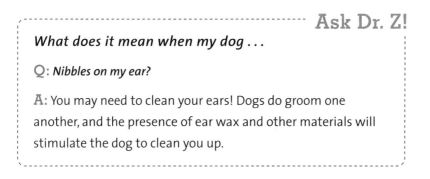

Toenails

WHAT YOU'LL NEED

Acrylic nail file (human-grade, from the drugstore, or a dog nail file from the pet store)

Nail trimmer with a file attachment

Kwik Stop powder

It's really important to keep your dog's nails short. You'll know it's time to trim them when: 1) he walks with uneven weight on his feet; 2) he makes click-click-click noises on hard floors; and/or 3) his nails begin to curl into his paw pads, which can cause bleeding or infection, and require possible removal of the nail. Walking on nails that are too long can be downright painful for dogs, especially if they break off in a way that's uneven and pokes into their feet. Trim toenails also prevent a dog from irritating his outer ear when he scratches with his back paws.

Your dog's nails will need to be trimmed every six weeks, though some dogs' nails grow faster than others'. You can either care for your dog's nails yourself or ask your groomer to do it for you. You can also choose to simply maintain your dog's nails between grooming visits, which is what most people I know do. In every case, you must ask your vet or groomer for a detailed demonstration. I'd even encourage you to practice the first few times under a professional's supervision. A dog's nail area is very sensitive: Most dogs hate having their feet tended, even if you desensitize them first. So the earlier you start to care for your dog's nails, the better, since using a nail instrument (either a file or trimmer) on your dog as a puppy will help him adapt more quickly than if you introduce these tools later in life. If you adopt an adult dog, try desensitizing your dog first using the tips provided.

Cindy at NSALA *highly* recommends filing over clipping your dog's nails; she says that if you file your dog's nails every two weeks, you won't need to trim them at all! Plus, your dog's paws are very sensitive, and there are too many ways to injure him if you get distracted or make an honest mistake by nicking a vein. So between or in lieu of grooming visits, try filing your dog's nails with a human-grade acrylic file, a dog-specific nail file, or a dog-specific professional filer like Pedi Paws pet nail trimmer (a dog's nails are too hard for an emery board). You can do it while hanging out on a Sunday or lounging in the sun— just try to keep the mood calm; a peaceful atmosphere and slow progression make all the difference. Let your dog smell the file to become comfortable with it, and work on one nail at a time to start. Reward each finished nail with a small treat and praise.

Note that every dog nail has a blood vessel inside it. On pale-colored nails, you can see the darker vein that travels to the nail's tip, called the quick. This makes it easier to file or clip the tip of the nail before the vein ends, but it's also really easy to nick the end of the vein if your dog squirms or you become anxious. Filing or clipping a dog's nails too short causes bleeding. Should this happen, apply a powder called Kwik Stop (sold at pet stores) to the nail's tip and press the area with your fingers until the bleeding ends. Similar liquids and gels perform the same function as Kwik Stop, but Cindy says they don't react as quickly as the powder.

Black nails are harder to groom than pale nails. When working on these, look for a small dot in the middle of the nail, which is the end of the vein. If you doubt your dog or yourself, just file—don't clip—your dog's nails every two weeks.

I use a Dremel tool with a sander attachment on Bianca's nails—though I should add that a lot of dogs are uncomfortable with the vibrations of a professional filer and grinder. Then again, if you begin using it on your dog as a puppy, he'll take to it much more easily. Talk to your vet or groomer about what he suggests for your dog, should you consider going this route or any of the others mentioned above.

General Tips for Nail Cutting

If you choose not to use a groomer for your dog's nail care, I'd *much* rather you file than snip, and so would your vet. But if you're comfortable with clippers, I've outlined some basic pointers below to make things easier. Please ask your vet or groomer for a tutorial before you trim at home, since it's easier to explain these steps live and in person than it is in a book.

▶ Nail growth varies with each dog based on his exercise routine, the surfaces he runs on, the shape of his feet, and whether his nails touch the ground. At a minimum, they'll need to be trimmed every six weeks.

▶ Use a nail clipper suggested by your vet or groomer. Clippers fall into two categories. The first resembles a scissor or hedge trimmer, with sharp blades that curve around a nail. The second is referred to as a "guillotine," and the nail fits into an opening that lets you squeeze the blade down onto it. I should add that while they're popular, I don't personally like these clippers, since they can pull a nail and make your dog jumpier than he already is. It takes a steady and cautious hand to use guillotine-style clippers without injury or concern.

▶ Blades should always be sharp, since dull blades add unnecessary pressure to a dog's nails. And never use a human fingernail or toenail clipper on a dog. These will push the nail flat, which causes pain. They also create a poor angle for nail growth and balance.

▶ Choose a time to trim nails when your dog is relaxed, possibly after a long walk or play session. The ideal trifecta: exhausted, in a tranquil setting, with few to no distractions. Make sure all hair has been trimmed away from your dog's feet before bringing out the clippers. This should happen during a separate grooming session.

▶ Settle into a position that's most comfortable for your dog. Some dogs prefer to get clipped while they lie on their sides in bed or on a rug, while others like to sit up or stand. Small dogs can sit on your lap or stand on a table.

▶ Spend time desensitizing your dog's paws for grooming before you start to trim. Never become upset or try to grab or control his feet. Your dog should be a willing participant in this process.

▶ Let your dog sniff the trimmer and enjoy a treat before you begin grooming him.

▶ Calmly pet and relax your dog, then take his paw in your hand. Do this without a clipper.

▶ Clip one nail at a time, and reward each clipped nail with a small treat immediately afterward. Allow yourself a few snips to finish a nail before moving on. There's no rush.

▶ If your dog squirms, tries to bite your hand, or seems at all antagonistic, stop all clipping and relax him with a soothing voice and touch. Give him a treat if he lets you pick up his paw to resume clipping.

▶ Always cut your dog's toenails at a diagonal, away from the toe itself, to avoid bleeding.

Wrinkles and Folds

- -

Disposable unscented wipes (use wipes made especially for dogs or hypoallergenic wipes made for babies)

Antibacterial, antifungal, and anti-inflammatory ointment (from your vet)

Cotton swabs and squares

Hydrogen peroxide

Unscented talcum powder (from a drugstore) or R-7 ear powder (from a pet store)

- -

Dogs with wrinkles and folds around their mouths and necks, like Bulldogs, Pugs, or Cocker Spaniels, need special grooming attention. Folds are a warm, moist environment for bacterial and germ growth; as a result, they need to be carefully washed, dried, and sometimes medicated.

Cleanse your dog's folds with a clean washcloth and shampoo during his bath, and be sure to rinse the area well. Between baths, clean your dog's folds every day, and always lift the folds of a dog's skin to check for redness, sores, rashes, or an unusual smell. Use a disposable unscented dog wipe or hypoallergenic baby wipe to clean inside all the crevices around the neck area. To clean facial crevices, you can use a cotton swab that's been dipped in hydrogen peroxide to sanitize the area. Depending on the condition of the folds, sprinkle an unscented talcum powder (great for white dogs) or a drying powder like R-7 ear powder to keep all folds free of moisture and deter bacterial growth.

When Bianca's folds get yeasty, I apply Otomax ointment (this is also good to use after cleaning your dog's ears); I use Panolog ointment on infected folds. Both of these are antibacterial, anti-inflammatory, anti-fungal ointments that treat infection. You can buy them from your vet.

How Often Should I Bathe My Dog?

How frequently you bathe your dog can depend on the dog, his coat, where you live, and his overall cleanliness. I bathe Bianca when she starts to smell gamey. Most experts suggest a bath either once or twice a month in the summer and less frequently in the winter, since cold weather and heated homes tend to dry out a dog's skin. Bathing your dog too often will also zap his hair's natural oils and cause his skin to dry and flake. Choose products that suit your dog's skin, coat, and how regularly you bathe him.

If your dog gets dirty between baths, spot-clean with no-rinse dog shampoo or disposable dog wipes. You can also wipe down his entire body with dog wipes every two days, to ensure he's always sanitary. Visual cues like a greasy or dirty coat are obvious signs that your dog needs a bath. Some groomers even say the paws of dirty dogs smell like corn chips or Doritos! Beyond the smell of party mix, always keep your nose open to unusual scents. Yeast infections in the ear or infections in your dog's eyes can yield a really bad smell (sometimes it smells like pungent cheese).

How to Bathe Your Dog

- -

Brush: Slicker brush (for all dogs) or wire pinhead brush (for long-haired dogs only)

Comb: For long-haired dogs

Detangler spray: For long-haired dogs

Three bath towels: One for the floor and at least two for your dog

Rubber bath mat: Helps prevent slippage inside a tub

Suction cup and restraint (if you bathe your dog in a tub): Here, one or more suction cups attach to the tub with a cushioned lasso-style collar on an elastic cord, or a dog's collar (use an inexpensive nylon collar for baths). A restraint is helpful when bathing your dog in a tub, but if your dog is cooperative or prefers showers, you might not need this.

Dog showerhead: Hand-held spray nozzle that connects to your showerhead or outdoor hose.

Rubber curry brush: Removes excess hair on short-haired dogs. Use before and after bath once your dog is dry.

Rubber bathing brush: Massages your dog's skin in the bath with rubber nubs that also help lather shampoo. (This isn't a regular brush, so you can use it when the dog's wet.)

Shampoo: Use only dog-specific shampoo. The brand and formula will depend on your dog's skin, coat, any health conditions, and how regularly you bathe him.

Conditioner: Use only dog-specific conditioner. The brand and formula will depend on your dog's skin, coat, any health conditions, and how regularly you bathe him.

Cotton balls: Protect dog's ears from infection.

Eye and ear products: Clean sensitive areas otherwise prone to infection.

Blow-dryer set on warm or cool (optional)

Until your dog gets used to the bath, tub time may not be that easy. I'm very fortunate that Bianca has always looked forward to bath time. As soon as I shout, "Let's take a bath, Bianca!," she runs to the shower and waits for me inside the stall while I gather her grooming supplies. Below, Artist, Jorge, and Dana suggest how to make the most of your dog's bathing routine.

BEFORE YOUR DOG'S BATH

▶ Brush your dog to remove excess hair and loosen any knots that would otherwise worsen when they're wet. Never brush a wet dog with anything but a rubber bathing brush.

▶ Use a slicker brush on a long-haired dog. Use a curry brush on a short-haired dog to remove loose hair and dirt. See Dana's list of tools for descriptions of each on page 351.

▶ If you notice your dog has small mats when you're brushing him, take him to the vet or professional groomer to cut them out. Mats are knots of hair that are usually too close to the skin for you to cut yourself. Matting often occurs on legs and bellies, around the groin, in the armpits, between toes, and behind your dog's ears. Because they're tight to the skin, mats can cause sores that become infected. As with tangles, washing mats makes them worse, and if a mat gets wet from even a puddle, it can develop mold. Regular brushing helps aerate the skin and spread oils to help avoid matting.

▶ Tangles, knots, and mats are big problems for long-haired dogs. For some, you'll need to use a comb *and* brush to smooth their coats before washing (brushing alone only untangles the hair's surface). Use a detangler spray like Johnson's No More Tangles for kids or a similar dog product. Jorge makes his own by mixing one part dog conditioner to two parts water in a spray bottle.

▶ Clean your dog's ears before and after his bath. The first cleaning is to remove wax and dirt; the second is to remove bathwater. An ear-cleansing solution from your vet will change the pH of the bathwater in his ears and stop bacterial growth. (You'll also want to use this after he plays in the rain, or swims in a pool or at the beach.)

▶ Dana suggests putting a cotton ball in each of the dog's ears before his bath to prevent water from seeping into his ears, to help avoid infections caused by water that becomes trapped during baths. Since the cotton creates a direct funnel to the ear canal, Dana likes dampening it with ear cleaning solution, which gives the cotton ball a dual purpose. to clean and to keep water out.

▶ Where you bathe your dog depends on his size. Smaller dogs do well in large sinks and tubs, and medium to large dogs can stand in a shower or outside. Use a showerhead attachment on all dogs so you can target specific areas all over his body (it's also a lot more time- and energy-efficient than dumping bowls or cups of water over his sudsy fur).

▶ Shut or gate off the room's entrance so your dog can't make a run for it.

▶ Guide your dog to his bath on a leash, since he may not come to you if he knows what's in store for him. The more calm you are, the more calm your dog will be. Maintain a relaxed and happy demeanor as you wash, rinse, and dry your dog. Bianca loves when I sing silly songs to her as she takes a bath. Sweet, reassuring tones are music to every dog's ears.

▶ Your dog won't always be squirmy in the bath. After a few sessions, he'll come to enjoy it!

DURING YOUR DOG'S BATH

▶ When tub-bathing, consider tethering your dog with a bathing restraint. This holds him still so you can really wash him. It also keeps him from licking himself and/or drinking the tub water.

▶ Always use warm water, never hot. If your dog has itchy skin, cool water can be very soothing.

▶ Start by bathing your dog's body. His head should be the last part of him that you wash and the first that you rinse.

▶ Use a dog shampoo *and* conditioner on your dog. No matter how good your shampoo is, it's intended to remove oil from human hair, because we sweat through our scalps. But dogs sweat through their paws, so our shampoo is too harsh for their skin. Dogs need to preserve their natural oils, and dog shampoos help them do this. I use Kiehl's For Your Dog shampoo and conditioner on Bianca. Royal Treatment and Dr. Shawn's Organic Shampoos also make great pet-specific products.

▶ Follow the instructions on the shampoo bottle about how much to use on your dog. Wash him with a rubber bathing brush to improve circulation. This also helps strengthen hair follicles and reduce shedding. Long-haired dogs should be massaged in the direction of hair growth. Use a circular motion with short-haired dogs. On all dogs, you can use your fingers to scrub between toes and under legs.

▶ It's very important to rinse your dog well after a shampoo to prevent bacterial buildup. Pay extra attention to rinsing between wrinkles and folds; you can clean these with a soft-head toothbrush.

▶ Use a dog conditioner or cream rinse after you've rinsed away his shampoo. Shampoo opens hair cuticles for cleansing, while conditioners seal them from excess dirt. Conditioner helps dogs stay cleaner longer, as its smoothing properties deter mats. Ask a vet or groomer about your dog's coat and skin needs to help you choose the right products: Greasy, sensitive, hypoallergenic, and moisturizing shampoos are just some options for special needs.

▶ Guide or lift your dog out of the tub, basin, or shower stall. Brace yourself for a good shake!

AFTER HIS BATH

▶ Place one towel on the floor near the bathtub. Wrap your dog in his second towel like a burrito (you may need a third to cover his body). Hold him still until the towel absorbs 60 percent of the water. Let him finish drying naturally, or use a blow-dryer (though your dog may resist this).

▶ Remove the cotton balls from the dog's ears. Be sure to get every strand if they break apart.

▶ If you think he's game for a blow-dry, turn on the dryer for a minute before using it; this will let him get accustomed to the sound and air temperature before actually feeling the breeze on his body. Blow-dryers should always be kept on a cool or warm setting. Hot dryers can burn a dog's skin. And like human hair, dog hair is flammable.

▶ When drying a short-haired dog, hold the dryer close to his skin and dry him in a circular motion while simultaneously using the curry brush until all hair is dry. When drying a long-haired dog, point the dryer in the direction of hair growth. You should also simultaneously brush him with a slicker brush in the direction of his hair growth to keep knots from forming.

▶ Ask your vet about rinsing your dog's eyes with saline solution after his bath. Some groomers suggest this, but it isn't necessary for all dogs (those with lots of eye discharge may benefit). Rinsing will remove debris and small hairs that are pushed into your dog's eyes during his bath.

▶ Wipe down your dog's outer ear with the corner of a dry towel to dry excess bathwater, and use an ear wash on his inner ear.

▶ Brush/comb your dog once he's dry. Use a curry brush on short-haired dogs to remove loose hairs. Use a grooming comb and slicker brush on long-haired dogs for a smooth and silky look.

▶ Give your dog a big rub on his belly. What a trouper. He's finally clean!

When Your Dog Hates Grooming . . .

▶ Practice positive desensitization techniques with lots of treats. Let him sniff the comb, reward him with a treat; touch various parts of his body with your hands and tools, reward him with a treat; move him into grooming positions, reward him with a treat . . .

▶ If a dog struggles when you groom him, don't give up, or he'll learn that fussing equals freedom!

▶ Don't butt heads with your dog by hovering, grabbing, or holding his body against his will.

▶ If you say, "I can't brush my dog. He won't let me!," then you're not trying hard enough.

Grooming a Dog That Sheds

Dogs with heavy coats shed all the time, though the main shedding seasons are in the spring and fall, when a new coat comes in. Brush these dogs often, and consider using a shedding blade (the tool isn't half as scary as it sounds!) to pull out dead fur (a groomer or vet can show you how) so it doesn't cover furniture and clothes; this process is called deshedding. Without regular grooming, an undercoat can mat down painfully against a dog's skin. A good deshedding is done during and after a bath, for the dogs that need it. In the interim, you can use a shedding blade or a product called the Furminator, which removes insane amounts of fur from your dog. Be careful and follow directions if you choose to use the Furminator's blade—it's sharp and should be used with extreme caution.

Long-coated dogs need regular maintenance and professional attention. Groomers always talk about how easily hair can tangle and mat, and both scenarios can become uncomfortable for your dog. Some owners of long-coated dogs like to shave their dog or keep his hair short in the summer. The problem is that a longer coat gives dogs insulation against the heat *and* cold, so shaving may make your dog more uncomfortable. Long-haired breeds have less hair in the summer anyway, since they drop their undercoat in the spring. If you like the look or maintenance of a shorter cut, groomers suggest choosing one coat length throughout the year, since the process of going from short to long to short can be a shock to the dog's system and throw off his equilibrium.

Just as nutrition affects human skin, nail, and hair health, experts say that this is also the case among our canine friends. With a poor diet, a dog can grow too much of an undercoat or wind up with unnaturally dry and brittle hair. Adding fish oil and omega-3, -6, and -9 supplements to your pet's dog food can help with shedding and shine. Ask your vet about doses based on his size, age, and health.

Ask Dr. Z!

What does it mean when my dog . . .

Q: *Paws at my hair?*

A: Dogs groom one another, so your dog may be echoing that type of contact with you (he doesn't think you're a dog; he is just demonstrating a familiar behavior). Dogs also solicit contact and play by reaching out with their paws.

Shaping and Clipping Your Dog at Home

Some breeds need their ears shaved close, while others need topknots shaped, bodies trimmed, legs and tails shaped, etc. I don't believe that untrained hands should use clippers on a dog. So if you have a dog whose coat requires shaping or clipping, and your dog needs a trim, see a groomer. Proper shaping requires expertise, and too many dogs get hurt when owners try to "learn" how to trim their dog's coat at home. Dogs can also develop clipper burn (which is not normal, contrary to what sloppy groomers may tell you) from aggressive clipping with a hot blade. When a dog's skin is irritated, his instinct is to lick or bite it, which only makes the situation worse and can lead to infections if not treated properly. If you don't want to spend the money for grooming, that's okay, but don't invest in a dog that requires this routine by nature.

Grooming Tools

When buying tools for your dog, it might help to bring him with you to the store. The wrong brush, for instance, can be too rough or gentle on certain animals' skin, and you never want to make grooming a bad experience for your dog. Dana suggests the necessary tools below for DIY grooming or maintenance between appointments.

Slicker brush: Buy a slicker brush with soft to medium bristles. Using a brush with coarser bristles can cause brush burn, a sore, reddened skin irritation caused by aggressive, repetitive brushing. When using a slicker brush on a dog's body, try it against the palm of your hand first to test the pressure. This is the best brush for all dogs, whether they have hair or fur; it's especially great for long tails and leg feathers.

Wire pinhead brush: Maintains long and short lengths of hair. You do not need to use this on fur.

Rubber curry brush: Use before and after a bath (when your dog is dry) to add sheen to a short-haired coat and massage his skin. This brush also helps remove loose hair and dirt found in his coat.

Rubber grooming brush: Great for shampooing and scrubbing both short- and long-haired dogs. Collects loose hair and provides a stimulating massage while conditioning the skin.

Shedding blade: Removes dead hair, reduces shedding, and prevents mats from forming. Use daily on short-haired dogs to maintain a healthy and shiny coat, especially during shedding season. Use this only on dry hair. The blade is a U-shaped piece of metal with a leather handle (it's not as dangerous as it sounds). The metal has blunt teeth on one side that catch and remove excess hair from the dog's coat. Deshedding helps keep hair off your furniture and clothes during shedding season.

Grooming comb: This comb's teeth have narrow and wide spaces to groom dogs with both long and short hair. Long teeth reach the hair's roots to make sure long-haired coats are free of knots.

Caring for Your Grooming Tools

Experts say that it's important to keep your tools clean at all times by removing excess hair and dirt after every use. Wash brushes, combs, and blades in warm soapy water, and use an alcohol astringent at least once a month. (Do not use a bleaching agent, as this will harm the dog's skin.)

BRUSHING TIPS AND FACTS

Though daily brushing is ideal, it's not always realistic. The general rule is that short-haired dogs should be brushed twice a week, and long-haired dogs should be brushed and combed every other day.

Brushes untangle the surface of a coat, while metal combs work the hair at its roots.

Never brush a wet dog, since it can damage his coat (plus, it hurts!). Instead, always brush him before a bath and after a bath, while he's drying.

Brushing your dog's hair eliminates knots and tangles, increases blood flow and circulation, reduces shedding, and spreads your dog's oils for a healthier coat.

Grooming Products

Shampoos

Even the best-quality human shampoos are bad for your dog, because the pH of your dog's skin is different than a person's. Most human shampoos are too harsh for dogs; that can include even baby shampoos for some breeds (ask your vet if this applies to your dog). To be safe, choose a dog shampoo that suits your dog's coat and skin type. Look for products with soothing ingredients like oatmeal, lavender, aloe vera, avocado oil, wheat germ oil, and tea tree oil already in the shampoo, or consider adding them to your dog's shampoo. (Do not mix oils.) Artist likes to add one drop of pure peppermint oil per ounce of shampoo, and blend. He says peppermint opens a dog's pores to clean them; plus, it soothes and cools the skin to relieve hot spots, scratches, scarring, or flea bites.

When it comes to ingredients, try to go all-natural unless your dog has a specific health need. Always follow your vet's advice when it comes to using a chemical-enhanced shampoo, since you're in no position to diagnose a skin- or hair-loss condition. Ingredients to avoid are alcohol, any sulfur-based silicone derivatives, and coal tar. As with human soaps and shampoos, a good all-natural shampoo may not lather too much—and that's okay. The absence of sulfate fillers is what causes this. Bubbles don't always equal clean!

White-haired dogs, as you might expect, can get dirty very easily. Though some groomers like whitening shampoos, Jorge doesn't suggest using them at home, since they're very strong and strip the dog's hair. However, if you choose to use one, know that these shampoos need to be coupled with a good conditioner and should not be used very often. Because they're so chemically enhanced, ask your groomer if he uses whitening shampoos (sometimes a groomer will do so without telling you), and request that he use them only on paws for discoloration. They should never be used on a dog's head.

Whitening the hair around a dog's eyes, which is sometimes browned by tear and face stains, is a bad idea. An inability to remove tear stains is not the sign of a shoddy groomer; they simply can't be removed without a bleaching agent (some groomers prefer to trim this hair back). See "Tear and Face Stain Solutions" on page 355 for more on this topic.

Conditioners

Be sure to condition your dog's hair or fur, since shampoos strip natural oils from your dog's skin and coat as they simultaneously get rid of dirt. For this reason, conditioning is a must even for short-haired dogs like Chihuahuas and Pit Bulls. Aesthetically speaking, conditioners also leave your dog's coat shiny, smooth, and tangle-free.

There are two types of conditioner. The first should be thoroughly rinsed out after a shampoo, and the second should be left in for an indefinite amount of time. A spray-in dog conditioner used between baths can prevent tangles between and during brushings.

Choose a conditioner with nonaggravating ingredients for your dog's skin and coat. Oatmeal, sunscreen, and natural oils soothe, shield, and cut down on static.

Fragrances, Balms, Gels, and Post-Grooming Products

Too much product can become an irritant to a dog, so most groomers agree that the fewer chemicals used, the better. I like to use all fragrance-free products and am not a fan of doggie perfume. Experts say that a dog's sense of smell is a thousand times more sensitive than a human's. So I don't think we should inundate him with scents that are foreign and unpleasant.

A number of groomers use dog-specific sprays, gels, and balms to promote shine and repel dirt. This is a great idea, but only if these products are used in conjunction with all-natural and/or fragrance-free shampoos and conditioners to limit the amount of chemicals and fragrances used in the dog's hair. Because most people don't take their dogs to the groomer more than every six to eight weeks, I can't see the harm. But I wouldn't do this after every bath, or during maintenance grooming at home, since these cause buildup.

Tear and Face Stain Solutions

White and lighter-colored dogs can get reddish-brown tearstains below their eyes (this is most common among Toy Poodles and Malteses). Experts say that tearstains come from too many tears, and when a protein in the tears causes discoloration, the overflow causes staining. This problem can be caused by abnormalities in a dog's tear ducts, which can be the result of a birth defect, infection, clogged ducts, and/or trauma later in life.

Ask your vet for an ophthalmic exam to determine the stain's cause and potential treatment in the form of meds or surgery. Some groomers recommend drops or a product like Angels' Eyes that you can add to your dog's food to neutralize his tears. But not everyone is in favor of chemical additives, so if you decide to use a product like this, do so judiciously.

Face stains, which resemble tearstains but appear on the dog's beard, can be caused by teething, ear infections, plastic bowls, color additives in food, and tap water (purified bottled water has been shown to help reduce this problem). As with tearstains, there is no easy fix, but you can check with your vet to make sure your dog's eye moisture and staining is at a normal level for him. Make no mistake: An inability to remove tearstains is *not* the sign of a bad groomer. The best he can do is trim back her hair with thinning shears or cut the hair away altogether, so the tears drain onto more skin than hair. Don't try this at home!

Flea and Tick Treatments, During and After Baths

Though a dog doesn't need to be clean to be treated against fleas and ticks, I like to use flea and tick treatments around the time I groom Bianca. (Note: most experts suggest waiting at least forty-eight hours after a bath for application.) Follow the instructions on a product's box for directions and dosage, and read the manufacturer's warnings carefully. And *never* use multiple flea products at once. It's usually fine to use a flea product with an all-natural concoction, like a homemade tea tree oil shampoo, but always ask your vet to be sure. Experts caution against using two commercial deterrents, like a topical from Frontline plus a flea collar, since this is a chemical overload for any dog.

Fleas and ticks can cause serious problems to your dog's health, though how extreme you are about guarding your home and pet against them can depend on the region you live in. Year-round use of treatments is not ideal, as a number of parasite products contain toxic ingredients that can damage a dog's organs, immune system, and nervous system. But fleas, for instance, reproduce year-round in many parts of the U.S. and can proliferate indoors even when it's cold out. And as the weather becomes less predictable thanks to global warming, it's become harder to define what was previously known as tick season (spring and summer). Your vet can advise you on the best course of action for your dog and your home during your very first appointment, but I think it's smart to do a little homework about your options first.

I personally find that products from Frontline and Revolution are really effective for flea and tick control. You can buy these from your vet or an online store (sometimes at a discount) and apply a monthly dose between your dog's shoulder blades. The topical liquid doesn't burn or startle a dog, and it's successful in keeping flea and tick dangers at bay.

Groomers and vets say commercial flea and tick shampoos are rather useless, since flea relatives and their eggs can live in bedding and carpeting long after they're washed out of your dog's hair. Artist, however, discovered an all-natural way to make your own flea shampoo that's particularly effective. He says this organic solution should be used in addition to, not instead of, chemical flea products about once a month: Add one drop of pure lemon oil, lavender oil, or tea tree oil (choose one, don't mix them) per ounce of shampoo. You can also squeeze an entire fresh lemon, lime, or orange into a sixteen-ounce bottle of dog shampoo, and mix thoroughly, for the same result. Make sure that your dog doesn't ever ingest citrus oils, since they can cause vomiting, and never put any oils directly on a dog's skin.

Check your dog's body for fleas and ticks each time you groom him, paying close attention to the areas between his toes and under his earflaps, since fleas and ticks like to hide in hard-to-find places. For more on fleas and ticks in general, see "Parasite Control" on page 202.

Canine Dental Care

Cleaning your dog's teeth isn't a choice; it's an investment in his comfort and long-term health. Your dog doesn't have a clear way to tell you that he has sore gums or a mouthful of plaque, so it's your job to stay on top of his dental care for him. As with people, your dog's dental health affects his entire body. Plaque builds up on his teeth and lets tartar develop, and this causes gums to become inflamed, bad breath to follow, and bacterial infections to surface that can enter your dog's bloodstream and become a danger to his overall health, including his vital organs (dental disease can lead to problems in the heart, liver, kidneys or other organs). I asked my friend Jennifer Jablow, DDS, a cosmetic dentist in New York City with whom I developed the pet dental care pen called Pawfect Smile (www.PawfectSmile.com), to address common questions about dental care.

Q: *How often do I need to clean my dog's teeth?*

A: As with humans, your dog's oral hygiene will likely require at-home and professional care. However, if owners start caring for their dog's teeth when he's a puppy, they may be able to decrease or avoid professional cleanings throughout the dog's life.

Biannual vet trips should always include a painless and anesthesia-free dental exam. Dental cleanings, however, will require putting your dog under mild anesthesia about once a year—though not every dog will need his teeth professionally cleaned this often. The need for dental cleanings varies from dog to dog, since regularity is due largely to the dog's natural defenses against dental disease (genetics) and how much care you provide at home.

A professional groomer should always brush your dog's teeth as part of his package, but *your* attention to dental care should be more frequent. Dog owners need to practice preventive dental care, which involves any or all of the following: toothbrushing, dental rinses added to your dog's water, protective gels, appropriate chew toys, or prescription dry food for dogs that amass more than a "normal" amount of tartar due to genetics, diet, or a combination of the two. Dental diets include a mild abrasive that helps clean teeth.

Try to brush your dog's teeth every day to avoid dental disease and tooth extraction and make it part of your dog's grooming routine. If you're late to the brushing game and your dog is no longer a puppy, don't worry. Do know, though, that home brushing won't mean a thing until your vet scrapes the plaque from his teeth. Then you can resume brushing and possibly even reduce how often he needs professional cleanings in the future.

Q: *Do dogs get cavities?*

A: No, but they can lose their teeth if they drastically decay. The number one reason for tooth loss in dogs is periodontal disease. When plaque isn't removed from a dog's teeth, his gums become inflamed, and the plaque eats away at the bone. This loosens rotten teeth, which become loose and can fall out or require extraction.

Dog teeth are shaped differently from human teeth: They don't trap plaque on the biting surface. If you open your dog's mouth, you'll notice that all of his teeth look like human canine teeth. They don't have molars like our molars, either. They have spaces between their teeth, so they don't get decay between them the way we do. Plaque on dog teeth accumulates primarily around the gum line. One of the signs that your dog's teeth are in bad shape is if there's a yellow ring around a tooth where it meets the gums.

Q: *What does a plaque-ridden mouth or a damaged tooth look like?*

A: Pull your dog's mouth up on one side, and examine the gum line and teeth from this angle. An unhealthy gum line will look angry: swollen, red, and puffy. It may bleed a bit on occasion, like when your dog's chewing on a toy. The base of a dog's teeth will also have yellow or golden-brown accumulation that looks like orange peel. For most, a healthy gum line is pink and tight.

A pinkish-purple tooth is a damaged tooth. Discoloration is usually the result of blunt trauma that causes the inner pulp of the tooth to become inflamed. Infection from a blood-borne disease, chewing on hard objects, or improper use of dental cleaning equipment can also cause damage. Vets suggest that discolored teeth be removed or repaired, especially in older dogs.

Q: *What should I use to brush my dog's teeth?*

A: Every dog's mouth (and temperament) is different. Use only a canine toothpaste and toothbrush that have been formulated for a dog's needs; human toothpaste can be extremely dangerous to dogs for various reasons. Some owners find rubber-finger brushes to be the easiest route with puppies, while others use a mini-toothbrush or a long swab on a stick that is specifically designed to fit inside a dog's mouth.

Beth and I developed a tool that combines the look of a tooth-whitening pen for humans with a dog's dental needs. The brush we created looks like a felt-tip pen with an angled tip to clean between crevices. It contains a peanut-butter- or vanilla-flavored gel that combats periodontal disease and bad breath. (No animal by-products for us!) The brush is also unintimidating to the dog. Bianca is a fan of the peanut butter one!

Q: *How do I brush my dog's teeth?*

A: Sit down with him on the floor or on your lap. Put a pea-size drop of dog toothpaste on your index finger and let him lick it so he becomes familiar with the taste. Next, gently move your finger around in his mouth until he becomes accustomed to the sensation. Pull your dog's lip up and angle the toothbrush into the gum line. When brushing, spend time in the area where plaque accumulates most: where the tooth and gum meet. Massage your dog's gum line, as well as his teeth, with the dog toothbrush.

Ask your vet how to hold your dog if he doesn't sit still. Medium and large dogs can have their teeth brushed on the floor or outside the house for a positive experience. With a smaller dog, you may want to place him on a countertop, with your arm wrapped around his stomach and his bum backed against the wall. This will limit his movement.

Q: *Can I feed my dog any foods with natural cleansing properties?*

A: Raw baby carrots act like a tiny toothbrush as they rub against plaque. They also don't stick to your dog's teeth, so most of them end up in his stomach. Some vets say that raw food diets also promote good dental hygiene, but most vets advocate both raw vegetables and safe bones as part of a healthy and balanced meal plan.

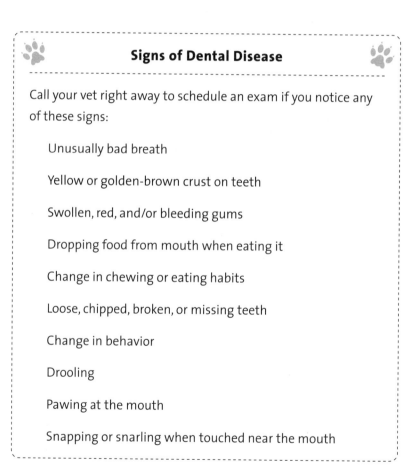

Signs of Dental Disease

Call your vet right away to schedule an exam if you notice any of these signs:

Unusually bad breath

Yellow or golden-brown crust on teeth

Swollen, red, and/or bleeding gums

Dropping food from mouth when eating it

Change in chewing or eating habits

Loose, chipped, broken, or missing teeth

Change in behavior

Drooling

Pawing at the mouth

Snapping or snarling when touched near the mouth

🐾 **What to Avoid and Look for in Canine Toothpaste** 🐾

Avoid products that contain even trace amounts of:

Xylitol: Fine for humans but fatal for dogs; a tiny amount of this sweetener can send a dog into fatal hypoglycemic shock

Fluoride: Can be poisonous for dogs

Sodium lauryl sulfate (SLS): Detergent used in human toothpaste that's dangerous for dogs

Purchase products that contain:

Cetyl pyrridium chloride (CPC) or chlorohexidine gluconate: Antibacterial ingredients

Baking soda: Polishes teeth and neutralizes breath

Silica: Mechanically polishes teeth and gently removes tartar plaque

COQ10: Powerful antioxidant known to fight periodontal disease

Chlorophyll: Naturally fights bad breath

Vegetable glycerin: Natural carrier for the paste ingredients

---

Professional Dental Cleaning

I know a lot of people who are hesitant to have their dog's teeth professionally cleaned. Some don't trust a process that involves anesthesia, and others find it expensive. What these well-meaning dog owners might not realize is how important teeth cleaning is to a dog's health, since periodontal disease is a gateway to even worse conditions. It's not a vanity issue by any means.

All dogs are at risk for dental disease, though small-breed dogs are in greater danger, since their teeth are closer together, and they seldom chew large bones or gnaw on toys as enthusiastically as larger dogs do. I like Kongs and non-edible Nylabones and treats from Bell Rock Growers as plaque deterrents and teeth strengtheners for dogs of all sizes.

For dogs that aren't candidates for anesthesia, there are some services that advertise professional dental cleanings without the drug-induced loss of consciousness. However, it can be a very painful, terrifying, and unsafe experience for a dog to be awake while a stranger meticulously examines his mouth. A dog's teeth need to be scraped, and vets can give a more thorough exam and cleaning when the dog is asleep.

Your vet should be able to administer cleanings or refer you to someone who specializes in dental care, though a solid veterinary practice should have at least one specialist or trained dental technician on staff. You can also find a canine dental specialist via the American Veterinary Dental Society (AVDS). Visit AVDS-online.org to search for one in your area.

Toothpaste Flavors

Dogs like . . .

Peanut butter

Vanilla

Chicken

Beef

Dogs don't like . . .

Believe it or not, mint!

Puppy Breath

Before a puppy reaches maturity, his breath has a very distinct smell. And while some find it heavenly, others think it's utterly offensive. Some say it smells like bologna while others detect the acidic smell of old milk. Either way, puppy breath is totally normal and lasts only until the puppy reaches about a year old.

Puppies should receive dental exams at every vaccination appointment and again at six months of age. Around this time, begin a daily toothbrushing regimen to freshen your dog's breath. If your puppy is healthy and toothbrushing doesn't normalize his breath as much as you'd like, look for all-natural breath-freshening dog treats and neutralizing drops to add to your dog's water.

If you notice a smell that seems off, experts say that puppy breath can also result from an impacted baby tooth, which causes the dead tissue and bacteria that surrounds it to yield an odor at the site.

Clean House, Clean Dog

Some of the cleanest dogs I know live in tidy homes. After all, someone who leads a conscientious lifestyle will help his dogs do the same. Dogs need less frequent baths if their owners regularly spot-clean their coats, and they smell better when the air in which they live is purified. Cutting back on allergens and preventing shedding in the house benefits owners, too. Dogs are innately clean animals that thrive in sanitary environments. Here are a few tips culled from the spick-and-span dog owners in my life.

- Wash your dog's bedding and toys once a month, though you may want to do it more often during spring and summer months. Fleas abound in warm weather and can lay eggs or infest the house.

- Use allergen-resistant covers on mattresses and pillows.

- Use air-purification devices to reduce allergens and household odors.

- Dogs typically shed their coats in spring and fall. Groom them regularly to help control shedding.

- Keep your home well ventilated.

- In general, tightly woven rugs and upholstery clean more easily than looser fabrics. Natural fibers like wool and cotton do not hold odor the way synthetic fibers do.

Ask Dr. Z!

What does it mean when my dog . . .

Q: *Sniffs in one spot and then rolls in it?*

A: When dogs find a smell they like, they want to enjoy it all the more—and even share it by rolling in the spot and letting others enjoy it as well. On the other hand, a dog can also roll on the ground after you've exposed him to a smell that he *doesn't* like, in an effort to rid himself of the scent. Dogs do this a lot when you spritz them with human perfume, for instance.

How to Fix a Grooming Disaster

Being a dog means stepping in paint and tangling with skunks. So when your dog is in a dire situation, always have a solution on hand. And if he finds himself in trouble on a regular basis, you may want to stash these items in your dog's first aid kit—within reach but far from edible kitchen supplies.

Chewing gum: Using your fingers, rub the area with a dollop of peanut butter or vegetable oil. You can also rub the gum with an ice cube to harden it, then break it off in small pieces. If these remedies don't work, cut the gum out of your dog's hair. (I'll never forget when Bianca stepped in a freshly spit-out wad of watermelon Hubba Bubba. It was so gooey and embedded in every crevice of her paw pad! Thankfully, peanut butter and a pair of scissors came to the rescue.) Always follow with a bath.

Silly Putty: A grooming comb and oil-based product like Skin So Soft, mayonnaise, or mineral oil should loosen this up. A spray-in conditioner may do the trick, too. Follow with a bath.

Paint: Clip the splattered area and get to a vet immediately. Your dog may want to lick or bite his coat, and paint is toxic. Never use turpentine or other chemical solvents on a dog. These are also toxic, not to mention flammable, and they irritate the skin. After a vet visit, you may want to ask your groomer to shave either the affected area or your entire dog. His hair will grow back evenly.

Skunk: Do *not* prepare this recipe ahead of time. It produces oxygen and will explode in a closed container! Mix one quart 3 percent hydrogen peroxide, one quarter cup baking soda, and one teaspoon liquid dish soap. Dilute with an equal amount of water, and rub into your dog's coat. Rinse many times with fresh water. This remedy may leave a faint smell, but nothing too offensive. Follow with a good shampoo and conditioner. You may also want to try a spray formula called Triple Pet Skunk Insurance, sold at OnlyNaturalPet.com, which destroys skunk odors on contact. The product breaks up the sulfur compounds so the odor doesn't return, even if your dog gets wet, and it works in fifteen minutes. Triple Pet Skunk Insurance eliminates skunk smells from fabrics and hard surfaces. (By the way, bathing your dog in tomato juice doesn't work. Your dog will just smell like a Bloody Mary that was sprayed by a skunk.)

Burrs: These rough, sticky seeds from plants always manage to find their way onto a country dog's coat. Burrs can cause pain, matting, and infection, so remove them immediately. The longer burrs stay on a dog's coat, the harder they'll be to remove. Look for them with the same precision you would when inspecting for ticks: After every outing, carefully run your fingers over

---

Ask Dr. Z!

What does it mean when my dog . . .

Q: *Rolls in poop?*

A: Dogs find aesthetic pleasure in many things that we may find repulsive. Bird poop, dead fish, cow manure, and a wide range of other items provide a perfume that many dogs find irresistible. Rolling in it allows them to have a full-contact experience and perhaps share it with many others.

---

your dog's skin. Remove burrs with either your fingers or tweezers (you may want to wear kitchen gloves to keep from pricking yourself). Don't get your dog wet, which will worsen the situation. If the burr is trapped in matted hair, pull the hairs apart and then brush out tangles. Oils and detangling sprays can also help. Give your dog a break every ten minutes—it can be a lengthy process.

Splinters: Most people recommend a DIY remedy that involves antibacterial soap, tweezers, and an antibiotic salve. But dog paws are too sensitive and too easy to damage, so I insist you take your dog immediately to the vet to have him remove splinters properly. He'll likely find other debris stuck between your dog's paws, too, so it's good to err on the side of being thorough.

Ticks: Whether you use fine-tipped tweezers or a special tick-removal instrument, do not squeeze the tick, which will force harmful bacteria from the tick into your dog's bloodstream. What's more, squeezing female ticks may disburse eggs into the house and onto your dog. To remove a tick properly, grab it by its head or mouth where it enters the skin. Do not grab it by its body. Pull firmly and steadily out—do not twist or jerk the tick as you pull. Contrary to popular belief, petroleum jelly, a hot match, or alcohol won't release the tick's grip; in fact, these approaches may cause the tick to deposit more saliva into the wound. Kill the parasite by drowning it in a jar of alcohol. Clean the wound with a disinfectant or triple antibiotic ointment.

7

The Bond

The bond I share with Bianca resembles that of a doting mother and her appreciative daughter. Bianca comes to me when she's scared, when she's hungry, when she's not feeling well, and I always make sure she's clean, well fed, and comfortable. Howard may take her for weekend beach walks and give her evening belly rubs, but Bianca really is my shadow. When I work at my desk, she sits at my feet; when I take baths, she sits near the tub; and when I bring her to photo shoots, she either watches off-set or is right there with me in the shot. Although Howard and I fell in love with her immediately, my bond with her is the most solid. It's as if we were meant to be together. And the more memories Bianca and I make, the stronger our bond becomes.

In this chapter, we'll explore what it takes to establish a special relationship with your dog and how your bond can grow throughout his lifetime. I'll cover communication tips, pampering suggestions, travel ideas, and ways to involve your dog in holidays and special occasions. We'll also hear from experts on how to keep your dog safe, stimulated, and entertained on a daily basis.

I've personally found that the trick to feeling really connected to your dog is treating every moment as an exercise in devotion. Bonding isn't a series of mushy stops and starts; it's a fluid rapport that begins with an early-morning walk and ends with a good-night hug. What makes me feel so in tune with Bianca is similar to what makes me feel close to Howard, family, and friends: Trust, affection, laughter, loyalty, mutual respect, and gratitude are the ties that bind us. I promise that if you make a real effort to connect with your dog, you'll reap the rewards of a faithful bond, too.

What Does It Mean to Bond with Your Dog?

According to Mary Burch, PhD, CAAB, an animal behaviorist with the AKC, a bond is the process of forming an emotional attachment between a dog owner and his pet. It's the feeling that there's a mutual connection between the two, and that once that bond is forged, a dog loves his owner more than anyone else on earth. In many ways, it's our need for this bond that prompted domestication in the first place. Dogs have always served a purpose in humans' lives, whether it's for companionship, hunting, or protection, and it's the bond between dog and owner that makes these relationships work.

A solid bond benefits more than the owner. A dog's allegiance can be seen in his wagging tail, twinkling eyes, and happy disposition. If he's excited to see you after a long day, or even a few hours apart, it's clear that he feels linked to you in more ways than one. As his owner, you have the ability to make a dog feel safe, secure, and loved. What a beautiful gift that is!

DOGGIE FUN FACT

The first animal to ever be domesticated appears to have been the dog, dating back to around 15,000 B.C. in East Asia. This preceded the domestication of other animals by several millennia.

EXPERIENCES THAT CAN DETER BONDING

Dr. Burch says there are five main issues that can negatively affect the bond between dog and owner. Noticing an obstacle before it really impacts your pet will help you overcome it sooner.

1. **Early experience.** If puppies are alienated from human contact (for instance, if they're kept in a backyard, away from people), they may have a harder time bonding with owners if placed with families later in life. Bonds will form, but they may require a little more work and flexibility on the owner's part.

2. **Developmental issues.** As you know, there is a critical period during which dogs should learn socialization—between four and twelve weeks old—but if puppies are not appropriately exposed to new people and experiences during this time, they may have a harder time bonding afterward.

3. **Breed differences.** Some breeds are simply more stoic or independent than others. Try as you might to soften one up, a Chow Chow may never be as mushy as a Golden Retriever.

4. **Training.** Without proper training, a dog will not feel as loyal to his owner as one who knows obedience. Also, when a dog recognizes his own boundaries, the relationship feels more rewarding to the owner, and the dog feels freer to behave in a positive way.

5. **Operant variables**. Food, walks, play, and training are just some variables that encourage bonds. If you're the one who provides most of these for the dog, you'll bond more quickly with him than others. Family members who ignore or reject the dog will not bond with the animal, but persistently friendly dogs may eventually convert the stubborn!

How Dogs Help People

What's in it for you? As we discussed in Chapter 1, studies show that dogs improve the health and well-being of their guardians. For instance:

Dogs help to reduce stress.

Dogs help to prevent heart disease.

Dogs help to fight depression and loneliness.

Dogs help to lower health care costs.

Dogs help to battle obesity.

Dogs help to strengthen children's immune systems.

Dogs help kids become more nurturing, empathetic, and socially competent.

🐾 Encouraging Your Dog to Like Someone Other Than You 🐾

Though your dog may technically belong to the entire family, Dr. Burch says he'll identify most with the person who provides the largest amount of reinforcement: food, walks, games, and so on. Assigning a guardian or role model early in the dog's life prompts this relationship, but constant nurturing and attention are what clinches it. If a new partner or (supervised) child wants to feel closer to your dog, suggest he/she feed and play with him a bit each day. Food and play are two of the strongest bonding motivators a dog can experience.

Quality Time Requires Quality Interactions

To bond with your dog, you must interact with him. Dr. Burch says that if you take your dog to an open field and let him run free, it might be a positive experience for the dog, but it doesn't count as bonding time, since you're not relating to him in any way. A dog needs to pair a close-knit activity with the person engaging in the activity in order for him to associate one with the other—and only then will he feel connected. For some dogs, this means playing on the floor together. For others, it involves being brushed in front of the television every night. In the evenings, I brush Bianca's teeth. She waits patiently for me to do it and even looks forward to it.

Meeting your dog's basic needs for food, clean water, bathroom breaks, and exercise help initiate the bonding process, since the dog will associate you with the pleasant activity or reward. Experts tell us that everything beyond providing these necessities will make your relationship that much stronger.

What does it mean when my dog . . .

Q: *Fetches toys but won't bring them back to me?*

A: Not all dogs play fetch like they do in cartoons, where a person throws an object and a dog brings it back. If a dog doesn't retrieve his toy and offer it to you, he's not being greedy with his goodies or acting anxious. This is social play, and he is trying to entice you into chasing him with the toy, or perhaps he simply needs to be taught how to play.

How to Schedule Bonding Time

The best way to bond with your dog is to integrate him into all aspects of your life. But for those of us with unpredictable schedules and multiple commitments, it may be easier to set aside a specific time to bond. Dr. Burch notes that this also gives you and your dog something to look forward to.

Dogs appreciate predictable schedules. Morning and evening rituals are an especially nice idea, because they cue your dog to realize that something good happens before you leave the house (share a piece of cheese), and something good happens when you return (go for a walk or play a game). Surprise bonding activities also activate the reward circuits in your dog's brain, so mix it up in between. You should spend at least a cumulative thirty minutes a day bonding with your dog.

Given our schedules, Howard and I split bonding time with Bianca. I am with her during the day, and Howard, because of his demanding work schedule, spends hours at night watching TV with her. This offers Bianca the best of both worlds. That said, we can tell that she loves nothing more than when the three of us are together. I swear we can see the smile on her face!

Bonding by Breed

Though dogs can be open to bonding activities outside their comfort zone, different breeds are innately prone to different types of bonding. The reason for this dates back to selective breeding, when owners bred dogs for certain purposes. Once you identify your dog's ancestry, it may be easier for you to create bonding dates that he'll seem most receptive to. The AKC recognizes seven major breed groups, with more than 160 breeds, divided according to the work originally done by the dogs in the group. Based on these generalizations, Dr. Burch and I have made suggestions for activities that might play in to your dog's nature. (If any of these classes or trials sound unfamiliar, see the activities list in "Classes and Competitions That Enforce Bonds" on page 381.) This doesn't mean that if your dog likes to watch movies, he won't also chase a stick—remember, every dog is unique, so try a variety of activities to determine those your dog likes most.

SPORTING GROUP

Examples: Cocker Spaniel, English Springer Spaniel, Golden Retriever, Labrador Retriever, Irish Setter, German Shorthaired Pointer

Bred to: Work with their owners, often as hunters, in a water and field setting.

Try: Going for runs together, swimming together, playing hide-and-seek games. Outdoors, ask this dog to fetch a ball and bring it back; for indoor retrieving activity, make it a stuffed toy.

Ask Dr. Z!

What does it mean when my dog . . .

Q: *Finds a stick and carries it home on his daily walks?*

A: Wild dogs may carry prey for long distances. For domestic dogs, especially those who have played catch or fetch with sticks, the sticks will act as a substitute for prey that they bring along. This instinct may be stronger in hunting dogs like Labrador Retrievers or Boykin Spaniels than, say, lapdogs.

HOUND GROUP

Examples: Pharaoh Hound, Norwegian Elkhound, Beagle, Basset Hound, Dachshund

Bred to: Hunt by tracking and chasing. Some use acute scenting powers to follow a trail; others are sight hounds. These dogs have great stamina, and some produce a unique sound known as baying.

Try: Hiking together, "find it" games (fun for scent hounds), agility training (great for fast-running sight hounds).

WORKING GROUP

Examples: Doberman Pinscher, Rottweiler, Siberian Husky, Great Dane

Bred to: Guard property, pull sleds, perform water rescues. They're strong, independent, intelligent, quick to learn, and capable animals.

Try: Attending any kind of dog training class together to learn manners, play training, agility training, rally trials, or sledding for arctic breeds. These quick learners also love to be taught new tricks.

TERRIER GROUP

Examples: Norfolk Terrier, Cairn Terrier, West Highland White Terrier, Airedale Terrier

Bred to: Hunt and kill vermin

Try: Playing chase games with squeaky toys. Some terrier breeds do very well in obedience and agility training, plus Earthdog training and trials.

TOY GROUP

Examples: Chihuahua, Yorkie, Maltese, Shih Tzu

Bred to: Spread delight. Some were originally bred to sit on the lap of royalty for company and serve as flea catchers, since the parasites preferred to land on these dogs more than their owners!

Try: Watching movies together, going on short walks, taking car rides, and playing with small toys in the house.

HERDING GROUP

Examples: Corgi, Border Collie, German Shepherd

Bred to: Control the movement of other animals. A Corgi, for instance, can drive a herd of cows many times its size to pasture by leaping and nipping at their heels.

Try: Agility training together, herding training and trials, obedience training, fly ball training.

NON-SPORTING GROUP

Examples: Chow Chow, Dalmatian, Boston Terrier, French Bulldog, Bichon Frise, Poodle, Llasa Apso, English Bulldog, Tibetan Spaniel, Chinese Shar-pei, Shiba Inu

Bred to: Be companions. This group is a catchall for a variety of breeds that no longer work in their original jobs. The background, personalities, and appearances of these breeds is so varied that they have little in common.

Try: A variety of tasks, based on the breed's physical characteristics and the activities the dog is most receptive to. Many of these breeds (English Bulldog, Shiba Inu) are nice companions and are happy watching movies with you, sleeping at the foot of your bed, or sitting at your feet while you work at your desk. The Bichon Frise would be thrilled to attend playdates with friendly, well-mannered dogs. Poodles excel at obedience and agility training. Sorry, no shortcuts here!

Ask Dr. Z!

What does it mean when my dog . . .

Q: *Climbs trees—and he's a Lab!?*

A: This is a rare behavior and may be the result of past experience. A tree-climbing Lab may have chased a squirrel up into a tree in the past and has continued the behavior.

Classes and Competitions That Enforce Bonds

Training classes aren't just for teaching your dog basic manners and obedience. Since they require teamwork between the dog and his owner, classes are also a great way for you to interact with your dog in a fun and active environment. If your dog becomes really good at a specific activity, like agility or flyball, he can even participate in professional trials and events. For specifics about each of the following classes, check with national and regional clubs and associations for seminars, standards, rules, schedules, and related information in your area. Here are just some of the classes you can choose from:

Agility: During a class or with a private trainer, a handler (you) helps the dog through an obstacle course of jumps, tunnels, ramps, teeter-totters, and more—in a race for time and accuracy. Visit the United States Dog Agility Association (USDAA) at USDAA.org and the North American Dog Agility Council (NADAC) at NADAC.com for more information.

Flyball: This is a relay race with four dogs per team, consisting of hurdles, a spring-loaded box, and a tennis ball. Dogs can compete, or owners can use it as a way to bond or socialize with other owners. Contact the North American Flyball Association (NAFA) at FlyBall.org for more.

Rally: Together, a dog and his handler (you) complete a course of designated stations, each with a sign that gives instructions about the next skill that a dog must perform. Visit AKC.org for more.

Play training: Uses gamelike techniques to teach basic and advanced obedience. Play training accelerates learning via positive associations. Ask your vet or trainer about classes in your area.

Earthdog: Earthdog tests offer breeders and owners of small terriers and Dachshunds a standardized gauge to measure their dog's natural and trained hunting and working abilities, like tunneling or scenting vermin. To compete in this sport, you must follow a rule book from the AKC. Visit AKC.org for more.

Herding: Herding taps a working dog's natural ability to herd sheep and other stock. The training, working, and partnership between an owner and his herding dog can have emotional and practical results. Visit the American Herding Breed Association at AHBA-Herding.org for more.

Field trials: Sporting dogs compete for recognition of advanced hunting skills; there are different trials for pointing dogs, retrievers, and flushing dogs. Visit AKC.org for more.

Ask Dr. Z!

What does it mean when my dog . . .

Q: *Loves having his bum scratched more than any other spot on his body?*

A: A dog has a hard time reaching the area around the base of his tail, so he likely appreciates the help! But if you're scratching your dog around the anal area and he likes it, then his anal sacs may be full, or his tush may feel itchy because of worms or an allergy. See a vet for either.

Bonding Activities That Every Dog Loves

No matter what the breed, all dogs can appreciate:

Being petted while you relax and watch television

Getting a canine massage (see page 414)

Being brushed in a relaxing way that makes the dog feel good (for example, some dogs like to lie on the floor and have only their belly brushed). This is different than regular grooming, which aims to clean and maintain the dog's appearance and well-being.

Playing indoors as you sit on the floor and throw toys for a game of fetch.

Running and playing outdoors while you throw the ball for your dog to retrieve. Bianca is a tomboy and likes to play football. She runs after it, jumps in the air, and grabs it like a New York Giant.

Taking car rides to a special place, like the park or into town to go shopping.

Having playdates with other dogs, if they most enjoy being with other canines.

Visiting friends and family, if the dog most enjoys being with other people.

> ### 🐾 When Dogs Like People Better Than Other Dogs 🐾
>
> Whether it's the result of a dog's nature or his limited social exposure to other canines during the four to twelve weeks in which he's most adept to learning socialization skills, some dogs are more comfortable among people than they are among dogs. If your dog is like this, organize activities that cater to his notion of fun. People-sociable dogs make great therapy dogs, and they can also be the life of the party at holidays, birthdays, and other dog-free gatherings. While experts say that there are benefits to dog socialization even among the most introverted canines, why force this dog to endure a dog park when he'd be happier at a (human) family reunion?

Doggie Playdates

Playdates for your dog should be enjoyable for both of you. Engagements can be either private (in your home) or more public (like a group hiking trip), but Dr. Burch says that you should always be involved if you want to consider playdates as a means to bonding. If you and your dog hit it off with another duo at a big event, you can make plans for a more intimate get-together later on. Bianca's best playdates involve circling the block with my friend Laura and her dogs Sydney and AJ. Bianca loves the company, with me by her side, and I secretly enjoy the walks because they make her use the bathroom faster (once the other dogs pee, she overpees to show that she's in control). Here are some activities that dog-sociable pets might enjoy:

Doggie day care: Great for exercise and socialization, this lets you leave your dog for a full or half day. Day cares are a nice way to meet other owners; they may also know about and organize owner/dog activities. See "Doggie Day Care" on page 164 for more.

Dog parks and dog beaches: Off-leash parks and beaches are great places for dogs to meet other canines in the neighborhood, as you interact with both your dog and other dog owners in a sunny setting.

Playgroups: Playgroups are organized for owners by dog type: puppy, small dog, big dog, breed-specific, etc. Go online to find activities and clubs in your area. Organized people groups, like those on MeetUp.com, often schedule trips to dog parks, doggie day cares, and other dog-friendly venues.

Online sites to meet other dog owners: Online sites are a fun way to find your dog his perfect play match. (Note: Even if you joke that you can find your dog's "boyfriend" or "girlfriend" this way, you should never breed your dog with a stranger's.) Some great sites include MyDogDating.com, Petster.com, DateMyPet.com, and Dogster.com. If you hope to meet someone for yourself *and* your dog, check out sites like LeashesandLovers.com.

Ask Dr. Z!

What does it mean when my dog . . .

Q: *Hides behind my legs at the dog park?*

A: The dog is looking for comfort and protection, and he knows it's safe behind his guardian's legs. This dog may not be properly socialized. To help him feel at ease in dog parks, introduce him to canines with similar temperaments in a less intimidating environment. Once he enjoys the company of other dogs, he'll feel more equipped to navigate a dog park with many personalities.

Playdate Tips

Organize playdates only with dogs that complement your dog's temperament.

Initiate activities that involve owners and are dog-specific for both bonding and socialization.

Playdates can be held one-on-one or in small groups.

If you host a playdate, find a space that allows all dogs to play without bumping into furniture. Rug-free zones are also ideal if you're afraid of accidents or excessive shedding from either dog.

Be careful when making people and dog introductions. See "How to Introduce Your Dog to Other People and Other Dogs" on page 86 for guidelines. Those who make bad impressions shouldn't get repeat invitations until they've learned how to play acceptably.

Volunteering with Your Dog

Enrolling your dog in a therapy program is a thoughtful and rewarding way to bond with your pet—and allow others to do the same. Therapy dogs visit nursing homes, disaster relief sites, libraries, children's shelters, and various hospital wards (oncology, psychiatric, pediatric). All therapy dogs need a handler (you), and all dog/handler teams require special certification. Here's how to get started:

- ▶ Consider your dog's attitude. Does he gravitate to seniors? Is he a sucker for kids? Therapy dogs should like to meet new people and approach them in a calm and friendly way. Fearful and aggressive dogs don't make good volunteers, but an enthusiastic dog can be trained to relax.

▶ Think about how he reacts to "new." Therapy dogs must tolerate unfamiliar faces, noises, settings, commotions, and other visiting animals. He should be able to acclimate quickly and reliably.

▶ Research the right facility. A library (with reading programs for kids), prison (with much older inmates), and psychiatric ward (with unpredictable patients) will prompt different reactions from dogs. Choose a facility that you think will solicit the most positive responses from your dog.

▶ Join an organization that can connect you to opportunities and educate you about certifications. Therapy Dogs International at TDI-dog.org and Delta Society at DeltaSociety.org review testing requirements and programs, venues, and related information. You can then volunteer, upon approval, at local hospitals, schools, nursing homes, assisted living facilities, etc.

▶ Apply for a Canine Good Citizen certificate from the AKC. To qualify, your dog needs to demonstrate good volunteer dog behavior. Visit AKC.org for more information.

NOTE: If you don't have time to formally certify your dog, he can still spread goodwill. Some volunteer directors at smaller facilities will create more casual arrangements with dog owners for their clients and residents. Sick and elderly neighbors always enjoy the furry company, too.

How Well Can Dogs Read People?

Dr. Burch says that some dogs can read us better than most humans, by merging basic instinct, an extraordinary sense of smell, and the ability to interpret subtle changes in body language. For this reason, dogs can be trained to detect a seizure before it happens by picking up on chemical changes in a person's body. Others are trained to detect cancer by relying on their sense of smell (many untrained dogs have been known to sniff and lick body parts stricken by breast, ovarian, and thyroid cancers, too). Dogs can also read our facial expressions and body language—this last skill was critical when wild dogs read other dogs that came into their pack to determine whether they were friend or foe.

Has your dog ever sat beside you, or licked you profusely, when you were feeling sick or even just bummed out? It's as if he can sense when you're happy and when you're blue, right? Bianca always waddles over to comfort me when I'm sad. Dr. Burch says that what may cue your dog is a change in body language and the noises you make. A flat voice, hunched posture, sniffles, and salty tears pouring from your eyes are four unusual cues that alert a dog to the fact that you're not acting as you usually do and something could be wrong.

Ask Dr. Z!

What does it mean when my dog . . .

Q: *Is happier on group family walks than alone with a leader or other single family member?*

A: Dogs are social animals, and the group is probably more dynamic and exciting with lots of activity. Take this as a compliment that your family is a functional unit for your dog!

When Dogs Misunderstand Your Intentions

Even with the best intentions, it's easy for your dog to misconstrue your emotional behaviors. So with Dr. Burch's help, I've outlined the most common misunderstandings that occur between dog and owner—and loving alternatives that might solicit a more welcome response. For many of these examples, like hugs and kisses, you can train your dog to appreciate them with positive reinforcement training. I've taught Bianca to tolerate my smothering hugs, so when I wrap my arms around her, she sits still and waits for me to finish (it helps that she gets a treat when the hug is over).

TERM OF ENDEARMENT: PATS ON THE HEAD

Why dogs don't love this: Touching a dog's head doesn't allow him to recognize your smell first. A fast-patting hand that reaches over a dog's head (often while you're leaning) can make him anxious.

Better option: Let a dog smell your hand, then scratch under his chin with the same cupped hand.

TERM OF ENDEARMENT: ONGOING CONVERSATION

Why dogs don't love this: Your dog may patiently listen to a monologue about your boss or vacation, but his perked ears are really listening for words he knows. Try not to use established cues like "sit" or "walk," which can confuse a dog when coupled and out of context.

Better option: Tell your dog about dinner as you make it; about the walk you'll take just before you take it; about the game he'll play just before he plays it. This will help your dog learn new words that are directly affiliated with an action and reward.

Term of Endearment: Hugs

Why dogs don't love this: Hugs aren't natural to dogs because they don't give them to each other. Some learn to like them, and others learn to tolerate them, but if your dog doesn't appreciate your hugs, don't take offense. They may interpret the hovering body language of a hug as intimidating.

Better option: Massage, tummy rub, scratches under the dog's chin or behind the ears.

Term of Endearment: Kisses

Why dogs don't love this: Dog kisses are licks, not sucking noises with pouty lips. Angling toward a dog with this facial expression and accompanying noise might startle him, since dogs don't do this to each other.

Better option: What's better than a kiss? We dole out kisses too often and intuitively to nix them altogether. Train a dog to enjoy this on every part of his body with positive reinforcement.

Ask Dr. Z!

What does it mean when my dog . . .

Q: *Lets my kids bang on his head in an attempt to "pet" him?*

A: This is a very tolerant dog, but the parent of a child who allows this shouldn't let the banging continue, since the next dog a child bangs on may not be as tolerant. Instead, teach your child to wait until you ask if the dog is friendly before carefully extending his hand so the dog can smell it. Next, show the child how to gently pet a dog under his chin and away from the top of his head, to be safe.

Travel Websites and Accommodations for Dog-Related Services

I can't get over how many pet-friendly travel sources are available online! I've pulled some national sites for you, but a search for your specific destination may yield the best options for RV parks and campgrounds, beach guides, parks and hiking, off-leash parks, city and country guides, and even outdoor dining. Once you reach your destination, hotel chains like Holiday Inn, Best Western, Marriott, Motel Six, W Hotels, Four Seasons, Westin, and Loews offer pet-friendly programs at select locations, some of which include turndown service for dog beds, new toys, dog walking, doggie robes, homemade treats, in-room massage, and gourmet menus. Some accommodations insist that you keep your dog crated when you leave the room, so find out if this will apply to you. You should always call ahead to learn about additional fees and regulations.

TripsWithPets.com

DogFriendly.com

PetsWelcome.com

PetTravel.com

FidoFriendly.com

DogTravelNetwork.com

About.com also has a comprehensive list of participating hotels from dog-friendly chains.

AAA'S PET GUIDE

AAA publishes a very practical pet guide called *Traveling with Your Pet: The AAA Petbook*. This book features pet-friendly AAA-approved and Diamond-rated lodgings and even lists the ten most pet-friendly cities in the U.S. and Canada. It's also full of travel tips and checklists for dogs on the go. The guide is available at AAA offices and national bookstores.

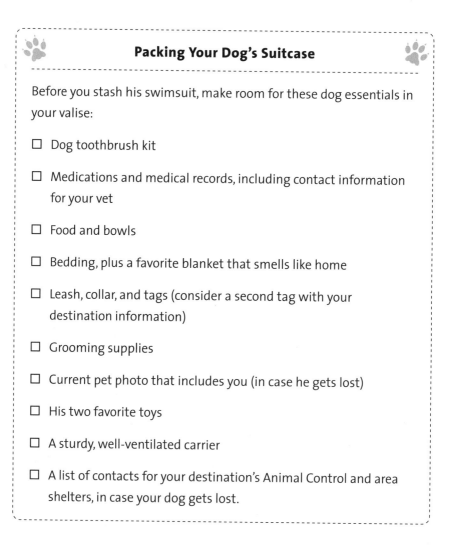

Packing Your Dog's Suitcase

Before you stash his swimsuit, make room for these dog essentials in your valise:

- ☐ Dog toothbrush kit

- ☐ Medications and medical records, including contact information for your vet

- ☐ Food and bowls

- ☐ Bedding, plus a favorite blanket that smells like home

- ☐ Leash, collar, and tags (consider a second tag with your destination information)

- ☐ Grooming supplies

- ☐ Current pet photo that includes you (in case he gets lost)

- ☐ His two favorite toys

- ☐ A sturdy, well-ventilated carrier

- ☐ A list of contacts for your destination's Animal Control and area shelters, in case your dog gets lost.

Safety Tips for Traveling with Your Dog

According to Bark Buckle Up, a travel safety group for pets that works with Greg Kleva, trainer and behavioral therapist for Bark Busters and host of the Sirius XM Radio show *It's a Dog's Life*, more people are traveling with their dogs than ever before. In fact, the group's studies show that 82 percent of dogs travel in the car and on vacations, and pet-friendly lodging has increased 300 percent since 2006. Let's run through typical modes of transportation and Greg's safety precautions for each. When it comes to traveling with your dog, the journey is just as important as the destination.

Car Safety

Securing your dog on a car trip is an important safety precaution. In fact, Greg says many states and provinces insist that pets be restrained in a moving vehicle. Check out the various restraints available; all can be purchased either online or at your local pet store.

Harnesses and restraint systems: These are available as doggie seat belts and/or tie-down attachments that hold your dog in place while the vehicle is moving. The best restraint harnesses are padded, adjustable, and designed to distribute weight evenly.

Carriers and crates: You can secure these with a seat belt or carrier restraint. Carriers and crates are available in a variety of shapes and materials, including mesh, nylon, and plastic. Some can also be used on planes and trains. In this case, the term "carrier" does not apply to a tote bag.

Pet car seats: Car seats involve a booster seat and restraint to allow your pet more mobility as you're driving (dogs can sit down, stand up, and look out the window). Booster seats attach to the headrest and give smaller dogs an elevated view. Most have built-in harnesses for restraint. Check the latches for a strong and secure fit. Metal latches are better than plastic ones.

Vehicle barriers: Barriers are made from metal or mesh. They create a barrier between the driver and the pet and allow you to harness and/or contain your dog in the back portion of the vehicle, often the cargo area, while occasionally keeping an eye on him via the rearview mirror.

Should Your Dog Ride Shotgun?

Think twice before letting your dog ride in the front seat. Because dogs sit with their heads forward, Greg says that they run the risk of striking their heads on the dashboard or windshield during sudden stops—not to mention becoming trapped or suffocated by an inflated airbag. The safest place to restrain a dog is in the backseat, either in the middle of the seat or on the passenger side of the car, where you can keep an eye on each other when you're at the wheel. Also, he should keep his head in the window, so he isn't hit by flying debris while zipping down a back road or highway.

FOUR GOOD REASONS
TO SECURE YOUR DOG IN A VEHICLE

1: Keeps pets from jumping out of the car through an open window or door. The impact of a collision can force car doors and windows to open, and following a car accident, frightened or disoriented dogs can escape and dart into traffic. They can be hit by other vehicles, cause other collisions, or flee and get lost.

2: Prohibits the dog from jumping around in the car and causing a distraction or accident. Even dogs that are normally well behaved can get spooked by something unusual and, out of fear, dive into the driver's lap or at his feet. Never ride with a dog in your lap.

3: Helps protect your dog and the occupants of your vehicle in case of an emergency brake or collision. In the event of a sudden stop or accident, a dog can become a flying projectile that may injure you or your passengers, or be thrown through the windshield. At just thirty miles per hour, a sixty-pound dog can cause an impact of 2,700 pounds slamming into a car seat, a windshield, or a passenger.

4: Facilitates the progress of rescue workers for whom every moment is precious. Following an accident, adrenaline and fear may cause a dog to guard the car or the injured owner and attack emergency rescue workers who are trying to help.

Some Cars Are Safer Than Others

Studies show that 50 percent of dog owners consider their pet's comfort when buying a car. Some SUVs even offer specialized pet travel gear, including crates, carriers, and a ramp. The next time you shop for any car, Bark Buckle Up brilliantly suggests that you consider the dog-related benefits of these common features:

In-floor storage bins: Keep crates and other gear secure

In-dash cooler: Stores water, medicine, and pet food

OnStar: A direct link to poison control for dogs that might ingest something toxic like antifreeze

Remote keyless entry: Helpful when hands are busy managing a leashed dog

Privacy glass and automatic climate control: Keeps temperatures cool in the back of the car

Sliding rear doors: Easy entry and exit for pets

Seat tethers and anchors: Helpful for restraint systems like dog car seats

Crash-tested vehicle barrier: Creates a barrier between the driver and pet and allows you to harness and/or contain your dog to the back portion of the vehicle. They're often sold separately, but some cars feature their own barriers that remain intact during a collision.

Train Safety

Before you hop on a train with your dog, call ahead to make sure he's allowed to come along. Once you have permission, review these tips to make your ride an uncomplicated one.

- ▶ If you own a small dog, ask a train representative where he'll ride. Some small dogs can ride with their owners in the train car, but most must ride in cargo, which has no climate control. Try to avoid putting your pet in cargo; if you must, do so only during spring and fall, when temperatures aren't too hot or too cold. Otherwise, take another mode of transportation.

- ▶ If your dog must ride in cargo, ask about taking him out for water and potty breaks.

- ▶ Double-check that your dog's ID tag can't get stuck in the carrier and that your contact information is on his collar. Make sure your cell phone number, and not just your home phone, is listed on the tag.

- ▶ Add a travel label to the dog's carrier with your name, permanent address, telephone numbers (cell, home, work), final destination, and where you or a contact person can be reached when the train arrives.

- ▶ Clip your pet's nails right before your trip to prevent them from hooking in the carrier's door, holes, and crevices.

- ▶ Give your pet at least a month before your trip to become familiar with his carrier. For at least fifteen minutes a day, leave him in the carrier—which should contain some of his toys—in another room. Work up to leaving him in it a few hours at a time.

▶ Do not give your pet tranquilizers unless they are prescribed by your vet. Make sure your vet understands that the prescription is for train travel and not another type of travel, like airline, car, or boat.

Airline Safety

If you decide to fly with your pet, you must decide whether you wish to carry him on the plane (and stow him under the seat) or send him with cargo in a designated area for dogs. Obviously, your dog's size and breed play a role in this decision, too, but if you're given a choice, make one that is wise for your pet. For more on each of these options, see "What to Know About Flying a Dog on Board, in Cargo, and on a Pet Airline" on page 401. Greg suggests the following safety tips for carry-on and cargo flights:

▶ Always travel on the same flight as your pet. If it makes you more comfortable when storing him in cargo, ask the airline if you can watch your dog being loaded and unloaded into the cargo hold.

▶ Book direct flights to avoid being separated from your dog during transfers or delays.

▶ Most airlines limit dog travel in certain temperatures to avoid weather extremes that can harm your dog while he's in transport. Should they not, take note: In the summer, travel in the early morning or late evening when it's cool. In winter months, afternoon flights are best, since the temperature is most moderate then.

▶ Spend at least a month getting your dog accustomed to his crate or carrier. This applies to cargo or onboard travel. Creating this haven in advance will minimize his stress during travel. Place favorite toys in the crate, and keep him in there with the door shut for a minimum of fifteen minutes a day. Incrementally lengthen the time to build up to the amount your dog will spend on the flight.

▶ At the airport, prior to putting your dog in his carrier and boarding the plane, spend fifteen minutes exercising his body and mind. A brisk walk and simple training exercises will provide him with enough stimulation to keep him calm and help reduce anxiety during the flight.

▶ Give your dog a chance to potty before entering the airport.

▶ When you board the plane, notify the head flight attendant that your dog is traveling with you or in the cargo hold. They may make special considerations or take precautions to ensure his comfort.

▶ Affix a travel label to the carrier with your name, permanent address, telephone numbers (cell, work, and home), final destination, and where you or a contact person can be reached as soon as the flight arrives.

Ask Dr. Z!

What does it mean when my dog . . .

Q: *Sleeps with his head on a pillow or robe?*

A: Can you blame him? It's comfortable and likely smells like his owner (especially the pillow, since your head lies on it for eight hours at a time). It makes him feel safe and close to you.

▶ Well-manicured nails will ensure that your dog's feet don't get caught in the carrier's door, holes, or other openings and crevices.

▶ Try to avoid giving your dog sedatives or tranquilizers before a flight, especially the snub-nosed breeds. These pharmaceuticals, combined with a high altitude, can cause breathing difficulties and can compromise a dog's balance. Consider more all-natural remedies, like Bach Rescue Remedy, which are formulated to reduce stress or anxiety. If you must give your dog something to help him relax, ask your vet to prescribe any remedies and make sure he understands that the prescription is for air travel.

▶ Do not feed your pet for four to six hours prior to air travel. Give him small amounts of water before the trip. If possible, freeze water in the tray attached to the inside of your pet's kennel, which will let your dog hydrate without spilling a water bowl and making his carrier uncomfortable.

▶ Avoid flying with your dog during busy travel times such as holidays and the summer. Your pet is more likely to undergo rough handling during hectic travel periods.

▶ Carry a current photograph of your pet. If he is lost during the trip, a photograph will make it much easier for airline employees to search and help you locate your dog effectively.

▶ When you arrive at your destination, examine your dog as soon as you are in a safe, quiet place. If anything seems out of the ordinary, get your pet to a veterinarian as soon as possible. Ask the vet to make note of the results of the examination in writing, including the date and time.

What to Know About Flying a Dog on Board, in Cargo, and on a Pet Airline

On board: If you want to fly with your dog, your best option may be to stow him under the seat. If you have a small dog, some airlines will allow you to carry him on for a fee. If you suspect that your dog may be above a certain size or weight limit, call ahead to learn about cargo availabilities, though they're seldom ideal; some airlines also have breed restrictions, so be sure to research all rules in advance. Weigh all costs against your dog's safety and alternative options like pet-specific airways and transport services, especially for very long trips, when cargo shipping is the only option available to you.

Cargo: Shipping your dog is the least desirable option, though it may be necessary if you're traveling a far distance, have a large dog, or own a dog that doesn't meet breed mandates. Before booking, ask about dog supervision, temperature changes, and designated cargo facilities for dogs—and whether they're separate from loose or shifting luggage.

Pet airlines: Pet Airways is the first airline dedicated exclusively to pets: Dogs fly in a main cabin that's lined with pet carriers instead of seats. Each pet is cared for by trained pet attendants who monitor and check the comfort of all animals during the flight. Visit PetAirways.com for more.

FIVE QUESTIONS TO ASK
YOUR TRAVEL AGENT OR AIRLINE REP

Are dogs allowed on board? If so, what are the restrictions for dogs in the cabin?

If pets are required to travel as cargo, what are the airline's restrictions and policies?

What health and immunization documents are required?

What type of pet carrier does the airline require or allow (soft crate, hard crate, etc.)?

What are the different costs for dog-related services?

Special Rules for Special Dogs

Never ship brachycephalic breeds, or pug-nosed dogs such as Pugs, Bulldogs, Pekingese, and Chow Chows, in the cargo hold. These breeds have short nasal passages that leave them vulnerable to oxygen deprivation and heatstroke in that type of environment. They are also at high risk for sedative or tranquilizer complications, since these pharmaceuticals, combined with the plane's high altitude, can cause breathing difficulties and compromise a dog's balance.

▶ Make sure your pet is wearing identification that cannot get caught in the carrier. Affix two pieces of identification on your dog's well-fitted collar: one that has the long-term permanent ID with your name, home address, and telephone number; and a temporary travel ID with the address and telephone number where you or a contact person can be reached.

TRAVELING OUTSIDE THE COUNTRY

When traveling outside the U.S., do your homework before deciding whether it's wise to bring your dog along, says Susan Nelson, DVM, assistant professor of veterinary medicine at Kansas State University, in Manhattan, Kansas. Here are a few tips for the internationally bound traveler:

▶ Start planning your trip at least six months to a year ahead of time, since many countries require special testing, like rabies titers (these test your dog's ability to fight disease). A quarantine, or isolation, period for several months after this titer may also be mandated. The quarantine time may be allowed to be served in your own country, or it may need to be done in the country of destination—or even a combination of the two. Your pet may also be required to have special dewormings or flea/tick treatments just prior to entering the country. Microchips are also typically required, and some countries will accept only those of specific frequencies. You should contact airlines, hotels, and quarantine facilities (if indicated) far in advance to research and secure your pet's reservation.

▶ Consider your dog's well-being: Is he healthy enough to travel far away? How will he adapt to his new environment? Is the trip long enough to justify extensive and stressful travel conditions?

▶ Not every animal is admitted into foreign countries. Contact the Animal and Plant Health Inspection Service (APHIS) to find out the regulations for the country you're traveling to and what you need to do to gain admittance (visit APHIS.USDA.gov for current guidelines). It's also a good idea to contact the foreign consulate or embassy of the country where you'll be traveling to get the most recent regulations.

> ### 🐾 Transport Services: A Travel Alternative for Dogs 🐾
>
> Transport services are a great option for dog owners who need to shuttle their dog solo for long or short distances. These services let you book a pet van, taxi, and even limo service to a local destination, or act as a delivery service from the airport to your home (and vice versa). Ask an airport or travel agent about these transports, or do a quick online search for your geographic area. Transport services are also a great alternative for owners who want to fly but are more comfortable with their dogs being driven to their destination. Transport sites for vacation needs aren't as common but do include TJR Pet Express at TJRPetExpress.com and USA Transporters at USATransporters .com. If you're relocating, versus traveling for vacation, try the International Pet and Animal Transportation Association (IPATA) at IPATA.com and the Animal Transport Association at Aata-AnimalTransport.com.

▶ Update your dog's vaccinations. At a minimum, he should have his rabies and distemper (DA2PP) vaccines. Many countries have strict rules for the intervals between vaccine boosters and the length of time between the last vaccines and entrance into the country. Some require at least two rabies vaccines before your pet may enter.

▶ Research flight accommodations, since not every dog is allowed to fly overseas. Airlines need to consider the health and disposition of the animal, proper health certificates, kennel markings (arrows and/or words that indicate how a kennel should be stored, such as "This End Up!"), and size when transporting dogs.

▶ Organize all paperwork mandated by the APHIS, including an international health certificate, which can be filled out by your regular vet but will also need to be endorsed by a USDA area veterinarian. There may be only one USDA vet in your state who can sign these, and their offices may not be open over the weekend, so good planning is a must to expedite the process. You can locate an area veterinarian on the APHIS website. Note that a certificate is good for thirty days; however, your airline or country of destination may require that it be issued within a closer date of travel: Ten days is typical. It's also a good idea to carry a valid rabies vaccination certificate and proof of other vaccinations.

▶ Check federal regulations about a puppy's age and weaning requirements for international flights. Most rules insist that a puppy be of a certain age and weaned from his mother for a given number of days before jetting off to his destination.

Boat Safety

While on a boat, all dogs should be under constant supervision. Here's how to make the most of your time on the water:

▶ Take your dog to the pet store for a well-fitted, brightly colored canine personal flotation device (PFD) before you embark. Even dogs that are good swimmers should wear these, in case they accidentally fall overboard or encounter rough waters. Most PFDs have a handle on the top of the jacket that can help you lift a dog out of the water during normal and emergency situations.

▶ Go for a trial swim while wearing the PFD to ensure it provides enough buoyancy. The attachment straps should be comfortable and shouldn't cut into your dog's skin.

- ▶ Dogs can get motion sickness, so ask your vet about meds or remedies that may address this if you've found it to be a problem in the past.

- ▶ Bring a generous supply of drinking water for your dog; you may want to teach him to drink out of a sports bottle to prevent spills.

- ▶ Help your dog find his sea legs. Give him time to adjust to the boat's movement and the engine's noises. Fiberglass boats can be slippery for dog paws, so provide better footing with a rubber mat.

- ▶ Try a short trip before you venture out for a longer sojourn. If your dog is prone to terrible seasickness or acts stressed on the boat, keep him on land in the future.

- ▶ For potty breaks, take him to land (and clean up his waste!). Or if you have a large boat, you can teach him to use the bathroom on a portable dog potty or in a specific spot on the boat that's easy to clean.

Water Safety

Greg warns that a pool, beach, hot tub, fountain, or pond can become a risk for dogs both while at home and traveling. Here are a few tips Howard and I learned from raising Bianca not far from the water:

- ▶ Never leave pets alone, either in or near a pool. Actively supervise dogs at all times near water.

- ▶ Put up a fence around a pool, pond, or spa. We have an in-pool safety alarm that makes a loud noise when it senses that an object has fallen into the pool. This is a great precaution for pets, children, or both.

- ▶ Keep rescue equipment, like a life preserver, near the pool. Have your cell phone nearby for close calls.

- ▶ Remove all toys from the pool after you're finished with them, so dogs aren't tempted to jump in after them when you're not around.

- ▶ Dogs should never have access to a pool that has only a metal stepladder to get in and out. Dogs don't know how to use these and can drown while trying to learn. Show your dog where the steps are in any pool, so he doesn't panic and try to claw his way out on the wall. Teach puppies and adult dogs to find the steps with the help of a trainer and positive reinforcement.

- ▶ Not all dogs are natural swimmers. Sign your dog up for swim lessons before throwing him in the pool and expecting him to doggie-paddle his way across. Also, keep an eye on very lean and well-muscled dogs; they are not buoyant and will become tired very quickly while swimming.

- ▶ If your dog falls into cold water and shows signs of hypothermia (for instance, his body temperature is below normal), wrap him in towels for warmth and take him immediately to the vet.

- ▶ Dogs can get leptospirosis, which is a potentially fatal bacteria, by drinking or wading in contaminated water. The disease is transmitted via the urine of an infected wild animal and is contagious in ponds, on grass, and in soil for up to six months. Leptospirosis can cause kidney or liver failure and even death. It can also be passed from animals to humans. You can vaccinate against this disease, but to avoid overvaccinating, keep your dog away from puddles, ponds, or muddy, stagnant water in the woods, and watch for symptoms that include appetite loss, fever, vomiting, listlessness, and increased thirst and urination. Treatment involves antibiotics and IV fluids.

GENERAL TRAVEL TIPS

▶ Never leave your dog in the car unattended. Even with the windows cracked, temperatures inside your car can turn it into an oven on the most seemingly pleasant days. Dogs have also been known to step on (and turn off) AC controls or close automatic windows, and temperatures in a car can quickly escalate and kill your pet within minutes. If you need to leave your dog in the car, he shouldn't have come on the trip.

▶ If your pet isn't fond of traveling, bring along a familiar item from home that will help create calming positive associations, like a favorite toy or blanket.

▶ Filtration, chemicals, or pH balance of water that's unlike what you give your dog at home may cause digestive upset. If he has a sensitive digestive system, carry a supply of water from your home tap while you travel, or use filtered bottled water that your dog is accustomed to during your trip.

▶ Keep your pet full and hydrated. On a trip, it's tempting to skimp on food and water to avoid pit stops. You may want to cut back for your pet's comfort on the go, but he should always have enough to drink or eat. If you're driving, plan for plenty of stops to walk and exercise your dog.

▶ After traveling with your dog, always have him tested for internal and external parasites like heartworm, roundworm, hookworm, fleas, and ticks. You never know what he might pick up.

Could Your Dog Have Cold-Water Tail?

A tucked tail is often a sign that a dog is afraid or lacks confidence. But vets say that among working breeds like English Pointers, English Setters, Viszlas, Foxhounds, Beagles, and Labrador Retrievers, it can also signal an uncomfortable condition known as "cold-water tail," "limber tail," or "dead tail." This happened to our friend Gary's dog, a Viszla named Murphy, who swam in his pool for too long. Gary thought his tucked tail meant that he was sad, but he was really sick.

Cold-water tail appears in young adult dogs as a flaccid tail that hangs down from the tail's base and is clamped to the body, or is held horizontally for three inches and then drops like an upside-down L. With cold-water tail, the tail remains in this position even when the dog moves. Experts say that cold-water tail may be triggered by hard workouts, heavy hunting, and bathing and swimming in water that is too cold or too warm. A high-set or very active tail, gender (males are more often affected), and nutritional factors are possible causes. Dogs with cold-water tail may seem uncomfortable or in pain, but owners should leave the dog's tail alone and call a vet. Recovery takes about two weeks, and the condition often recurs during activity. Anti-inflammatory drugs recommended by your vet and warm packs at the base of the tail may help to relieve the resulting pain.

Ask Dr. Z!

What does it mean when my dog . . .

Q: *Rolls over with his tummy facing up?*

A: Rolling over is a submissive gesture, but many dogs also find getting a belly rub enjoyable. Their belly is sensitive, with little hair to cover it. And their paws are rough and have nails, which can be abrasive on that surface. It is also hard for dogs to reach their bellies, so you can do this for them.

Be a Vacation Volunteer

Does bonding with other animals sound like your kind of vacation? The Best Friends animal sanctuary welcomes thousands of volunteers each year to help clean, groom, pet, brush, walk, or sing to the dogs at their facility in Kanab, Utah. Call ahead to speak with a volunteer coordinator about the extent of your duties and how to best plan your visit. Though the sanctuary doesn't offer day care for your pet, you can spend as much or as little time at Best Friends as you want—and spend the rest of the trip sightseeing with your own dog. Visit BestFriends.org for more.

Celebrate Special Occasions with Your Dog

Including and honoring your dog during parties, holidays, and special occasions further solidifies his place in your family. Short of having her own room, Bianca is treated to all the perks of living in the Ostrosky-Stern household. Consider:

Giving your dog a gift on holidays like Christmas or Valentine's Day.

Inviting your dog to be your maid of honor or ring bearer at your wedding. (Bianca wore a pink satin dress to our family wedding celebration when I married Howard.)

Dressing him as the host of your cocktail party.

Making a pin-the-tail-on-[your dog's name here] poster for a child's birthday party.

Taking him trick-or-treating in a bona fide Halloween costume for dogs. Bring fruits and vegetables for the other dogs in the neighborhood. No candy for canines!

Inviting friends to a dog-themed movie night and watching with your pets. (Bianca hosted a screening of *Marley & Me*.)

Customizing holiday, thank-you, and greeting cards with your dog's image. All of our holiday cards and notecards feature a picture of Bianca.

Ask Dr. Z!

What does it mean when my dog . . .

Q: *Stops an arm's length away or circles and stops beside me instead of in front of me when I call him to come?*

A: He may be playing and hoping to entice you into a chase-and-run game. He may also be a soft-tempered dog who prefers to sidle up near you instead of approaching you head-on. And that's okay, too.

Happy Birthday, Dear Doggie

When your dog's special day rolls around, invite your friends and their dogs to throw a party in the birthday dog's honor. (If you don't know your dog's birthday because he came from a shelter, NSALA designated August 1, aka "Dogust the first," to be the universal birthday of shelter dogs.) This should be amusing for you *and* for the dogs, so strike a balance between people and dog fun.

PARTY IDEAS *(all or just some of the following make for a terrific day):*

Send out formal invites or a customized Evite to announce your dog's birthday

Designate a dress code based on a theme: beach party, T-shirt contests, bow ties and bows

Hold the party in a fenced area that welcomes pets: a park, doggie day care, a pet store, your home, or the home of a friend or family member who loves dogs

Greet human guests with a glass of wine from Mutt Lynch Winery, Château La Paws, or Les Compagnons

Set two hors d'oeuvre tables: One for dogs and one for humans (that's out of a dog's reach)

Serve dog-friendly bite-size cupcakes or birthday cake (see our delicious recipe on the following page)

Hire a dog psychic or canine massage therapist for guests

Stuff goodie bags full of surprises like all-natural treats, squeaky toys, and a *Benji* DVD

Take lots of photos and start an album you'll enjoy for years to come

Carrot Zest Birthday Cake

Elise DiRuggiero, owner of Preppy Pup, a water park for dogs with indoor and outdoor country pet boarding in Summit, New Jersey, loves to host birthday parties at her facility. She passed on her signature recipe for a healthy and dog-friendly carrot cake that you can enjoy as well. (I helped myself to this, and it's delicious!) For more recipes from Elise or information about her space, call her at 877-Go-Fetch or 877-463-3824.

Serves 12

1 cup honey

½ cup crushed or chopped pineapple, drained

2 cups firmly packed, finely grated carrots (about two large carrots)

Juice of one large orange

2 teaspoons vanilla extract

¼ cup light olive oil or flaxseed oil

¾ cup chopped Turkish apricots (unsulfured, dried)

1 cup unbleached white flour

1½ cups whole-wheat pastry flour

2 teaspoons baking soda

1 teaspoon cinnamon

½ teaspoon ground allspice

1. Preheat oven to 350°F.

2. Heat honey in the microwave for thirty seconds, or until it's liquefied.

3. Drain the pineapple of all its juice, then give it a good squeeze in a paper towel.

4. In a large mixing bowl, stir together carrots, orange juice, vanilla, olive or flaxseed oil, honey, and pineapple.

5. Mix in the apricots.

6. Blend the dry ingredients into the carrot mixture, stirring until just mixed.

7. Pour the batter into a nonstick square baking pan and bake for 45 to 60 minutes, until a knife inserted into the center comes out clean.

8. Allow cake to cool for about 15 minutes, then cut into 12 pieces. Enjoy!

Ask Dr. Z!

What does it mean when my dog . . .

Q: *Sits on my stomach or lies on my back in the mornings?*

A: Dogs and other social animals enjoy the comfort of contact. This does not mean a dog is trying to dominate you because he's sitting on top of you. The dog may simply be a snuggler and appreciate the warmth of your body next to his.

Canine Massage

A professional canine massage therapist can promote healing and relaxation. But for special bonding time at home, you can provide a similar service. Massage can help you calm your dog, build confidence and trust, and have fun in the process. To see real benefits, it's not enough (and can be harmful) to randomly rub your dog's ears, snout, joints, and paws. You'll need to learn a series of careful hand positions, strokes, and pressures. To that end, I suggest buying a book, CD, and/or DVD that can teach you how to rub your dog the right way. PetMassage, Ltd., lists a number of products and training workshops at PetMassage .com. Descriptive illustrated books like *The Healing Touch for Dogs* by Michael Fox and *Stretch Your Dog Healthy* by Racquel Wynn are also great. The DVD *Therapeutic Holistic Dog Massage* with Elsa Valdez has a more curative approach and comes with a set of canine anatomical parts to help you follow along. Some day care facilities even teach classes on this technique.

Benefits of Canine Massage

Improves general health by increasing circulation and enhancing all the body systems

Corrects damage from inactivity due to injury, surgery, illness, age, or obesity

Treats athletic injuries and improves performance in speed, strength, and stamina

Helps eliminate waste and improve skin and coat

Corrects hidden structural imbalances

Relieves pain and discomfort, plus muscle spasms

Improves muscle tone, increases flexibility, and decreases inflammation and pain in joints

Speeds rehab after surgery, illness, or emotional and physical trauma

Modifies anxiety and depression and improves sleep patterns that can help with behavior

Helps you keep a close eye on your dog's physical condition

Ask Dr. Z!

What does it mean when my dog . . .

Q: *Sleeps splayed out like a bearskin rug?*

A: Spreading out can help with cooling, especially if the dog is able to lie on a cool floor on a warm day. It may also be comfortable for him to stretch out his muscles and joints. This is usually the sign of a relaxed and comfortable dog.

Doggie Style

If style is an important part of your life, then it will likely become an integral part of your dog's life as well. Just use common sense when buying your dog a beautiful bed or dressing him in trendy clothes by remembering that his needs as a dog are different than ours as humans. Does a dog need to wear underwear or a wig? Nope. But would he benefit from booties and a sweater in the winter? Absolutely. Below, I've listed my dos and don'ts for dog shopping sprees, plus brands and retailers that I like for each category, though most sell more than one type of item. Use them to shop around.

SPLURGE: *Dog clothes*

Do: Dress him in cotton fleece, nylon, cotton, and knit blends that feel soft and breathe easily. Consider water-resistant coats (for warmth and protection against the elements) and booties (for traction and protection against toxic salts) during cold and icy weather.

Don't: Dress him in polyesters, which retain heat during warm months. Wools naturally breathe and repel water, but some dogs have wool allergies. If you see signs of a contact allergy during or after use (see "Allergies" on page 230), call your vet. As with people, cashmere blends cause fewer problems.

Shop: BowWowsBest.com, PinkPuppy.com, RomyandJacob.com, RalphLauren.com

SPLURGE: *Dog fragrances*

Do: Use all-natural scents if you want to fragrance your dog's fur. Adding natural oils to your dog's shampoo smells good *and* repels fleas. See "Grooming Products" on page 353 for a recipe.

Don't: Use a perfume enhanced with chemicals or alcohol, which can be found in people perfume and dog perfume. These eau de toilettes and perfumes can irritate a dog's skin and eyes, plus overwhelm his senses. Experts say that a dog's sense of smell can be a thousand times more powerful than ours!

Shop: SheaPet.com, CanineEarth.com, OliveGreenDog.com

SPLURGE: *Collars, Harnesses, Leashes, and Leads*

Do: Choose items made from cotton, nylon, and leather. For more on fit and function, see "Shop for Your Dog Before He Comes Home" on page 56.

Don't: Buy a fabric or material that simply looks stylish, like faux leather, that can irritate a dog's skin.

Shop: TrixieandPeanut.com, CanineAmerican.com, DublinDog .com, EarthDoggie.com

SPLURGE: *Dog bed, floor pillow, blankets, and other sleeping arrangements*

Do: Buy a bed that's easy to clean (most have covers that zip off to wash). Stain-, moisture-, and odor-resistant fabrics are a plus.

Don't: Choose a bed with small pillows that can be mistaken for chew toys. Find one without buttons or other details that can be easily torn or chewed off. Be careful with goose-down filling, which can poke through the fabric and into your dog's skin or eyes. Bianca's favorite beds are from a company called Bessie + Barnie.

Shop: BitchNewYork.com, BlueBloodPups.com, CallingAllDogs .com, IntheCompanyofDogs.com, FetchDog.com

SPLURGE: *Style accessories like barrettes, collar charms, bandannas, socks, neck warmers, etc.*

Do: Monitor your dog when he's wearing any kind of accessories.

Don't: Go overboard. Small items are easy to swallow, and those around the neck shouldn't constrict his airflow. Neck warmers and bandannas, for instance, should remain relatively loose.

Shop: HeartofMyHeartPets.com, FunnyFur.com, TeaCupPuppies .com

SPLURGE: *Carriers and bags for your dog*

Do: Choose a carrier that restricts movement but allows for maximum breathing room. If you carry your dog in a bag, he should fit snugly inside, with just his head poking out for ventilation.

Don't: Mix your dog among wallets, water bottles, loose makeup, and other items that can cause a bumpy ride. Instead, provide height and support with a folded shirt or blanket between the dog and other items in your purse or tote.

Shop: FetchDog.com, Kwigy-Bo.com, ReadytoWag.com

SPLURGE: *Bowls, place mats, treat jars, food tins, and other feeding accessories*

Do: Buy items that promote freshness and sanitation. Bowls should be stainless steel or porcelain. Canisters should always have a lid, so your dog isn't easily tempted to see what's inside.

Don't: Choose unpractical items. Designers have a lot of fun with this category, but a place mat made from Astroturf may confuse a dog about what he's supposed to do near his bowl.

Splurge: IntheCompanyofDogs.com, WhinerandDiner.net, MichaelAram.com

SPLURGE: *Toys*

Do: Buy interactive, indestructible, and natural toys: See "Three Types of Toys to Buy" on page 60.

Don't: Give your dog the same toy or all his toys at once. Rotating them keeps him interested, as in: "Which one will you give me next?" It heightens his interest to keep him guessing.

Shop: Dog.com, PlanetDog.com, HauteDiggityDog.com

SPLURGE: *Pet art (photography, commissioned portraits, etc.)*

Do: Capture your dog's image in a tasteful piece of art.

Don't: Hesitate to commission art students or create a DIY photo or painting to save money.

Shop: ChristopherAppoldt.com, PaintingaDay.com, PopArtPet .com

SPLURGE: *Treats for you like dog-related jewelry, notecards, home goods, welcome mats, etc.*

Do: Show your love for dogs with fun items for you and your home.

Don't: Get carried away. From a taste perspective, dog items are best used in moderation.

Splurge: Blingbone.com (My Beth O. Bling Bone design proceeds benefit NSALA!), FineStationery.com, BitchNewYork.com, Decorati.com, HelenFicalora.com

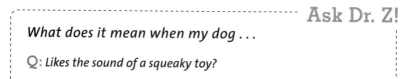

Ask Dr. Z!

What does it mean when my dog . . .

Q: *Likes the sound of a squeaky toy?*

A: One theory is that the squeaks are similar to the sounds of small prey animals, such as mice, and the squeaky toy stimulates their predatory play behavior.

When Your Dog Resists Pampering

Dogs don't always appreciate a doting effort to the extent that we wish they would. To avoid disappointment, never forget that your dog is an animal, not a doll or a person, so he may not be as happy in a baseball cap or Louis XIV bed as you want him to be. (Bianca hates her rain slicker because the Velcro closure refuses to hold: She's too pudgy!) And if you notice that your dog is licking, tugging, itching, panting rapidly, or showing other signs of discomfort while wearing a fragrance or bow, don't force him to be miserable in the name of looking cute. Leave him alone.

Bonding Ideas: Pass 'em On!

I love asking dog owners how they bond with their pets, especially since they offer new ideas about how I can spend time with Bianca! A selfless dog owner is always happy to share bonding tips with friends, which is why it's no surprise that Howard's listeners let me in on some of their favorites. I hope that the suggestions below inspire you to enjoy quality time with your pet.

Why Not . . .

Go camping with your dog

Sing him a song

Set aside a full day to spend together

Cuddle in bed together

Take a nap

Go on a road trip

Dance with your dog

Take him to a street fair

Wrestle on the floor

Bring your dog to work on a half day

Take long walks on the beach

Go fishing

Play Frisbee

Race him down the street

Participate in charity walkathons

Share a slice of whole-grain toast in the morning

Give belly rubs while listening to Howard on the radio

Ask Dr. Z!

What does it mean when my dog . . .

Q: *Licks or "kisses" me? Is this really a sign of affection?*

A: Licking or kissing is a normal part of a dog's social greeting. This is most common when puppies greet an adult dog— or you, as his guardian. In wolf packs, puppies lick near their parents' mouths in the hope that they'll barf up some food for them to eat. (No, your dog doesn't expect you to do the same for him; nor does this mean he's hungry!) As dogs were domesticated, adult dogs retained some of the behaviors of juvenile dogs. This is called neotany.

Are You a Good Dog Parent?

An admirable dog parent takes responsibility for the dog in his/her life. That's why the AKC created a vow called the Canine Good Citizen Responsible Dog Owner's Pledge that holds owners to their word about caring for and bonding with their pet. The pledge can be found at AKC.org, but I've summed up its points below. You know you're a good dog parent when . . .

▶ You meet your dog's health needs. You provide vet care, updated vaccines, adequate nutrition, daily exercise, regular bathing, and careful grooming.

▶ You keep your dog safe. You build fences where needed, leash him in public, provide proper identification, and supervise all dog-and-children interactions.

▶ You don't allow him to infringe on other people's rights. You don't let him run loose in the neighborhood, become a nuisance by barking, or poop without picking it up and disposing of it.

▶ You enhance your dog's quality of life. You make sure your dog understands basic training, receives adequate attention and playtime, and is the recipient of a commitment grounded in time and love.

When It's Time to Expand Your Canine Family

Is there more than enough love to go around in your home? Then maybe you should consider getting another dog! Greg and Dr. Burch shared their thoughts:

IT'S A GOOD IDEA TO GET A SECOND DOG IF . . .

▶ You can meet the needs of your current dog *and* a new dog. These include health, safety, and quality-of-life needs. Did you learn that you're a great mom or dad from reading "Are You a Good Dog Parent"? If so, you may be ready for a new dog.

▶ Your routine is consistent and your life is stable. This means that it will not significantly change in any foreseeable way in terms of structure, home location, family members, etc.

▶ You feel that losing your first dog would be too damaging without a second for comfort.

▶ You choose two dogs whose ages are spaced out. Otherwise, it may be a lot to manage two old and ill dogs at the same time. This can be a financial, practical, and emotional burden on owners.

▶ Your first dog lost his mate and he's pining. A second dog may help him emotionally recover.

IT'S A BAD IDEA TO GET A SECOND DOG IF . . .

▶ You're expecting a baby. A new child introduces change that disrupts the entire family unit. Do the psychological math: New child + displaced first dog + adjusting new dog = total chaos.

▶ You're moving. You may have more space, but wait until you're settled to bring a dog into this environment. All family members will be too distracted to help both dogs feel at home.

▶ You have a new job. Late hours and an erratic schedule can prevent/hinder proper training and bonding. Each dog needs individual attention, both at home and away from the house, without the other dog. This is important to a dog's emotional health and to the bond you are establishing with them.

▶ You're at an inconvenient life stage. See "Make Your Life Stage a Priority" on page 23.

▶ You're having problems with the dog you already own. Some people think you can correct bad behavior by getting a dog a playmate. Not true. Anxieties can spread from one dog to another, and aggressive and predatory behavior toward animals will influence other dogs in the family.

Ask Dr. Z!

What does it mean when my dog . . .

Q: *Sniffs and licks another dog's bumhole?*

A: Think of bumholes as fingerprints for dogs. From them, a dog can find out everything he needs to know about another dog with a quick sniff and a lick. Dogs explore the world with their noses and remember the dogs they meet according to scent characteristics. In females, the urinary tract exits near the rectum, so sniffing can also provide clues about the reproductive status of the female—like if she's ready to mate. Submissive dogs are more likely to let other dogs sniff their butt.

PROS AND CONS OF RAISING A SECOND DOG

PROS

Your current dog will have a friend to relate to, play with, and exercise with on a regular basis.

Two dogs may really enjoy bonding with each other.

Watching two dogs interact can teach you about dog behavior and help with training.

Two dogs provide twice as much love and emotional satisfaction.

When you go on a trip, the dogs may help each other feel more comfortable in an unfamiliar place.

In some situations, adding a second dog can aid the first dog's confidence.

A new dog can teach responsibilities to other family members.

CONS

Not every dog is happiest in a pack, so research your breed's preferences. Your dog may not like sharing you!

A second dog can weaken your connection to the first.

Dogs can become possessive with their space, food, toys, and you. To help understand dog behavior, you can easily observe it during playdates and with other people's dogs.

Two dogs are twice as much work and money spent on food, bills, toys, and pet care.

Travel is easier and more flexible with one dog than with two. If the dogs stay home, boarding is more expensive.

A nervous dog can damage the confidence of a housemate.

How to Choose a Second Dog
That Makes Your First Dog Happy

If you'd like to add another dog to your family, it's essential to find one that can live in harmony with your current dog. The dynamics in your house will change when you bring another canine into the mix, so try to make the transition as easy on your current dog as possible. Greg recommended some tips for successfully adding a pet:

1. Find a dog with a temperament that's compatible to your current dog's. Attitude overrides age, breed, and size, to some extent. If you have an elderly dog, you don't want a wild dog that can hurt him. If you have a wild dog at home, you may not want to introduce a fragile breed. Use common sense, and talk to a breeder or shelter about temperament-testing to find a new dog to fit into your existing dynamic.

2. Ask the breeder or shelter if you can bring your old dog to meet the new dog to watch them interact. This is a great time to ask questions and request tips. Two dogs need a lot of supervision when they first interact at home, so initiate a meeting before you force them into the same environment.

3. Choose a spayed or neutered dog of the opposite sex to avoid behavior problems. Experts unanimously say that opposite-sex dogs get along better than same-sex dogs.

You've Decided to Get Another Dog? Here's How to Prepare

▶ Think very carefully about the time, energy, costs, and exertion you spend on your current dog—and then double it. Make sure you're ready for doggie number two!

▶ Talk to friends and family members who have two dogs about the challenges and rewards.

▶ Reread Chapters 1 through 3.

▶ Vow that you won't show preference for the new dog over the old dog. Both should have the same rules, regardless of size, breed, and attitude. Dogs sense favoritism and can act out in retaliation.

▶ Make an appointment with a trainer to determine specific ways for each dog to feel individually cared for and valued. The trainer will also help you adjust training techniques to suit multidog homes.

▶ Establish that each dog will have his own bed, toys, treats, food, and space to avoid dominance issues. Buy these items in advance, so your new dog feels immediately at home when he arrives.

▶ Designate a role model or guardian who will take the reins for the second dog. Assign other, small responsibilities to various family members, so everyone knows their chores in advance.

▶ Take a deep breath, and open those arms wide. You're about to bring home a new doggie!

8

Emergencies,
First Aid, and
Saying Goodbye

There's nothing scarier than feeling overwhelmed or ill prepared for an emergency. And when your dog needs immediate care, unlike a child, he can't tell you where it hurts, whether he's bleeding, and how long he's been suffering. This means *you'll* need to recognize the abnormal behavior of your sick or injured dog and take the necessary steps to get him help.

The best way you can help your dog now is to prepare for emergencies before they happen, so you're ready for action when and if they do. Keeping a first aid kit on hand (see "Dog First Aid Kit" on page 208 for a list of contents), creating an emergency plan for disasters like fires and earthquakes, and learning how to conduct CPR on your pet are a solid start. In this section, I'll cover those points, along with first aid for other situations that require urgent attention. With the help of emergency care experts, particularly Deborah C. Mandell, VMD, DACVECC, an emergency and

Emergency Supply Kit

Always keep an emergency supply kit on hand for natural and human-made disasters for your dog as well as yourself. (This includes a first aid kit, plus other essentials; if items overlap and feel excessive, use your judgment to remove what you don't need.) All contents should be kept in an easily transportable duffel bag that's filled with sturdy waterproof containers. The dog supply kit should include:

▶ Dog first aid kit (either use the same one you keep in your home or create a second).

▶ Sturdy and comfortable carrier that's large enough to accommodate each dog for several days. Be sure your dog can stand up and turn around in the carrier.

▶ Medications, medical records, and care instructions stored in a waterproof container. This should include vaccination records, descriptions of your pet's medical conditions, your vet's name and phone number, and other special concerns. Include your dog's rabies certificate with an up-to-date license number, plus his tattoo or microchip number.

▶ Leash and/or harness.

▶ Five-day supply of food and bottled water. Don't forget bowls and, if your dog eats canned food, a manual can opener.

▶ Blankets or towels to keep your dog comfortable and warm.

▶ Toys and treats to reduce stress and provide comfort.

▶ Cleaning supplies: newspapers, plastic bags, disinfectant, paper towels, etc.

▶ Current photos and descriptions of your dog in case you're separated.

> ▸ Current list of emergency contact numbers, including those of your vet, animal shelters, friends, and relatives (see "Before a Disaster" on page 433 for specifics).
>
> ▸ Label all of your belongings with a permanent marker.
>
> Note: If you have a big dog like a Great Dane or Mastiff, buy a collapsible crate. During an emergency, you can transport it in its collapsed state and then open it when needed (with a small dog, a crate that you can carry might be more helpful). Though the crate may eat up space in your basement now, it will be very useful if you need to take your dog to a facility that doesn't have enough cage space but might make an exception for your pet because he brought his own.

critical care specialist at the Matthew J. Ryan Veterinary Hospital of the University of Pennsylvania in Philadelphia, and pet care adviser for the American Red Cross, I've included tips on how to handle the basic needs of a sick or injured dog, like one that has a cut or hot spot. As you read, you'll notice a common theme: in a dire situation, check your dog's vitals (body temperature, mucous membrane color, heart rate, respiration rate), do CPR if needed, check for shock, and take your dog to the vet or veterinary emergency hospital right away. This last point is very important. Emergency action should always begin with a call to your vet or veterinary emergency hospital (you can do CPR in the car if you need to, but obviously, someone else should be driving!) and end at a professional facility.

In addition to owning *Oh My Dog!*, I encourage you to buy a guide called *Dog First Aid*, developed by the American Red Cross, and keep it in your dog's first aid kit; in fact, this invaluable reference is where the majority of this chapter's research was done! *Dog First Aid* describes many injuries, illnesses, and medical emergencies, discusses how to create a disaster plan, and provides first aid suggestions for dog owners. It also comes with a DVD that demonstrates how to do some of the more challenging techniques that benefit from a visual. The guide is available through any local Red Cross chapter or at RedCrossStore.org (all proceeds go to the American Red Cross). You can also elect to take a class with the American Red Cross; it will give you hands-on practice with dog mannequins, plus the supervision of a trained professional. I found this course so informative, and I highly recommend it. In many ways, I think that careful preparation could be the best first aid you'll ever do.

At the end of this chapter, I'll review end-of-life options for dogs that suffer from long-term illness or die suddenly. This is a difficult topic to discuss, but one that deserves attention. I won't blame you for skipping it, but if you want to plan ahead, I think it will really help.

When Natural Disasters Strike

Natural disasters can strike at any time, so if your area is prone to earthquakes, floods, tornadoes, or severe weather conditions—and/or if you live in a hazardous zone, like a floodplain or a wildfire- or hurricane-prone area—it's essential to be vigilant about an action plan. Of course, natural disasters aren't the only emergencies that wreak havoc: fires, terrorism, and other human-caused catastrophes (like a toxic spill) may require a fast response, too.

After Hurricane Katrina, NSALA rescued hundreds of dogs that were separated from their owners during the storm. The scene was so devastating, and the dogs were so frightened, that it made me realize how imperative it is to plan ahead for such events; this way, you'll know exactly what to do before, during, and after an emergency. Below are a few tips that NSALA advises you to do when preparing for an emergency. It goes without saying that if your family evacuates, your dog goes with you.

Before a Disaster

▶ Realize that depending on the type of disaster, you may need to either 1) stay home or 2) follow an evacuation order. Plan for both options. Updates on the radio and TV will provide guidance during a disaster; you can also check online for information and instructions from authorities.

▶ Even if you don't live in a disaster zone, think about how you will deal with impending emergencies like fires. Run your family, with the dog, through a 911 drill to ensure safety.

▶ Stay current with your dog's vaccinations, and keep all paperwork accessible in a supply kit (see "Emergency Supply Kit" on page 430). Emergency dog shelters may require proof of vaccinations.

▶ Always keep a collar with an ID and rabies tag on your dog. I strongly recommend having a microchip implanted in your pet, since tags can fall off, and he may get lost.

▶ Spay or neuter all pets so your dog can't become pregnant or impregnate others if he/she gets lost during an emergency.

▶ Most emergency shelters designated for people won't allow animals—except service dogs—to stay there. Decide where to take your dog(s) during an emergency so you don't feel harried in the moment. If you have more than one pet, you may need to house them separately.

▶ Make a contact list that includes the following names, and keep it in your emergency supply kit. Call them while you're in planning mode to confirm that they provide emergency shelter during a disaster:

Pet-friendly hotels and motels in your area

Friends and family you can rely on during a disaster

Helpful dog resources, including animal shelters, vets, boarding facilities, and emergency clinics

---

Make Arrangements for Multiple Dogs Before Emergencies Strike

Dr. Mandell says that most people don't even think about where to leave their dogs during disasters, or expect to leave their dogs at shelters, which is one reason shelters fill up during emergencies. So in all homes, but especially multiple-dog homes, she suggests making arrangements other than planning to leave your pet at a local shelter. To do so, you can contact hotels and motels that are outside of your local area (but are still nearby) to check their policies on accepting pets and restrictions on number, size, and species. You can also ask if "no pet" policies can be waived in an emergency. Multiple-pet owners should also be prepared to ask friends, relatives, or others outside the affected area whether they could help shelter animals. Another option is to check with local boarding facilities and veterinarians that might shelter animals in an emergency; your local Humane Society may also provide referrals and resources. But again, the key is to find out now and be prepared, since phone lines and websites aren't always dependable during an emergency.

During a Disaster

▶ At the first sign of an emergency, bring your dog inside and confine him so you can take him wherever you go. Don't wait to bring him in from a storm, hurricane, fire, etc.

▶ Never leave a dog tied or chained up outside during a disaster.

▶ Always have your emergency supply kit accessible. (This includes, but is not the same as, your first aid kit.)

▶ If you need to evacuate, never leave your dog at home by himself. If your house is damaged, he may run away, and he'll be left to fend for himself. If this happens, he can become a victim of exposure, starvation, predators, contaminated food or water, or accidents.

▶ Always use recommended evacuation routes, and leave early to avoid traffic or gridlock.

▶ If you're at home during a disaster, identify a safe area where you can stay with your pet. Keep him on a leash or in a carrier, and make sure he is wearing proper ID.

▶ Make arrangements with a neighbor who will be responsible for your dog if a disaster strikes and you're not home when an evacuation is issued. Give him a copy of your house key, and be sure he has your contact numbers. Ask him to secure your dog and then meet you at a specified location with your dog.

▶ Dogs can become frightened by unfamiliar noises. Keep your pet within sight to reassure him.

▶ Never tranquilize your dog. It will inhibit his natural survival instinct to escape potential danger.

After a Disaster

▶ If you're forced to evacuate, wait until authorities say it's safe for you and your dog to go home.

▶ Reorient your pets to their home by walking them around on a leash. They may feel confused and lost if landmarks and familiar scents are altered.

▶ If he seems disoriented, keep your dog on a leash and/or in a carrier inside the house for a few days. Try to establish a calm environment and help him back into a normal routine.

▶ Be on the lookout for downed power lines, debris, and reptiles that could cause your dog danger.

▶ Don't let your dog drink water or eat food that may be contaminated.

▶ Dogs can become aggressive or defensive after a disaster. Monitor your dog's behavior and contact your vet with questions if problems do not subside after about a week.

▶ If your dog is missing, contact your local animal control officer to find out where lost animals can be recovered. Bring a recent picture of your dog, tattoo number, or microchip number to the facility.

What to Do if Your Dog Gets Lost

Even though your dog should always live indoors and remain under your supervision while outside, dogs can get lost during emergencies—or simply on a random Tuesday. That's why dogs, even if they have a microchip or tattoo, should wear collars and up-to-date medical identification and owner contact information tags at all times (see "Your First Trip to the Vet" on page 91 for more on IDs).

If your dog gets lost, don't wait for him to come home on his own. To begin your search, call your local animal control officer—who is usually employed by police departments, sheriff departments, or parks and recreation departments in a municipality—immediately upon learning that your dog is missing. You should also contact area animal shelters and pet stores, hang signs in the neighborhood, and call surrounding vets and the police. If your dog has a microchip, you should contact the company that manufactures it for additional resources. (Home Alone, for example, sends out e-mail alerts and supplies posters to put up if your dog has one of their chips.) Some states mandate that shelters hold on to strays for a certain number of days, in order to give the dog's owner time to find him. Local radio and TV stations may offer to help you find a lost friend. Howard has been known to come to his fans' rescue, and it makes me so proud when he does.

Ask Dr. Z!

What does it mean when my dog . . .

Q: *Whimpers, runs in place, or lets out a stifled bark in his sleep?*

A: The jury is out about how or what dogs dream when they're asleep, but this may be a reflex of some sort, or a result of spontaneous brain activity while sleeping.

Ask Dr. Z!

What does it mean when my dog . . .

Q: *Vomits—and then eats it?*

A: Wild canids feed pups by eating at a kill, then coming back to the den and vomiting for the puppies. So this behavior is a normal part of the canid repertoire. Of course, this doesn't mean you should let your dog eat his puke if you see him do it. Distract your dog with a firm clap and then praise him when he walks away from it.

Your Dog's "Normal" Can Help Determine an Emergency

Dr. Mandell says that the best starting point for assessing whether a dog needs emergency medical attention is to know the degree to which he's acting abnormal. In Chapter 4, I suggested that you write down your dog's normal heart and pulse rates, breathing rates, temperature, mucous membrane color (color of gums or inner eyelids), and capillary refill time—and compare them against average readings (see "Know What Is 'Normal' for Your Dog" on page 220 for more). Keep this record of your dog's "normal" in your dog first aid kit, and if his behavior and normal rates ever seem irregular, call your vet to alert him to the situation.

Emergency Conditions

The American Red Cross considers the following situations to be medical emergencies that require immediate attention. If your dog has any of the following conditions (I'll review most signs and symptoms later in the chapter), head straight to your vet or a veterinary emergency hospital. If your vet provides emergency care, call him before you go to his office. Always contact your vet or veterinary emergency hospital with questions, from how to transport a dog to how to comfort him in the car. No question should go unasked when your dog is in a life-threatening situation.

In the list below, I've put an asterisk near conditions that I think are too dangerous for you to treat at home before heading to your vet's office or a veterinary hospital—though many are covered in *Dog First Aid*, since most if not all of the following emergencies can be life-threatening. Remember to always check the dog's ABCs (Airway, Breathing, Circulation) and perform CPR if necessary (see "Administering CPR" on the following page), and contact your veterinarian immediately to learn how to proceed.

Birthing problems*

Bleeding

Breathing difficulty

Burns

Cuts and gashes that expose internal organs or wounds with visible bone or tissue damage

Enlarged painful abdomen*

Heatstroke

Paralysis*

Poisoning

Profuse diarrhea or vomiting

Seizures (especially first seizures, seizures that last longer than two minutes, and seizures that repeat one after the other)

Shock

Snake bites

Straining to urinate*

Trauma (being hit by a car, falling from a dramatic height, being shot by a gun)

Unconsciousness

Ask Dr. Z!

What does it mean when my dog . . .

Q: *Randomly snaps in the air as if there were bugs flying around his head?*

A: This is called fly catching and may be a neurological problem best examined by a vet, as it can be a compulsive disorder or attributed to partial seizures. Fly catching predominantly affects seizure-prone breeds like Bull Terriers and German Shepherds and can respond to anticonvulsant therapy (such as medicines used to treat seizures).

Administering CPR

Cardiopulmonary resuscitation (CPR) should be used to treat a dog that isn't breathing and has no heartbeat or pulse. It consists of checking the dog's airway, rescue breathing (mouth-to-snout or mouth-to-mouth), and chest compressions. Taken from the first letters in the words "airway," "breathing," and "circulation," these principles are known as the ABCs of CPR.

When considering whether CPR is necessary for a dog, you must remember two things:

1. Do not assume that there is no heart rate or pulse* because an animal is not breathing. You can check your dog's pulse on his upper inner thigh, where it meets the body; just above the middle pad of the underside of the dog's paw; or just below his ankle. You can feel his heartbeat at the point where his left elbow touches the chest, near his fifth rib.

2. Do not start chest compressions before checking for a heartbeat. (If the animal is conscious and responds to you, then his heart is beating.) If you're at all confused by the written explanations of how to administer CPR, I suggest watching the DVD from *Dog First Aid*.

*Note: Heart rate and pulse rate are the same number in an animal when he does not have a problem like cardiac arrhythmia. In fact, the way vets diagnose an arrhythmia is by noticing if the heart rate is different (usually much faster) than the pulse rate. So while your dog's healthy heart and pulse rate are the same number, a change between the two indicates a problem.

TWO MUZZLES AND A SNOUT WALK INTO AN EMERGENCY . . .

The terms "muzzle" and "snout" can be confusing when they're used interchangeably and with various definitions. To clarify:

Muzzle (first aid device): This looks like either a wire basket or a soft piece of fabric that fits over the dog's snout; it is used during an emergency to prevent biting. If you don't have one, keep plenty of rolled gauze in your first aid kit to create a makeshift muzzle.

Muzzle (anatomy): The area from below the dog's eyes to the tip of his nose.

Snout: The area from below the dog's eyes to the tip of his nose. Interchangeable with "muzzle."

STEP 1: CHECK AIRWAY

Open a dog's airway and check the throat and mouth for foreign objects by doing the following:

Lay the animal down on his side.

Tilt his head slightly back to extend the neck and head.

Pull his tongue between his front teeth.

If the dog is unconscious, use your finger to check for and remove foreign material, including vomit, and take care not to push the object farther down into the airway. Do not put your fingers inside the mouth of a conscious animal.

STEP 2: CHECK BREATHING

After opening his airway, check to see if the dog is breathing. If he is breathing, let him stay in a comfortable position, and pay attention for any unusual sounds to tell the vet about later. If he isn't breathing, begin rescue breathing according to the directions in the chart below. *Do not attempt CPR on a conscious dog.* Continue to breathe for your dog until he starts breathing on his own; until you arrive at the vet's office or veterinary emergency hospital; or until you have given twenty minutes of artificial respiration. Beyond twenty minutes, there is little chance of reviving your dog.

For small dogs and puppies: Cover and seal the dog's entire snout with your mouth, and gently exhale until you see his chest rise. Give four to five rapid breaths, then check to see if your dog is breathing without help. If he begins to breathe but it is shallow and irregular, or if the breathing does not begin, continue giving him rescue breaths until you reach the vet hospital, or for up to twenty minutes.

For medium, large, and giant dogs: Hold the muzzle closed. Place your mouth over the dog's nose and exhale until you see his chest rise. Give four to five rapid breaths, then check to see if your dog is breathing without help. If he begins to breathe but it is shallow and irregular, or if the breathing does not begin, continue giving him rescue breaths until you reach the vet hospital, or for up to twenty minutes.

When to Administer Rescue Breathing Only

Dr. Mandell says that rescue breathing is doing mouth-to-snout or mouth-to-nose breathing when an animal is not breathing or not breathing effectively. You should administer rescue breathing on its own when a dog has stopped breathing but his heart is still beating (if his heart isn't beating, you should do breathing with compressions). For instance, this might happen when a dog has something blocking his airway like a foreign object, a swelling, or an underlying disease that would cause this symptom. If the dog's airway is blocked, you'll need to unblock it to administer effective rescue breaths. Ideally, you'd try to unblock the airway, but if you can't, then performing rescue breathing will get at least some air to his lungs. Rescue breathing is also helpful on the way to the vet, since you're giving your dog oxygen and essentially breathing for him.

STEP 3: CHECK CIRCULATION

Is there a heartbeat or pulse? If not, perform chest compressions. Use the chart below.

CPR FOR SMALL, MEDIUM, AND LARGE DOGS

For small dogs

Breathing position: Cover and seal the dog's entire snout with your mouth. Exhale until you see his chest rise.

Breaths/compression ratio: One breath, then five compressions

Breaths per minute: 20 to 30

Compression position: With your dog lying down and his chest facing you, place one hand over and the other hand under his ribs, behind his front legs. Compress the chest about one half to one inch each time, making sure the force is coming from your palms and not from your fingers.

Compression rate per minute: 100 to 120 (2 to 3 per second)

For medium and large dogs

Breathing position: Hold the dog's muzzle closed. Place your mouth over his nose and exhale until you see the chest rise.

Breaths/compression ratio: One breath, then five compressions

Breaths per minute: 20

Compression position: With your dog lying down and his chest facing you, extend your arms at the elbows. Cup one hand over the other, with the palm of one hand placed on top of the other hand. Using the palm of your bottom hand (you can lace your fingers together, if that makes it easier), compress the dog's chest at the widest part or at the point where his left elbow lies when pulled back to the chest. Compress the chest about one to three inches each time.

Compression rate per minute: 100 (2 per second)

For giant dogs

Breathing position: Hold the dog's muzzle closed. Place your mouth over his nose and exhale until you see the chest rise.

Breaths/compression ratio: One breath, then ten compressions

Breaths per minute: 20

Compression position: With your dog lying down and his chest facing you, extend your arms at the elbows. Cup one hand over the other, with the palm of one hand placed on top of the other hand. Using the palm of your bottom hand (you can lace your fingers together, if that makes it easier), compress the dog's chest at the widest part or at the point where his left elbow lies when pulled back to the chest. Compress the chest about one to three inches each time.

Compression rate per minute: 100 (2 per second)

CPR Size Key

Small dogs: under 30 pounds

Medium and large dogs: 30 to 90 pounds

Giant dogs: over 90 pounds

DOGS BITE WHEN THEY'RE SICK OR IN PAIN

No matter how gentle and loyal your dog is when he feels well, there's a good chance that he will bite you when he's sick or in pain. Dr. Mandell says that this has nothing to do with you; it's just the way your dog expresses that he's hurt. To avoid injury to yourself, always muzzle a dog before administering first aid (unless, of course, you need to do CPR).

First Aid for Dogs

For this section, I researched medical emergencies, injuries, and illnesses that could benefit from first aid before you reach your vet or a veterinary emergency hospital. Always call your vet or emergency clinic before administering any type of first aid, unless the injury or illness deems immediate action necessary. Use your best judgment. Deciding whether to rush your dog to the hospital or vet is a lot like deciding when you should go to the ER for a human problem. There are certain conditions that require it (heart attack), others in which it's smart (sudden pain), and still others when it's a wise precaution (an unusually high fever).

For each condition below, I've asked experts to help me identify the signs of each situation and how you can administer first aid until you reach the vet. None of this advice will fully treat a problem, and all scenarios require a call to the vet to schedule either immediate or next-day care.

Bianca's Close Call

Thankfully, I've had only one emergency situation with Bianca. A few years ago, I woke up in the middle of the night to find her panting excessively. She couldn't move and had a fever of 104.5—which is extremely dangerous, especially for her breed (remember, normal is 100 to 102.5 degrees). I called the vet, who immediately came over to administer IV fluids. It turned out that she'd had a reaction to a tick bite and was in the early stages of Lyme disease. We treated her condition with antibiotics, and she recovered soon after, but it was a really frightening moment.

Shock

Shock is the body's response to a change in blood flow and oxygen to organs and tissues, and it often results from the sudden loss of blood, a traumatic injury, heart failure, a severe allergic reaction, organ disease, or an infection circulating through the body. You should know what shock looks like in its early, middle, and terminal phases. A dog that is in shock, or that you suspect may be in shock, should be taken to a veterinary hospital immediately. Cardiopulmonary arrest may follow shock, so be prepared to perform CPR.

SIGNS OF EARLY SHOCK: *When the dog's body tries to compensate for the decreased flow of fluids and oxygen to its tissues*

> *Body temperature that is lower or more elevated than normal*
>
> *Mucous membranes (color of gums and inner eyelids) are redder than normal*
>
> *Capillary refill time of 1 to 2 seconds*
>
> *Increased heart rate*
>
> *Normal to increased intensity of pulse*

SIGNS OF MIDDLE SHOCK: *When the dog's body has a hard time compensating for a lack of blood flow and oxygen*

> *Cool limbs*
>
> *Hypothermia (body temperature is lower than 98 degrees)*
>
> *Increased heart rate*
>
> *Depressed mental state*
>
> *Prolonged capillary refill time*
>
> *Pale mucous membranes*

SIGNS OF END-STAGE SHOCK: *When a dog's body can no longer compensate for lack of oxygen and blood flow to vital organs—often leads to death*

> *Depressed mental state or unconsciousness*
>
> *Slow heart rate*
>
> *Prolonged capillary refill time**
>
> *Slow respiratory rate*
>
> *Weak or no pulse*

HOW YOU CAN HELP:

▶ Assess ABCs and perform CPR if necessary.

▶ Control bleeding if present (see "Bleeding" on page 453).

▶ Wrap the dog in a warm blanket.

▶ Slightly elevate his hind end by placing a blanket under his rear. Do not do this if you suspect a broken back or neck.

▶ Take your dog to the veterinary hospital immediately.

NOTE: To determine your dog's capillary refill time, press lightly on his gums or inner lip. The color should go from pink to white to pink again, and in a normal dog, this should take one to two seconds. But if the pink color returns in under one second, or over three, this is an emergency.

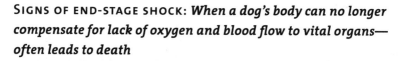

Ask Dr. Z!

What does it mean when my dog . . .

Q: *Snorts like a pig?*

A: Snorting is most common in short-muzzle dogs, or in dogs that are very intent on a particular scent. This dog may be excited that he discovered something good with his nose!

Allergic Reactions to Stings and Bites

A bee sting or spider bite can cause an allergic reaction in some dogs. It's not the sting itself that is problematic (though obviously, it's unpleasant for your dog), but the potential repercussions. A severe allergic reaction can lead to anaphylactic shock (a severe reaction that affects a number of different areas of the body at one time), either immediately or over a few hours.

SIGNS:

Collapse

Redness, discoloration, or hives around the site (sometimes they spread)

Pain, itching, licking at the site

Difficulty breathing

Red bumps on the dog's abdomen, back, and/or legs, vomiting, and diarrhea. Swelling at the sting site may spread and include the face, especially around the eyes and neck.

HOW YOU CAN HELP:

▶ If your dog's neck and face are swollen, check his ABCs. If he cannot breathe, try rescue breathing. If he is breathing but it's irregular, shallow, noisy, and labored, take him to the vet immediately and perform rescue breathing, if necessary, until you reach the veterinary hospital.

▶ Check for signs of shock.

▶ If the stinger is still in his skin, scrape it off with the edge of a credit card or your fingernail. Do not use tweezers, since this can release more toxins into the dog's system.

▶ Apply a cold compress, or an ice pack wrapped in a towel, to help control swelling.

▶ Call the vet and take your dog to a veterinary hospital. If your dog has hives from the sting, or if his face or lips are swollen, your vet may ask you to give him a Benadryl (diphenhydramine) before you arrive. Give oral medicine to your dog only if your vet approves it and your dog is conscious, able to breathe, and not vomiting.

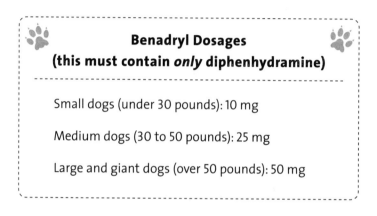

**Benadryl Dosages
(this must contain *only* diphenhydramine)**

Small dogs (under 30 pounds): 10 mg

Medium dogs (30 to 50 pounds): 25 mg

Large and giant dogs (over 50 pounds): 50 mg

Broken Back or Neck

A broken back or neck is very serious and may cause your dog a great deal of pain. Be gentle and patient with your dog, and don't forget to muzzle him so you aren't bitten.

SIGNS:

Front legs may be stiff and extended

Dog is in extreme pain

Anus is open

Dog can't move head, hind legs, or both front and hind legs

Dog may dribble urine or feces

You may see a divot or step on the spine that appears lower than the rest of the back. This may be hard to notice, but generally speaking, the spine will not look straight.

HOW YOU CAN HELP:

▶ Check ABCs and perform CPR if necessary.

▶ Stabilize your dog: Place a board flat on the floor or ground along the back of your dog. For small dogs, you can use a cutting board or kitchen tray; for medium dogs, try a snowboard or boogie board; for large dogs, use an ironing board or shelf from a bookshelf.

▶ Slide the dog, keeping his spine in alignment, onto the board while keeping his head and body still. Ask a friend to gently hold the dog's head, chest, and legs to keep him from moving. (The dog should be muzzled.)

▶ Secure the dog to a board by wrapping tape around his body and the board, depending on where he is hurt.

▶ Take him to a veterinary hospital immediately.

Ask Dr. Z!

What does it mean when my dog . . .

Q: *Salivates profusely?*

A: Lots of saliva could be the result of many things, like a dog's unnecessary anxiety or a foreign object lodged in his mouth. In both situations, you should consult a vet to resolve the problem.

Bite Wounds

Bite wounds can look minor but may be very serious, so if your dog is bitten by another dog or another animal, take him to the vet immediately to prevent infection. Note: If your dog gets caught in a dog fight, try not to break it up yourself, because you could be bitten. An animal control officer would be the best person to handle this situation. For what to do if the fight and/or your dog demands immediate help, see "How to Break Up a Dog Fight" on page 165.

SIGNS:

Small skin wound (you may be able to see the puncture marks)

Bleeding

Bruising

Signs of a bite wound infection include fever, lethargy, loss of appetite, and pain when the area is touched.

If the wound is not obvious, the injured dog may develop an infection or abscess, which is a soft swelling around the wound, one to two days after being bitten. He may also have internal injuries. If there are internal injuries, you'll notice other signs, like difficulty breathing, shock, bruising and swelling in large areas over the chest or abdomen, and potential collapse.

HOW YOU CAN HELP:

▶ If the wound is bleeding, control it (see "Bleeding" on page 453).

▶ Check ABCs and perform CPR if necessary.

▶ Check for shock.

▶ Shave the area surrounding the wound with grooming clippers, flush it with warm water or saline, and bandage.

▶ Administer basic wound care (see "Cuts and Tears [Major and Minor Lacerations]" on page 460).

▶ Contact your veterinarian.

Ask Dr. Z!

What does it mean when my dog . . .

Q: *Looks at a dog from the corner of his eye?*

A: When dogs stare, it can be a type of threat. When they want to observe another dog without provoking a fight, they will turn their head to the side and observe sideways.

Bleeding

Bleeding can be the sign of a larger problem, but it should always be handled when you first notice it. Call the vet or rush your dog to a veterinary hospital if you notice severe bleeding. Direct pressure is the safest way to treat bleeding until you reach a hospital.

SIGNS:

Arterial bleeding looks like rhythmic spurting blood. It is rapid and profuse, and it is difficult to stop. Venal bleeding is slower and can be less profuse than arterial. It is usually easier to stop and less dangerous. Know the difference between these two types of bleeding so that you can explain the pattern to your vet.

HOW YOU CAN HELP:

▶ Wash your hands.

▶ Put on nonlatex, powder-free disposable gloves (they should be in your dog first aid kit).

▶ Hold a piece of gauze, a washcloth, or other clean material over the bleeding site and apply direct pressure. If the material soaks through, do not remove it—it will stick. Apply another cloth over it.

▶ If the bleeding on a limb has not stopped and is spurting, apply direct pressure to the wound and gently press down on the area just above the wound with your hand in an effort to close off the blood vessel. If blood is flowing heavily but not spurting, hold the area just below the site to close off the blood vessels. This technique applies to a bleeding limb, and not other bleeding areas of the body, since you can only apply direct pressure to wounds on the body.

▶ If this doesn't stop the bleeding on a limb, wrap gauze or other material around the wound, just tightly enough to stop the bleeding. Do not make it too tight, and secure it with tape.

▶ If you wrap a limb and notice swelling, or if any of your dog's toes have become cold, this means the bandage is too tight. Loosen it. If the limb doesn't seem to be broken, elevate it above the dog's heart. Continue pressure.

▶ Take your dog to the vet immediately.

Burns

Burns are classified by severity, based on how deep the burn is and the extent of the body that is burned. The most severe burns can cover large areas, penetrate tissues, lead to shock, and place your dog at risk for infection and possibly death. All burns require veterinary care.

SIGNS OF SUPERFICIAL BURNS: *These heal with veterinary care.*

Loss of fur

Reddened skin

Swelling

Tenderness or pain

SIGNS OF DEEP BURNS: *These heal well with vet care, but your dog may experience scarring.*

Loss of fur

Redness

Swelling

Tenderness or pain

Blisters

SIGNS OF DEEP BURNS INVOLVING BLOOD VESSELS: *These eventually heal but result in a lot of scarring.*

Intensive care and surgery may be required.

Loss of skin

Skin is no longer sensitive to touch

Swelling under the skin

SIGNS OF BURNS IN WHICH TISSUES AND SKIN CELLS ARE DESTROYED: *These cause severe scarring. Intensive medical and surgical care is required.*

Area looks black and leathery

How you can help:

▶ Check for signs of shock in the case of deep or extensive burns.

▶ Apply cool water to the burn to decrease pain and further penetration of heat into the tissues.

▶ If the burn involves only one body part, immerse your dog in a cool bath (with no grooming supplies).

▶ If more than one part of the body or a large area is affected, do not use this technique; a dog is more prone to shock when large areas of his body are cooled too quickly and at once. Instead, run cool water directly over the areas, or place cool compresses on the affected areas.

▶ Do not use ointment, butter, or petroleum jelly on burns.

▶ Place a sterile nonstick pad or a clean moist cloth over the burned area to keep it sanitary.

▶ Take your dog to a veterinary hospital immediately.

Car Accidents

If your dog is hurt in a car accident, you may be able to momentarily help him, but he should be rushed to the veterinarian to check for internal injuries.

Signs:

Dog is in the middle, or on the side of, the road and looks injured

Most commonly, injuries occur for the following reasons:

Dog jumped, fell, or was thrown from the bed of a pickup truck

Dog was run over while someone was backing out of a driveway

Dog ran into the path of a moving car

Dog got loose from yard or leash

How you can help:

▶ If you witness the accident, notice where on the dog's body he was struck—and whether he was hit, driven over, or thrown in the process. Sometimes a dog will get up and walk away, but this doesn't mean that he is not severely injured. Dogs instinctively respond to danger by running away.

▶ If traffic has stopped, move the dog to the side of the road—the dog may not be able to move because of a spinal injury, severe internal injury and/or possible shock—and put a muzzle on him. (You may also need to put a muzzle on him *before* moving him. Remember to grab your first aid kit as you run out the door, or keep one in your glove compartment as a precaution.) Keep the dog as still as possible, and try not to worsen obvious fractures or limb displacements.

▶ If traffic hasn't stopped, alert drivers that you're approaching the scene, and take the dog to the side of the road before examining him. Use a muzzle and/or board if you have one, and if not, simply drag the dog by the fur on top of his body while trying to keep him as still as possible.

▶ Write down the position of the dog when you found him, plus the presence of any blood, urine, and/or feces. Your vet will want to know these details when you get to the hospital.

▶ Check the ABCs and perform CPR if necessary.

▶ If your dog is alert and can stand, notice if he's limping or favoring one side. Look for blood, open wounds, bruising, or limbs hanging in abnormal positions.

▶ If the dog is bleeding, do your best to stop it (see "Bleeding" on page 453).

▶ Check for shock.

▶ Any dog that's been hit by a car should be taken directly to a veterinary hospital. Trauma injuries may not even show up for twelve to seventy-two hours after the incident, so do not assume that everything is fine if his external injuries are minimal. Internal traumas can include the slow leakage of blood from internal organs, rupture of the bladder or other internal organs, and air or blood leaking into the chest cavity. Since the dog's body will try to compensate for trauma, early shock may be hard to identify.

Choking

A dog can choke on his own vomit, a foreign object, or even his swollen tongue when he's suffering from an allergic reaction. Choking can also be the sign of a trauma to the dog's throat or neck area, or even an upper respiratory disease. You obviously can't use a muzzle when helping a choking dog, but beware of biting in this situation, especially if the dog is conscious or semiconscious.

SIGNS:

Anxiousness

Stops breathing

Blue or white gums

Loud breathing sounds

Pawing at the mouth

Struggling or gasping to breathe

How you can help:

▶ If your dog can still breathe and the object, vomit, or foreign material is visible, pull the tongue forward and remove the object with your finger. Don't spend a lot of time trying to remove the obstruction if it's not easy to reach, since you can inadvertently push the object farther down the dog's throat.

▶ If you can't remove the object, place one hand on either side of the dog's rib cage and apply firm, quick pressure to try to squeeze out the object. This will push air out of his lungs sharply, and hopefully push the obstruction out of his throat. Repeat this until the object is dislodged or until you can get to the veterinarian's office.

▶ If you can put your arms around the dog's rib cage, you can administer abdominal thrusts: Hold the dog with his back against your stomach, and place your fist in the hollow immediately beneath his rib cage. Using a strong, quick, thrusting action, push in and up toward your stomach to force the object out.

▶ If the pet stops breathing or collapses, check the ABCs and start CPR if necessary. Get the animal to a vet immediately.

Cuts and Tears (Major and Minor Lacerations)

If your dog has a wound that cuts or tears through his outer skin to the deeper layers of his body, you may notice veins, arteries, nerves, muscles, or even bones. I realize that this can be scary, but these require immediate treatment and veterinary care, especially if the area is bleeding heavily.

SIGNS:

Bleeding (there may be a lot of bleeding if an artery is cut)

Licking or limping

Open wound (you may see ligaments or muscle)

FOREIGN OBJECTS

Foreign objects can become lodged in a dog's paw pads, skin, eye, mouth, nose, and throat. These objects range from sticks caught in the roof of a dog's mouth to a piece of glass that becomes embedded in his paw. The most obvious indication of a foreign object is irritation around the site and related abnormal behavior. A dog with a splinter in his pad may limp, or a dog with a blade of grass in his nose will sneeze excessively. Depending on the problem, the area may bleed and cause your dog pain.

In your dog first aid kit, you have the tools to remove foreign objects, but I don't recommend that you attempt it without a veterinarian or a vet tech on the phone to guide you. Objects could break or split into fragments, which means you'll cause more harm than good. The object may also be severely embedded and cause infection (redness, swelling, discharge, and pain). I don't think it's your job to differentiate between a serious puncture wound and a shallow glass injury, so call your veterinarian as the first line of defense. He will want you to come in.

How you can help:

▶ Check the ABCs and perform CPR if necessary.

▶ Check for shock.

▶ Stop the bleeding as best you can (see "Bleeding" on page 453).

▶ Even if there is no bleeding, cover the area with a clean cloth until you get to the vet.

▶ Take the dog to a veterinary hospital, since many deep cuts and tears require stitches.

Frostbite

Your dog's tail, the tips of his ears, and the pads of his feet are the areas most susceptible to frostbite. After a winter walk, clean your dog's feet to remove chemicals, salt, and ice particles. The causes for frostbite are the same as those for hypothermia, but these conditions are not the same; extreme hypothermia *causes* frostbite.

Signs:

Frozen area looks discolored. Skin looks pale or even blue in the beginning, then turns black and dead in later stages.

No pain or sensation at the affected area; or a lot of pain, especially when the area starts to warm.

Ask Dr. Z!

What does it mean when my dog . . .

Q: *Chews on the tip of his tail?*

A: This could be due to injury to the tail tip, or even anxiety. If tail chewing becomes a compulsive behavior, consult a behaviorist. Check for fleas, mats, or ticks in case the dog has an irritation.

▶ Remove your dog from the cold.

▶ Spray the affected area with warm, not hot, water.

▶ Do not rub or apply pressure to the area, which could worsen the condition.

▶ Apply a warm compress to the area.

▶ Immediately take your dog to a veterinary hospital.

Heatstroke (Hyperthermia) and Heat Exhaustion

Hyperthermia occurs when your dog's system isn't accustomed to a warm temperature. Dr. Mandell says it's common on the first hot and humid days of the year, when the dog is either running outdoors or living in an un-air-conditioned house. Heatstroke can also happen if a dog has prolonged seizures, has a thick coat in a warm climate, or is left in a parked car during warm weather. Some dogs, such as those with short snouts, are more susceptible to heatstroke. If the condition doesn't advance beyond a body temperature of 104 degrees, you can help your dog recover. The goal here is to decrease his body temperature to about 103 degrees in the first ten to fifteen minutes after he exhibits symptoms. Once you reach this temperature, stop the cooling process because the body temperature will continue to decrease and can plummet dangerously low.

Note: Even if you successfully cool your dog down to 103 degrees, you must still take him to the vet right away because the consequences of heatstroke may not show for hours or even days. Some conditions, like kidney failure, blood clotting disorders, destruction of the digestive tract lining, abnormal heart rhythms, respiratory arrest, and neurological problems, can be fatal if not medically treated in a prompt way. Ask your vet to check for symptoms when you see him.

SIGNS:

Body temperature of 104 degrees or above

Very quick capillary refill time

Collapse

Increased heart rate

Increased respiratory rate

Mucous membrane color is redder than normal

Salivation

Bloody diarrhea or vomit

Excessive panting and/or difficulty breathing

Depression, stupor, seizures, or coma

HOW YOU CAN HELP:

▶ Remove your dog from direct heat.

▶ Check for shock.

▶ Take a rectal temperature (use thermometer from the dog first aid kit).

▶ Spray your dog with cool water for two minutes. Take his temperature a second time.

▶ Place water-soaked towels on the dog's head, neck, feet, chest, and abdomen.

▶ Turn on a fan and point it in your dog's direction.

- Dab rubbing alcohol on the dog's foot pads to help him cool down. Do not use large quantities of alcohol, since it can be toxic if a dog ingests it.

- Take your dog to the nearest veterinary hospital immediately.

Hot Spots

Hot spots are areas that have become irritated by a sting, external parasite, foreign object, scrape, or allergic condition that the dog then licks, bites, or scratches excessively. Food allergies are common culprits, too.

SIGNS:

Bleeding in the area

Red or pink bald patches

Discharge or foul odor from the area

HOW YOU CAN HELP:

- Shave the area with grooming clippers, or ask your vet tech to shave the area for you.

- Clean the entire affected area with warm water.

- Look for a foreign object, like an insect stinger or flea. Remove it right away.

- Apply the topical triple antibiotic ointment from your dog first aid kit to the area.

- Consider an E-collar (cone) for your dog to avoid further irritation (he may want to lick the hot spot).

- Call your vet about further medical treatment.

Hypothermia

Hypothermia occurs when a dog's body temperature drops drastically because he's been exposed to frigid temperatures for too long. Hypothermia can result from shock; a fall into cold water; his fur getting wet from a cold, windy environment; an inability to regulate body temperature (in old and young dogs); or an underlying illness. The consequences of hypothermia include neurological problems, heart problems, kidney failure, slow or no breathing, and frostbite.

SIGNS:

Body temperature is below 95 degrees

Shivering

Decreased heart rate

Pupils may be dilated

Pale or blue mucous membranes

Weak pulse

Stupor or unconsciousness

HOW YOU CAN HELP:

► Remove your dog from the cold.

► Check the dog's ABCs and perform CPR as needed.

► Check for shock.

► Take a rectal temperature (use thermometer from the dog first aid kit).

► Wrap your dog in a blanket.

▶ Place warm water bottles, wrapped in towels to prevent burns, next to the dog.

▶ Take the dog to a veterinary hospital immediately.

Poisoning

See "Poison Control" on page 219.

Ask Dr. Z!

What does it mean when my dog ...

Q: *Licks the car window?*

A: He's not in love with the window. It may be damp or cool and feels really good on his tongue.

Scrapes

Scrapes that affect only the top layer of a dog's skin may be shallow and heal easily, or they can be large and more serious. Immediately take your dog to the veterinarian if his abrasion is larger than a quarter, seems painful, is red, does not heal after two days, oozes yellow or smelly discharge, or you're uncertain about its depth or severity.

HOW YOU CAN HELP:

▶ Wash your hands.

▶ Put on non-latex, powder-free gloves (these should be in your dog first aid kit).

▶ Apply a sterile, water-soluble lubricant to the wound, so the dog's hair doesn't contaminate the wound while you execute the next step.

▶ Clip the hair around the wound with grooming clippers.

▶ Flush the wound with warm water or saline solution to remove the skin lubricant.

▶ Gently wash the wound with water or saline to remove any remaining dirt or debris.

Seizures

Seizures are frightening to watch. They can be caused by epilepsy, an infection in the brain, inflammation in the brain, scar tissue in the brain, a tumor, an abscess, or a malformation of the brain. A dog's first seizure warrants a trip to the vet as soon as possible for an exam. If this isn't your dog's first seizure, and it lasts longer than two minutes or manifests in a cluster of multiple seizures, take your dog to the vet immediately—this is a medical emergency. See "Epilepsy and Seizures" on page 245 for more.

SIGNS:

Before the seizure, the dog looks dazed and anxious. He may also retreat to a safe place. During the active seizure, he may:

Fall over

Twitch

Urinate and defecate

Drool

Not recognize you

Become stiff and rigid

Stare into space

Bite invisible flies

After a seizure, a dog may be disoriented, walk into walls, or seem blind. He may also behave normally, so always call your vet if your dog seizes.

How you can help:

▶ Make sure your dog is away from a staircase or furniture.

▶ Record how long the active phase of the seizure lasts.

▶ Keep a log of your dog's seizures to share with your vet. Include the date, time of day, time after a meal, and how long the seizure phase lasts. Videotape them if you can.

▶ Keep your hands away from the dog's mouth. Do not attempt to hold his tongue. He may bite.

▶ Do not disturb your dog during and after his seizure. He is not himself.

▶ Take your dog to the vet as soon as he seems stable, post-seizure.

▶ If he is having multiple seizures or the seizure is lasting longer than two to four minutes, take your dog to the vet immediately (even while he is seizing).

Venomous Creatures

Bites from snakes and scorpions, jellyfish stings, and contact with poisonous toads are very real problems. Some of these creatures are more indigenous to certain regions than others, so find out which live in your geographic area, and try to keep your dog away from those natural habitats.

Snakes

Poisonous snakes in the U.S. include pit vipers like copperheads, rattlesnakes, cottonmouths, and coral snakes. If, based on the signs below, you suspect that your dog is suffering from a snake bite, call your vet immediately. It could be fatal.

Non-poisonous snakes may also bite, which can cause an allergic reaction. Still, take your dog to the vet immediately. The situation is not one that you're equipped to really assess.

Signs:

Bleeding puncture wound (potential fang marks)

Blood doesn't clot

Breathing stops

Bruising or shedding of skin around the bitten area

Neurological signs, like twitching or drooling

Pain

Reddening

Shock

Swelling of the bitten area; this can be severe and continue for longer than a day

How you can help:

▶ Try to identify the snake, but don't get too close. If you've killed the snake, take it with you to the vet to be identified. Be very careful! The fangs on a decapitated snake's head may be venomous for up to one and a half hours.

▶ Check the dog's ABCs and perform CPR as needed.

▶ Check for signs of shock.

▶ Try to keep the dog still and calm.

▶ Put on powder-free, non-latex gloves and wash the wound with mild soap.

▶ Do not cut the wound open or try to suck the venom. Do not use ice on the area or a tourniquet.

▶ Carry your pet to the car. Any movement may cause the toxins to spread faster.

▶ Immediately take your dog to a veterinary hospital.

NOTE: If you are afraid of snakes and their venom, as I am, you can also call your local fire department to pick up the snake.

Scorpions

Few scorpion bites are deadly (a sting from the more rare bark scorpion can be fatal), but being bitten is an emergency. If you suspect that your dog has been stung by a scorpion, get him to the vet right away.

SIGNS:

Accidental urination and defecation

Breathing problems

Pain

Paralysis

Swelling

Dilated pupils

Drooling

Tearing from eyes

Collapse (and potential death)

How you can help:

▶ Take your dog to the veterinarian immediately.

Toads

Most toads aren't poisonous—but exceptions include the Colorado River toad (found in the Southwest) and the giant brown toad, or marine toad (found in Florida, South Texas, and Hawaii), which can kill a dog within thirty minutes. The poisons on a toad's skin can cause discomfort or paralysis to most dogs. If you notice the remains of a toad in your dog's mouth or near his bed, or you witness your dog eating or licking a toad or its remains, call your veterinarian immediately.

SIGNS:

Collapse

Diarrhea

Excess salivation

Fever

Pawing at the mouth

Seizures

Vomiting

Weakness

HOW YOU CAN HELP:

▶ Rinse the dog's mouth out with water.

▶ Check for shock.

▶ Take your dog to the vet immediately.

Jellyfish Stings

Dogs can be stung by jellyfish in the water or onshore. Your dog won't die from the sting, but he will be in a lot of pain. This can be treated at home, with your first aid kit, but I suggest calling your vet to assess the situation after you've initially treated your dog.

SIGNS:

>Pain
>
>Stingers at site
>
>Swelling

HOW YOU CAN HELP:

- Pour rubbing alcohol on any tentacles left in the skin to help stabilize the toxins.

- Use sticky tape to remove any jellyfish tentacles from the dog's fur.

- Make a paste of baking soda and water, and apply it to the area to soothe it.

- Contact your vet to ask if you should bring the dog in or take additional measures. He may ask you to give your dog Benadryl (see "Benadryl Dosages" on page 450 for more).

End-of-Life Considerations

It hurts my heart to talk about how to face the sudden or impending death of any dog, much less yours or mine. When I think about how healthy Bianca is, I'm really grateful that she's had so few serious problems and seems bound for a long, happy life. But I think that knowing what to expect during a dog's decline, before death actually comes, helps remove some of the shock and confusion when the time arrives.

Sudden Death

Sudden death occurs when a seemingly healthy dog passes unexpectedly. Most commonly, it occurs when a dog suffers from conditions like undetected heart problems, stroke, bleeding from tumors, blood clots, aneurysms, and infections from parasites like heartworm (prevention is key!). These dogs can pass in their sleep, during a walk, at the groomer's, or on their own while you're at work. Sometimes bloat or gastric torsion, if fatal, can be considered a sudden death as well (see "Twenty-one Most Common Medical Conditions and Diseases" on page 230 for more). Traumas, like a car accident, can cause death, too. Though these are not technically considered "sudden death," it is a passing that you can't possibly plan for.

Sudden deaths and traumas are tragic and worrisome. If you return home to find that your dog is no longer alive, call your vet immediately, and he will suggest the next steps. He may send someone to retrieve the dog's body, or he may ask you to bring it into the office yourself. Your vet may also give you the option of an autopsy to determine the cause of death, but do know that not every condition can be determined through this procedure, and it can be very expensive.

If your dog dies away from your home, go to the closest vet or animal hospital.

Prolonged Illness

Dogs with chronic illnesses may undergo months or years of treatment, though there will come a time when your instincts tell you that it's time to talk to your vet about euthanasia. When a dog becomes very sick, euthanasia is the only humane option. It involves injecting an overdose of anesthesia or barbiturate into your dog to relax him and bring about a quick and painless death. It's a merciful way to pass, especially if the dog has been in a lot of pain during his final years.

When euthanizing your pet, ask your veterinarian about the best time of day to do this, since early in the morning or later in the day may be the most private time at the office. You may also want to arrange for the veterinarian to come to your house for the procedure. Growing up, my mom took our three rescues to the vet when it was their time. My brothers and I always stayed home, because we were too scared and sad to witness their passing.

Decide in advance whether you and/or other family members would like to be present during euthanasia. A pet's passing is a solemn time, so don't involve more people than you need.

How to Memorialize Your Dog

After your dog has passed, you'll need to choose whether you'd like to cremate or bury your dog in a pet cemetery, unless you'd like to bury him near your home. Realize, however, that burying your dog outside of a cemetery is illegal in some states. Check with your local bylaw offices to learn how pet-burial restrictions and local zoning laws affect you.

Cremation

Cremation provides a way for you to keep your dog with you or scatter his ashes in your yard, the ocean, or his favorite place. (It is also less expensive and more environmentally friendly than burial.) Your vet will be the last veterinary care professional to see your dog, so ask him about cremation. He has established relationships with crematoriums and will make arrangements for the service to pick up your dog's body. Cremation comes with options:

1. Private Individual Cremation: After your dog is cremated, his remains are returned to you either in an urn or in a small bag so that you can transfer them to an urn. During cremation, your dog shares space in the chamber with other pets; however, these animals are separated, so you can receive only your dog's remains since their ashes don't mix with others'.

2. Communal (Mass) Cremation: Your dog is cremated with a number of other pets, and his ashes aren't able to be separated. Ashes are seldom returned to the pet owner.

3. Viewing Cremation: This is similar to a private cremation, but friends and family are invited to be present during a service in the viewing room. This is not available at all crematoriums.

The prices for these options vary, so ask for details before you make this emotional decision. If you've asked for your dog's ashes to be returned, they will be sent to you or your veterinarian. At this point, you or your vet can transfer them into a permanent urn, vessel, or memory box. Your vet or crematorium can suggest places to buy these items, though there are various online retailers as well.

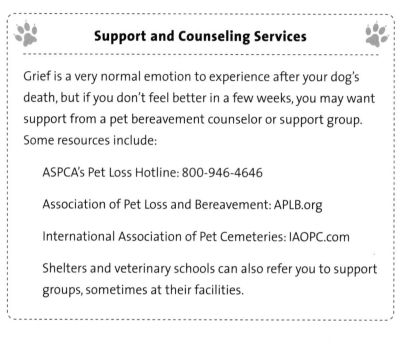

Support and Counseling Services

Grief is a very normal emotion to experience after your dog's death, but if you don't feel better in a few weeks, you may want support from a pet bereavement counselor or support group. Some resources include:

ASPCA's Pet Loss Hotline: 800-946-4646

Association of Pet Loss and Bereavement: APLB.org

International Association of Pet Cemeteries: IAOPC.com

Shelters and veterinary schools can also refer you to support groups, sometimes at their facilities.

Burial

There's something to be said for the comfort that comes from visiting the resting place of a loved one. Pet burial costs vary, depending on your dog's size, whether he requires transport from your vet or home, and other services. You should also consider how you'll contain your dog's body (you'll need to select an appropriate vessel) and what items you may want to bury with him. Your pet cemetery can direct you to retailers that sell vessels.

Visit the International Association of Pet Cemeteries at IAOPC.com for more on how to bury your dog. Its member list can point to cemeteries in your area, plus counseling for owners.

Celebrating Your Dog's Life After He's Gone

When it's time to honor your dog's memory, either at home alone or with friends at his burial service, remember the funny, sweet, and enduring memories that have brought so much pleasure to those around him. Telling stories and keeping your dog's favorite toys nearby will surely lift your spirits. You might also want to spend time with a friend's dog (your friend would love the help) or volunteer at a shelter (they can always use an extra set of hands). Bonding with other dogs and pet owners in your community will help you remember everything you loved about your own dog. It might also persuade you to get a new dog sooner than you think!

The Lessons Dogs Teach Us

When my friend Michael's dog Aggie died from cancer, he forwarded an anonymously written e-mail to me and a few other friends, which I saved. The message is about the valuable life lessons that dogs teach us, whether they realize it or not. I've reprinted it here, since I think it's so moving. (I especially like the one about lying on the grass on a warm day. Bianca and I can relate!)

When loved ones come home, always run to greet them.

Never pass up the opportunity to go for a joyride.

Allow the experience of fresh air and the wind in your face to be pure ecstasy.

Take naps.

Stretch before rising.

Run, romp, and play daily.

Thrive on attention and let people touch you.

Avoid biting when a simple growl will do.

On warm days, stop to lie on your back on the grass.

On hot days, drink lots of water and lie under a shady tree.

When you're happy, dance around and wag your entire body.

Delight in the simple joy of a long walk.

Eat with gusto and enthusiasm. Stop when you have had enough.

Be loyal. Never pretend to be something you're not.

If what you want lies buried, dig until you find it.

When someone is having a bad day, be silent, sit close by, and nuzzle them gently.

Always be grateful for each new day.

ALL ABOUT MY DOG!

The best thing about dogs is that no matter how many you decide to own, each one is a unique and special friend. Fill out the following questionnaire about your furry companion and keep it for posterity. I've written one about Bianca below as an example. Now it's your turn!

Name (Dog's): Bianca Jane Romijn-Stamos-O'Connell

First night home: October 3, 2003

Perfect day: Running in the snow in Central Park

Best friend: Sydney Lackner, our best friends' Yellow Lab

Archnemesis: Ticks!

Preferred grassy area: Anywhere she can find it; rolling on her back in grass is bliss

Favorite body of water: The ocean behind our house; Bianca loves waves splashing on her belly (no swimming, though!)

Hiding place during a storm: Wherever Mom is

Favorite snack: Slice of cheese

Best outfit: Does her red harness count?

Worst habit: Getting under people's feet (she's so quiet—people always step on her)

Favorite trip: Weekends at the beach house

TV time: She watches all the reality shows with Howard and me!

Favorite dog movie: Marley & Me

Naptime: In her bed in my office

Happiest: When Mom and Dad are together with her, watching TV

Messiest: After rolling in sand while wet

Beloved chew toy: Blue Nylabone

Biggest accomplishment: Cover model for Mom's book

Dog bed or your bed? Dog bed in every room except our master bedroom (she snores!!)

Role model: Meatball Sandler (may he rest in peace)

My dog is: Love

Name (Dog's):

First night home:

Perfect day:

Best friend:

Archnemesis:

Preferred grassy area:

Favorite body of water:

Hiding place during a storm:

Favorite snack:

Best outfit:

Worst habit:

Favorite trip:

TV time:

Favorite dog movie:

Naptime:

Happiest:

Messiest:

Beloved chew toy:

Biggest accomplishment:

Dog bed or your bed? Role model:

My dog is:

Name (Dog's):

First night home:

Perfect day:

Best friend:

Archnemesis:

Preferred grassy area:

Favorite body of water:

Hiding place during a storm:

Favorite snack:

Best outfit:

Worst habit:

Favorite trip:

TV time:

Favorite dog movie:

Naptime:

Happiest:

Messiest:

Beloved chew toy:

Biggest accomplishment:

Dog bed or your bed? Role model:

My dog is:

AFTERWORD:
NOW PUT DOWN THIS BOOK,
AND GO LOVE YOUR DOG!

———

Congratulations! You've officially earned the right to dole out dog care advice to friends, family, and strangers who now know significantly less than you do. So spread the word about your favorite tips in this book—plus those you've gathered as an owner—and start a dialogue within your community about how to make the most of canine companionship.

When researching *Oh My Dog!*, I was as diligent and comprehensive as I could be—especially considering that ideas, products, studies, and philosophies are constantly changing. These topics can also be incredibly subjective and sometimes controversial. So if I missed a point that's related to your dog, use the opportunity to research the topic and speak to your vet or other dog care professional about how to responsibly handle the situation. If I learned anything while writing this book, it's that there's always something new to learn if you reach out to the right people. I feel very lucky to have such a great network of dog experts in my life, and I really encourage you to create a similar group of professionals in your world. I don't think raising a dog is something you should ever do in a bubble, so the more input you can collect, the better.

If you'd like to connect with me, please visit BethO.com. I won't be able to respond to every note, but I will try to address your questions through the work that I do so others can benefit from your thoughts and concerns. I hope you like the book—and that your dog appreciates it, too!

ACKNOWLEDGMENTS

Thank you, Kristina Grish, for being such a godsend throughout the research and writing process. Thank you, also, for sharing my passion for animals and being my partner in this journey!

Thank you, from the bottom of my heart, to the following experts, without whom this book would not have been possible:

Stacy Alldredge

Jorge Bendersky

Cindy Bressler, DVM

Steve Brooks

Mary Burch, PhD, CAAB

Dana Cironi

Irene Deitch, PhD

Elise Di Ruggiero

Nicholas Dodman, BVMS

Jennifer Dorsch

Kenneth D. Fischer, DVM

Tamar Geller

Martin Goldstein, DVM

Robert S. Goldstein, DVM, and Susan Goldstein

Kim Guerin

Isabell Hamel

Susan LaCroix Hamil

Jen Jablow, DDS

Katenna Jones, CAAB, CABC, CPDT

Paul W. Kinnear, DVM

Greg Kleva

Artist Knox

Mike Malloy

Deborah C. Mandell, VMD, DACVECC

Sylvia Mariani

Shawn Messonnier, DVM

Melinda Miller

Susan Nelson, DVM

Lisa Peterson

Julie Shaw

Brandon Solotoff

Robert Tornello

Cindy Ventura

J. J. Wen, DVM

Stephen L. Zawistowski, PhD CAAB

The American Humane Association (AHA)

The American Kennel Club (AKC)

American Legacy Foundation

The American Red Cross

The American Society for the Prevention of Cruelty to Animals (ASPCA)

The Association of Pet Dog Trainers (APDT)

Bark Buckle Up

The Humane Society of the United States

North Shore Animal League America

Thank you, my wonderful family—

My mom, whose dream it was for me to write a book. Here you go.

My dad, always my biggest fan.

My brothers, Dave and Doug, my heroes.

Aunt Christy, for your friendship.

Grandma Adele, for being so proud.

Grandma Sweetpea, thank you for watching over me.

Thank you to:

Kelly, my bestest.

Katie Lee, for introducing me to the wonderful Jen Bergstrom from Gallery Books.

My amazing friends, you know who you are.

Also to:

Emily Westlake and the Gallery Team.

Laura Lackner.

Richard Basch.

Joanne Yohannan and NSALA family.

Christopher Appoldt.

Maribeth Edmunds.

Rachael Ray.

And to all the rescued animals who have been a part of my life and inspired me—Suziedog, Kitty, Lizzie, Gibson, PJ, Maow, Lucy, Russell, AJ, and Apple.

Finally, above all, to the two loves of my life, Howard and Bianca.

INDEX

ABOUT THE AUTHORS

Beth Ostrosky Stern's love for animals is her passion in life. She is the proud spokesperson and a volunteer for North Shore Animal League America (NSALA), the largest no-kill rescue and adoption organization in the world; she also writes a monthly column for their website Animal-League.org. Beth lives blissfully with her husband, Howard, her beloved Bulldog, Bianca, and rescued cat, Apple, in New York City and Southampton, New York, where she is also involved with the Wildlife Rescue Center of the Hamptons. She recently performed her own wildlife rescue on the streets of New York City, where she transported a hurt saw-whet owl to safety and released him back into nature after his successful rehabilitation. Visit her at BethO.com

Kristina Grish is the author of four books, including *The Joy of Text: Mating, Dating, and Techno-Relating* (Simon Spotlight Entertainment, 2007). Her writing has appeared in *Marie Claire, Real Simple, Cosmopolitan,* and *Redbook,* among other women's magazines. She lives in New York City with her husband, Scott, and their feisty Shih Tzu, Izzy.